The Monument F

CW00553704

HUMANE JUSTICE

What role do kindness, hope and compassion play in the criminal justice system?

Edited by
LISA ROWLES & IMAN HAJI

CONTENTS

Foreword
Edwina Grosvenor   ix

The Monument Trust into the future
Mark Woodruff   xi

Introduction: Humane Justice
Lisa Rowles and Iman Haji   1

Section 1
The voice of lived experience   5

Random acts of kindness
The Tartan Con   9

Home is Where You Are
Low Newton   11

The Light of Compassion Will Shine Brightest In the Darkest Places
Jayne Richards   12

Hope – the exit ramp from crime to healed offender
Callum Hutchison   20

Kindness, hope and compassion: A matter of life and death for
those in prison
Brenda Birungi   26

A Kind Prison
Nick Moss   29

My Hidden Hero
Anonymous   36

Only hope and kindness can save us
Amanda Visconti   37

The Nurseries of Crime – finding kindness, hope and compassion
Malcolm Carter   38

Kindness, hope and compassion in the criminal justice system:
Is it worth it?
Alan Jermey   45

Everyone Needs Good Neighbours
HM Prison Northumberland   52

Hope – Above All, Give Us Hope
Graham Johnson   53

Talking About Listening
Simon Kenny   56

Shining a light on good practice
John Dodd   63

It is always darkest before the dawn
HM Prison Wandsworth   70

Section 2
Examining the system   71

A parallel universe a mutated imitation of normal
Anonymous   73

Home is Where You Are
Low Newton   74

Casting off the gilded blindfold: The role of judges in
creating a fairer, more rehabilitative, justice system
His Honour John Samuels QC   75

Binding our wounds: Compassion and hope in tackling
racial disparity
Phil Bowen   83

Kindness and Accountability: Lessons from the City College
Basketball Scandal in New York
Greg Berman   88

Hope, compassion and kindness: reflections from the scottish violence
reduction unit
Niven Rennie   92

Police Officers as Peace Officers: the role of Kindness in Policing
Dr Peter Neyroud CBE QPM PhD   100

A practical reflection on global perspectives of youth justice –
how kindness, hope and compassion deliver effective youth
justice systems
David McGuire   104

Window of Opportunity
HM Prison Isle of Wight (Albany)   110

The Butterfly Effect
Mr Gee   111

We are doing the best we can with a very bad system
Marianne Moore   114

Compassionate custody?
Dave Nicholson   121

A brighter future: the role of hope in women's rehabilitation
Olivia Dehnavi   130

Understanding and changing the narrative
Shola Apena Rogers   137

After A Mild Rebuke
Anonymous   145

Ensuring restorative justice goes viral – time for a second surge?
Dr Belinda Hopkins   146

Restorative justice, putting the heart into the criminal justice system
Pete Wallis   155

Section 3
The frontline practitioner perspective   165

Grab the opportunities
Idris Jaulin   167

The Mask
HMP Dovegate   168

Charity, kindness, hope and compassion
Anne Fox   169

Kindness in prisons
Gerard Lemos   177

Meeting Shame with Kindness, Hope and Compassion
Charlie Rigby   183

Kindness: A compelling virtue in the criminal justice and desistance trajectory
Revd Dr Carver Anderson   189

Love Actually: Why we need love and empathy in services and systems
Sarah Wilkinson & Anne-Marie Douglas   195

A Window of Turbulence
HM Prison Holme House   203

Circles of Support and Accountability: reducing shame, bringing hope and preventing further victims of sexual abuse
Riana Taylor, CEO of Circles UK   204

Coaching: Tough Questions, Brave Answers
Ben Amponsah, Clare McGregor & Jules Roberts   212

The complexity of compassion
Alice Dawnay   221

The transformative power of recognising suffering
Jo Hobson and Keziah Poultney   228

Window of Opportunity
HMP YOI Parc   237

Supporting people to be out, out
Tracy Hammond   238

Compassion in the Criminal Justice System
John Bayley   246

Seeing the person
Tanjit Dosanjh   250

Free
Guernsey Prison 253

On kindness as "being solid": visible presence and icons in
institutional caring
Father Richard Rene 254

Searching for hope, kindness and compassion in the
Criminal Justice System? Find your local women's centre
Angela Collins 258

A peaceful oasis in an unforgiving desert
Deborah Murphy 266

Ward B11
HMP Low Moss 274

Lessons on kindness, hope and compassion from a Philippine prison
Trevor Urch 275

Hope: the role of the law in motivating change
Juan Periago Morant 281

A Personal Journey of Kindness, Hope & Compassion
Gary Stephenson 290

Lighting up my sky
Anonymous 295

How can kindness and compassion shape probation?
Rhian Metcalfe 296

A therapeutic lens on compassionate care:
Encountering the inner child in a forensic mental health setting
Belinda Sherlock 304

Twisted trolls or special souls?
HMP Low Moss 313

Be me to understand me
J Storell 316

We Will Meet Again
HMP The Verne 317

Contributors 319

References 337

RESISTING THE TIDE – HOPE IN THE FACE OF INJUSTICE AND OPPRESSION

Mark Alexander

If there is hope in prisons, it is found in the individual men and women struggling to survive each passing day. Having already spent a decade behind bars for a crime I did not commit, I see hope as a form of resistance in the face of injustice and oppression. At its heart, 'hope' engenders a refusal to accept the nature of one's present condition as somehow inevitable, final, and irredeemable. The desire to change one's circumstances really amounts to a belief that change is both necessary and possible.

Certain academics have described how prisoners simply learn to "swim with the tide", "yielding to rather than opposing the flow of life", but this does not reflect my own experience. Casting prisoners in the hopeless, passive role of a submissive subject, unquestioningly resigned to their fate, is – in the most part – a mischaracterisation. Hope is alive and well in prisons, embedded in the very process of coping and survival itself. Above all, hope is a positive act: resisting the tide and asserting one's autonomy, rather than being swept away.

FOREWORD

Lady Edwina Grosvenor

The penal apparatus world wide, ensnares millions of human beings who are unfortunate enough to get caught in its web and sadly, more often than not, they will emerge more damaged than when they first arrived. This of course is not what anyone wants, yet it is where we are. It is absolutely within our gift to change this but it will require a colossal mindset shift which prioritises qualities that many see as weak in a hyper masculine system.

A wide range of experts explain why it is of *vital* importance that we encourage live saving qualities and behaviours such as kindness, compassion and hope to infiltrate our Justice system at every level and at every juncture. The route to doing this is illustrated so beautifully in the collection of essays in this book.

Human transformation and change so often happen in deep moments of connection with others. Every interaction has the ability to be an intervention and this should never be overlooked. We must bring emotional intelligence to the fore and be led by its positive force, by warmth, care, love and patient understanding.

We need to encourage those who need our support to understand that they, like us, have a past to work with, but also a future to work towards. Where you go in life and how you get there is dependent on knowing where you have been and how that has shaped you. To ignore this knowledge and personal history is to carelessly throw away the solutions. We must provide an ecosystem within which humans can grow and flourish, where they can be seen and heard, not ignored and discarded onto the scrap heap of souls. Through reading this book you will undoubtedly finish it feeling thoroughly reassured and optimistic about the fact that it can, and in so many instances, is already being done.

I leave you with a question from a wise man I once had the pleasure of working for, the Bishop James Jones, Bishop of Prisons England and Wales:

"Do we want our prisons to be warehouses for the incorrigible or green houses for the redeemable?"

THE MONUMENT TRUST
INTO THE FUTURE

Mark Woodruff

Simon Sainsbury and Stewart Grimshaw established The Monument Trust in 1965, and in 2018, twelve years after Simon died, it awarded its last grants. Amid the enduring contributions that the trustees wished to see left behind, the most tangible are in the fields of arts & heritage and health. But what of Monument's work with people on the edges of society?

From the outset, Simon and Stewart were concerned for social renewal and a fair chance for those in Britain's disadvantaged communities, the homeless and those who fall on the wrong side of the law. But after the Home Secretary in 1993 declared, "prison works", promoting incarceration as the remedy for crime, social breakdown, violence and the illegal drugs industry, it soon became clear that "short, sharp" retribution to "get people off the streets" was making problems worse and multiplying their harmful effect. Numbers in prison steadily rose and, with inadequate investment in treatment, education and training, many people were released in a worsened position than before, reoffended, and went back inside, further overstretching what solutions there were. By the late 1990s, Monument was devoting a quarter of its resources each year to breaking this cycle, concerned "to keep young people out of prison and, if they do err, to ensure that they never go back". For twenty years, we invested in scores of projects, programmes and research in action to improve on what prison do positively, and, even better, to reanimate the older wisdom of prevention and motivating people with a higher vision of their future.

Time and again we found that those with no positive idea of themselves gained a sense of who they could become, because a prison worker, volunteer, teacher, therapist, coach or artist showed some belief in them. We found that cooking and baking, arts, music and performance, horticulture, enterprise, workplace skills - from making spectacles and stonemasonry to printing and design - reconnecting families, making amends to a victim, all demonstrate where someone could find they belonged in life and what they could achieve. In a word, this all comes down to kindness.

We are still too good at convicting people and locking them away, rather than addressing the underlying problems that they face in themselves and which then take their toll on others. But the trajectory of rates of reoffending has been downward for a long time, and we are thankful, by investment in such good examples, to have played our part. We believe that serious crime requires the punishment of liberty withdrawn. But we now know better ways than custody of dealing with most traumatised young people and women offenders. We know that triaging offenders to ascertain the true level of harm they risk causing, and deploying community policing to resolve trouble, then putting individuals onto the intervention they were lacking, or using the tools of reparation and restorative justice, can not only stop the problems but significantly improve a communities' strength and future prosperity. Justice services are more willing than ever to work with organisations in wider society and absorb their learning about humanity, as well as connect with the community that is vital to cementing someone's resettlement and leaving a traumatised and traumatising past behind for ever.

Five years ago, Monument realised that, while its arts, heritage and health work would endure, the powerful memory we held alongside so many charities around our foundational aim of social renewal for people might fade away. So we invited eight bodies working at the eight decisive points along the potential "Journey of an Offender" to form the core Monument Fellowship:

- Restorative Solutions, deploys Restorative Justice in the hands of police, communities and courts
- The Centre for Justice Innovation supports courts to be problem-solving, by using effective community sentences and relying less on counter-productive short sentences
- Diagrama UK brings a fresh "re-upbringing" approach to young people in care and custody
- The Good Prison, run by Lemos & Crane, enables governors and staff to rethink how they operate and harness potential already embedded in the community
- CLINKS is the strong network of organisations working in prison and after release towards the permanent resettlement of ex-offenders
- The National Criminal Justice Arts Alliance represents Monument's conviction that arts and creativity elevate the spirit and can transform people's future
- Koestler Awards develops and recognises the artistic achievement of those in custody, reshaping a prisoner's sense of who they can aspire to be
- Khulisa UK presents a person's place in a society renewed, showing "what it looks like when it's fixed", by anti-violence, hope and a stake in it to the exclusion of none.

We began with a manifesto not to criticise, or wring our hands, but to concert our efforts and distil all the wisdom from an even wider body of tested practice in the charities and services that we have worked with, as well as the crucial lived experience of those who have gone through the system. Could we provide a comprehensive response to public anxiety about offending and the criminal justice system? Conscious of a responsibility to do so, each year we have asked ourselves and our networks an open question, and then assembled the diverse and compelling responses in a book. So far we have asked, "What do prisoners and ex-offenders need to learn?", "How can we be a less violent society?", "What should happen to people who commit criminal offences?" and this year we have asked "What role do kindness, hope and compassion play in the criminal justice system?" Next year, we shall come full circle, to Monument's abiding concern for keeping young people out of the matrix of crime and punishment and prison. Monument's hope was that this unique series capturing the experience and truth of those with whom we have worked, directly and indirectly, will serve as a standing, lively account of what we have been hoping to see happening with and for people, across more than five decades.

Thirteen years ago I went to a prison to see a play performed by a mix of professional actors and prisoners. It was a revelation. When it was over and prisoners were led back to their cells, the audience gasped when the two leads joined them. We realised the human toll on prisoners, families, normality, not forgetting the victims of their harmful crimes, when human potential is wasted. Nowadays both work in theatre as professionals using drama and imagination for keeping young people away from gangs, crime and violence. Recently, two of these young people began careers in the TV and film industry. Kindness received, kindness passed on, kindness to be recycled.

We are grateful to the Fellows, especially Khulisa UK who have curated 2020's question and responses for this volume, as well as to all the contributors who have, once again, produced a remarkable collective witness statement out of the depths of direct experience and years of reflection. In her foreword, Edwina Grosvenor, brings the considered view of a long-time ally in this field of philanthropy: that our justice system is less than what we want it to achieve, wherever it loses faith in the human capacity to make good through connection and, more decisive in the end than anything else, a change of the heart.

Mark Woodruff
The Monument Trust 2000–2019

INTRODUCTION: HUMANE JUSTICE

Lisa Rowles and Iman Haji

This is the 4th curated volume in the Monument Fellowship series that poses key questions about best practice within our criminal justice system. This year we address a fundamental cross-cutting theme, namely the application of humane values and whether they effectively underpin the system. In light of the year that was 2020, there could not have been a better theme for us to highlight.

When we began curating this book in January 2020, the strain on the system was already apparent. Her Majesty's Prison and Probation Service (HMPPS) was operating with a budget 12% lower than in 2010-11[1] and the average custodial sentence length was the highest in a decade.[2]   Staff shortages and overcrowding meant prisoners spending less time engaged in purposeful activity – in some cases, locked up for over half of the working day.[3] Self-inflicted deaths were over six times more likely in prison than in the general population[4], and in the community, suspended sentences accounted for just 3% of all sentencing.[5]

And then COVID-19 hit, exacerbating these issues and more. All social visits in prison were halted, prisoners confined to their cells 23 hours/day, having to choose between a shower or time in the open air[6]. Her Majesty's Inspector of Prisons warned of "a real risk of psychological decline among prisoners."[7] At the same time, COVID-19 related restrictions significantly impacted our court system (both Magistrates and Crown Courts)[8]; resulting in an increased remand population,[9] together with a drop in both community orders and suspended sentence orders.[10] Inevitably the impact of this crisis will continue to be felt as we continue to navigate these challenges with increasing fatigue and minimal resourcing. With the system stretched to crisis point, never has the question posed by this book, about the humane values of kindness, hope and compassion, been more appropriate to the emotional and physical safety of so many.

You will read here about the critical need for kindness, hope and compassion within our system; as well as witnessing people's stories, confirming that these very values are physically saving lives on a daily basis. Our authors speak to our shared experiences this year, to take stock and reframe our approach to life, to justice; about developing new perspectives towards the importance of hope, kindness and compassion within our society.

The book is in three key sections. First we hear the voices of those with lived experience of the system; second the authors with a wider view on how the criminal justice system operates here in the UK and globally; third and finally we hear from the frontline practitioners working within and for the system. We've aimed to create a flow, where artwork and poems from those with lived experience consistently punctuates the narrative. Despite contrasting views and methods of expression, the golden thread is a focus on the life-changing impact of kindness, hope and compassion on those who live and work within criminal justice.

Our authors with lived experience provide first hand accounts of how hope heals; how kindness both reduces the shame that incapacitates potential and promotes desistance; how compassion can be the difference between life and death. These authors cite a lack of investment in prisoners' education and rehabilitation, which ultimately results in the high recidivism rates we continue to endure.

Our 'systemic' contributors – with insights from England, Scotland, Spain, USA and Brazil – highlight that the current system of enforcement is both unsustainable and obstructive to effective rehabilitation. Authors advocate for strengths-based approaches, community participation, restorative justice, problem-solving courts and improved relational health in rehabilitating offenders. This section explores the power of compassionate community policing in preventing harm, together with the opportunity the Black Lives Matter movement provides for a communal commitment for healing.

In our third section, frontline 'practitioners' explore different operating environments (including Spain, Canada and The Philippines); yet share the commonality of hope as a critical factor for change, borne out of kindness and practical compassion – attributes without which the system cannot function effectively. These personal accounts highlight that self discipline nurtures desistance, empowered through co-created communities of care; battling to break down perceived dichotomies between victim and offender that continue to preclude progress and promote shame.

We hope that this book inspires, challenges, empowers and encourages the reader to take action in support of justice reform, desistance and enabling effective rehabilitation. We hope that you feel moved to make personal and institutional changes. If this book enables you to shift yours and/or others perspectives on the importance of humane justice (hope, kindness and compassion) within the criminal justice system and beyond; if it helps you to understand how to make changes to achieve this, we will have succeeded in our message. Our invitation is to share this message widely.

Acknowledgements

We would like to express our deepest appreciation to all our contributors without whom this book would not exist. Thank you for your commitment, enthusiasm and patience; and for trusting us to share your heart-felt narrative to a wider audience. It's an honour to share all of your stories. We are especially proud to share contributions from people in prison, many of whom answered our call for essays from prison during a pandemic.

We are also extremely grateful to all of our colleagues within the Monument Fellowship for their support and introductions to many of this years' contributors. In particular, we extend our gratitude to Mark Woodruff, of the Woolbeding Charity (formerly known as the Monument Trust) for his encouragement and advice, which has been indispensable to us in curating this volume. Sincere thanks also to colleague and Fellow, Sally Taylor of Koestler Arts for the incredible artwork and poetry shared here from applicants to this year's Koestler Awards.

We would also like to acknowledge Soruche Sajeedi of the Prisoner Policy Network at the Prison Reform Trust, who played an instrumental role in keeping us connected to prison-based authors during this process; Tom Keates-Miles for the design of this year's book; Lady Edwina Grosvenor for taking the time to write our Foreword; Jo Farrar, Frances Mapstone, Raphael Rowe, Max Rutherford and James Timpson, who each took the time to read and endorse this book and finally to our colleagues at Khulisa who supported us this year in completing this curated volume.

From our hearts to yours – Thank you.

SECTION 1

THE VOICE OF LIVED EXPERIENCE

KINDNESS IS A WELCOMING
SMILE AND A SLICE OF CAKE

Anonymous

Before I went to prison, I associated them with big grey cell blocks, guards on every landing and of violence everywhere. Coming from a fortunate, close knit and eccentric family, my mother taught me to never judge and to treat people how I'd like to be treated: with the utmost respect.

48 hours into my sentence, and after puddles of tears, I was scared to even show my face on the wing. Four days in, a 6"4 inmate entered my cell and closed the door behind him. All my worst feelings crept in. My body tightened, my emotions were in a flurry and I prepared myself for a welcome beating.

To my surprise, but not my mum's, I realised that I had judged too early and jumped to my own conclusions. I was simply being welcomed with a slice of cake and a subtle smile.

Within the next 3 days, I got to know everyone on the wing and gained the respect of my respectful and considerate inmates. I was taken under the wing by another prisoner who had been there longer than I had. I saw my upbringing reflected in this prisoner, he echoed the kindness I learned and developed through my childhood.

When he left prison, I used this experience to help prisoners new to the wing feel welcomed and safe. A simple hello and engagement in conversation goes a long way in a place so dark and shallow.

Everyday civilians cannot picture putting the words kindness, hope and compassion in the same sentence as the word prison, but truth be told the right people use these expressions every day in the Criminal Justice System.

RANDOM ACTS OF KINDNESS

The Tartan Con

I am an ex-prisoner.

In my time in prison I witnessed, and was the beneficiary of, so many random acts of kindness by both my fellow prisoners and staff alike. I have no deeper belief than this: not only can compassion and kindness help those in prison find their path to rehabilitation kindness, kindness and compassion can save lives. Their impact cannot be under-estimated.

In this chapter, I cite two personal experiences as evidence of this.

During my time in prison, my form of self-harming was to starve myself. I had stopped eating, save for one price of dry Ryvita (other cardboard is available!) and my BMI went to an almost critical level. During this time, my fellow prisoners celebrated Ramadan. At the end of Ramadan, the festival of Eid took place. This is where those involved in Ramadan met in a hall and celebrated Eid where food, of all sorts was plentiful.

After the feast, prisoners were allowed to take leftover food back to their cells with them. This celebration took place during one of the times I was starving myself as a means of self-harm. I had not gone outside in the fresh air for over 9 months and had not left my wing for an equal amount of time.

I lived on an open wing. At the end of the evening of celebration, I heard someone walk past my room. There was a knock on the door. I left my bed to go and answer it. Upon opening the door, I found no one there. I looked down and found a tray of food left for me. No name, no message, just the food. That was a random act of kindness and compassion I had never experienced before. For the first time in many months, I smiled that night. Someone, I still do not know who, had taken their food and given it to a fellow human being who they knew to be suffering. Their compassion was humbling to experience.

My second experience of kindness came from the other side of the door.

I decided to end my life and picked the exact time and the method. It was to be one morning in May of a certain year. The day before, my personal officer had come to see me as he heard I was struggling. *"TC, I am busy right now, but I will come back and see you later,"* he said. He did not.

I felt worthless and decided to press on with my plan to commit suicide at 06:00 the next morning.

However, it was thwarted by such an amazing act of compassion. At 05:30 that morning, the duty officer said there was a call for me in the office. Anxiously, I opened my door.

"Don't worry its nothing bad, you can take the call if you want," he told me. *"I will just leave your door open."*

I went to the office on the wing, picked up the phone and said a very tentative *"Hello?"*

"Hi XXXX," came the reply. *"It's XXXXX, sorry for no seeing you again yesterday. Listen it's my day off, would you like me to come in and talk to you?"*

THAT... that act of kindness is what allowed me to be here and write this to you today.

To the question of what role does compassion play in the criminal justice system, I say this: it saves lives.

Home is Where You Are, Low Newton

Image courtesy of Koestler Arts

THE LIGHT OF COMPASSION WILL SHINE BRIGHTEST IN THE DARKEST PLACES

Jayne Richards

A Voice from the Inside

July 18, 2005. I was sitting in an upright coffin, a tin can sweatbox, with several other similar caged animals, heading to our respective holding pens. I felt numb, nauseous and unable to face the reality of what was happening.

I could hear others shouting angrily at the security team or comparing notes on their cases. All I could think about was the baby son that I might never see again, the pain in my parents' eyes as judgement was passed, the hell my actions put people through. It was all too much to process. I felt the deepest sense of self-hatred. I shut down. When I was finally deposited in the prison reception, I was stopped in my tracks by the television showing the latest news on BBC news channel. My once soulmate smiled brightly in an old photograph as the reporter explained the verdict in my case.

I screamed – at least I think it was me who screamed – and my legs sagged. Immediately, one of the prison officers demanded the TV be switched off as she helped me to my feet, gently leading me to a processing area. She fetched me water. I was not prepared for kindness, having heard such terrible things during my trial. I did not believe that I deserved compassion, but I was shown it, and that is when I finally let the tears tumble down my cheeks.

I arrived at HMP Styal at a time that coincided with the BBC filming the documentary 'Women on the Edge' following a significant increase in suicide and self-harm rates. My days were peppered with alarm bells, my nights filled with tortured screams, the occasional fire and a few hostage situations. It disturbs me now, that we were all so used to the everyday horrors that we became oblivious to it. It was normal; seeing the mess some women made of themselves with a makeshift blade, the daily battles staff had to save lives, anguished screams followed by other inmates' demands to 'Shut the f--- up' were routine. After three months, I was relocated to a lifer unit in the South of England.

I was housed in a block with 39 other life-sentenced women, which is when reality finally hit me. Three months after being incarcerated, I mentally imploded. My new focus was how to succeed in taking my own life. Anyone that I thought would try to prevent me from achieving my goal became an enemy. I would not engage. I trusted no one and so I became more isolated and non-communicative.

An uncomfortable truth

Eventually my mental state became too staff-intensive to manage on the unit, so I was moved to the healthcare wing. It was here, with the support of both psychiatrists and healthcare staff, with enormous patience and compassion that things began to change. It came to a head during a call to my mother, who at that time was caring for my beautiful son. I sobbed and stammered about how much I had taken, that I wanted to be at peace and stop the demons and that I didn't deserve to be alive. Her reply to me was the catalyst for change, like someone switching on a bright light at the end of a very long dark tunnel, she said, "Please don't do this… don't leave this gorgeous little boy an orphan in this world".

It was time for me to start thinking of others, to try to make a better person of myself, to focus on getting back to my son and family.

Contrary to popular belief, there is no stereotypical female prisoner. Of course, much like the male estate there are a proportion of women who have almost grown up in prison and are caught in the 'revolving doors' cycle of the criminal justice system. However, they do not make up the majority. Not all women sent to prison have substance misuse issues or are repeat offenders. Many, like me, have never had so much as a parking ticket prior to their first offence. Many are professional, have careers, young families and have appeared, on the surface, to be well-balanced individuals prior to committing that offence.

In going to prison, I cared nothing for myself. I hated myself and couldn't come to terms with what I had done. However, in the early days, when my ageing parents would bring my baby son to a prison visit, it would be more torturous than any sentence a judge could pass. My son would grip his tiny fists around my prison issue sweatshirt tightly and scream to a pitch that would pierce my heart, as my sobbing mother tried to prize him away when all visitors were asked to leave. I had to help pull his tiny fingers away from me and say goodbye when everything in my being wanted to cling to him and never let him go.

This is not an isolated case. A huge proportion of women and girls in prison have children at home. Children often - through no fault of their own - end up being moved around the care system, struggling to express their own fear and their need for love. Many of their mothers behind bars have gone through the exact same childhood trauma. This cycle can continue unless someone helps guide these young women away from the paths their circumstances have led them to; often the victims of abuse - be it physical, sexual, psychological, emotional or financial – and whilst *still children*.

Not every woman or girl who experiences abuse goes on to commit a crime of course. Many choose another option ... suicide. I myself have attempted this on many occasions, both prior to and after I committed my offence. Paradoxically, rather than being relieved that I didn't succeed, I felt shame and frustration that I couldn't even get that right. I don't say this lightly, as several of my friends in prison have been successful in taking their lives. The only way out they felt they had.

You see, simply locking these women away - alone in a cell or with other women with complex needs for 23 hours, a day, with nothing but their tormented thoughts for company - will never fix what went wrong in their lives.

The transformative impact of kindness, compassion and hope

If that were the end of the story, I would not be writing this now. My first experience of a criminal justice charity was with Only Connect, at HMP Holloway. I did not make it easy for Emma and Danny, the founders of the charity, to get through to me. Nevertheless, with gritty determination and unyielding faith in humanity, they dragged me from that bottomless pit and helped me view myself differently. Not by telling me but by believing in me, having faith in me and allowing me to see for myself what I was capable of.

From those first tentative steps, gradually came strides and from strides came leaps. All because someone had the patience and belief that I could do it and enabled me to see myself through different eyes. There are other people, whose care and compassion for others, despite their circumstances, are perhaps unknowingly huge influences on those in their care, turning their lives around. Prison staff, governors, offender supervisors, psychologists, chaplains and tutors all play their part. Not everyone who works within the CJS has these qualities unfortunately. Some can be cruel, but the kindness of those who have these qualities, can far outweigh the impact of those who do not.

That is something that is evident in all who work for the third sector in the criminal justice system. I count myself fortunate as one of those passionate people, blessed to work with some amazing, caring and non-judgmental people at Catch22.

However, this supportive attitude towards those of us within and exiting the criminal justice system is not commonplace. There is a palpable anxiety amongst women, who really want to make a better life for themselves and their families, about being accepted; a fear that they will always be judged by their past and will never truly serve their sentence, despite their rehabilitation. Mainstream employers also generally have a negative view of ex-offenders, irrespective of the work that those individuals may do to improve their chances of employment and a better life upon release. Did you know that more than 11 million people in the UK have a criminal record? That is a huge amount of people potentially frozen out of the workplace. Add to that the element of stigma, shame and precarious self-worth; it's not surprising that some go back to the same behaviour they exhibited before committing their offence. I was fortunate enough to have been employed by Only Connect whilst still in custody and attending work on ROTL; and although some women will also be supported into work as part of resettlement, this does not always mean that the job continues upon release.

The year of my release from prison, I graduated, achieving a BA (Hons) alongside being awarded an arts scholarship. I am not saying that it was easy studying in prison or that it did not at times seem an insurmountable challenge; but those first steps working with Only Connect planted a seed in my mind to go after the dreams I had when I was young, despite my situation.

So here I am, living proof that this method works. That even the most troubled amongst us can turn their lives around and play our own part in making our communities safer and happier places to live in. Many women in my situation arrive at the prison gates broken - but not irreparable. Most can be helped way before they enter the criminal justice system if only someone would listen, understand and support them. I am not suggesting that the road to a better life is easy for these women, or that they won't face challenges along the way, but with the right support networks and sense of purpose, it will be achievable.

I'm delighted that I am now able to help others through working for Catch22 Justice. The wonderful feeling of seeing tangible evidence that faith is well placed in those we support swells the heart and feeds the soul. Better still, is the effect it has on the individual, how proud they become of their achievements and becoming assets to their communities.

It is not easy writing this and baring my soul to you, but it is most definitely something I choose to do, with a belief that it might enable you to hear the reality of those blighted by bad choices and living with the consequences every day of their lives. I have chosen to speak at many events, not only through the Catch22 family but also for HMPPS, Prisoners Education Trust, Koestler trust and Lifelines, as well as through Amnesty International. My reasoning is always that it might open people's minds to the potential of those that have been in prison. To not write us off, to not talk about "criminals" dismissively as though we are all one group with one motivation. From my perspective, most often, we are a group of people with no voice, looking for support to take the next step.

Steps to change: Creating a kinder, more compassionate and hope engendering system

We all share a unique commonality: our humanity. We have the same basic needs, whether man, woman or child. I believe these fundamental principles apply to all and are intrinsic to reforming our criminal justice system. These will enable people, through support, to lead safer and more fulfilled lives, contributing positively to their communities, and - at its most basic level - reducing the burden on taxpayers and our overpopulated prisons. Healthy relationships, employment and criminal justice system involvement are interrelated and can have substantial effects on one another. Essentially, there are 3 overarching components to the success of the rehabilitation of the individual:

- Strong and meaningful relationships with good people who care;
- A good place to live in a community where we feel safe and belong and we are able to focus on positive changes in the rest of our lives;

- Something meaningful to do, using skills and opportunity to make an honest living

On this basis, and from personal lived experience, I can summarise the critical factors:

1. Be more human

If we treat a person like an animal, we should not be surprised if they act as one. Instead, treat everyone with the same basic principle of human dignity irrespective of his or her mistakes, flaws, class, race, gender, abilities or anything other than them being human.

2. Put relationships at the heart of rehabilitation

All evidence shows that strong, consistent and meaningful human relationships, based on mutual trust, understanding and empathy, lead to good outcomes. Their absence leads to bad outcomes.

3. Intervene early, in the community

Early interventions are proven to reduce the likelihood of a person developing criminal behaviour. We are all responsible for ensuring the developing child has a positive self-image, a sense of belonging and feels safe in their environment.

4. Engage communities

We all need to feel a sense of belonging. Often fear can lead to the way we consider those that have committed a crime. If as communities - instead of judging people by their past – we stand by and support them, as they move into their future, we will enable them to change and become assets not liabilities to these communities.

5. Help businesses realise the benefits of employing ex-offenders

We know that unemployment leads to a significant risk of re-offending. However, ex-offenders who want to gain employment are often impeded from doing so by the distrust and stigma associated with having a criminal record. In order, to counter this, it is essential that businesses are educated, perhaps even incentivised, to play an essential part in breaking the cycle of criminal behaviour by investing in those who are marginalized by their past.

Where there is light, there is hope

I would like to finish by commending charities like Catch22 and Khulisa, on behalf of those they support for having faith in them and working with them to realise their potential to have better lives. I would not have been able to share my story with you were it not for some incredibly kind and inspirational people who saw something in me I could not see myself. I am often humbled by the fact that they retain their open minds and hearts, despite at times dealing with particularly harrowing cases. We all work towards a common goal of making our communities safer places and helping others come to terms with a trauma in their life, so they can go on to lead happier lives.

It is no exaggeration to say that kindness, hope and compassion saved my life. And it has the potential to save many more, even when it may seem the situation is hopeless, and people cannot be rescued.

As Harvey MacKay said,

"If you get a chance, take it. If it changes your life, let it. Nobody said life would be easy, they just promised it would be worth it."

'HOPE – THE EXIT RAMP FROM CRIME TO 'HEALED OFFENDER'

Callum Hutchison

When I think of kindness, hope and compassion I do not automatically think of the justice system. For me, that is the problem. Our justice system is built to find the truth about a crime that has been committed. I believe that is necessary. But what comfort does it bring to a victim of crime if the offender is incarcerated for a period and returns to the community to commit the same offence? The justice is short lived and is nothing more than a sticking plaster for a wound that is far deeper than it may appear on the surface. What if we treated the addict who was a prolific shoplifter for his addiction? And in addition to that provided trauma counselling and a blueprint to treat his addiction instead? It would give the offender an opportunity to get clean and sober, live an honest and responsible life without the need to shoplift again. Surely, this is a far better outcome than a 12-month prison sentence, after which the person is returned to the same environment with the same tools and unhealthy coping strategies. How can we expect them to have learned their lesson and stop offending? We have been doing this for centuries now and I'm yet to see the evidence that it works.

I am not for a minute suggesting that we allow crimes to go unpunished. If you break the law there must be a consequence. However, when we house offenders in prison what are we actually doing with them to ensure - when they return to the community after a custodial sentence - that they will not offend again? What hope are we providing the public that an offender for assault has taken an inventory of his behavior and will not commit a similar offence again? I have navigated the Justice system since I was 16 years old. My previous convictions are all for violence and absolutely every time I committed a violent offence I deserved to be in prison. Yet there was always a common denominator in my offending and that was alcohol. I have never committed an offence sober minded. I have been through both the youth custodial estate and the adult prison system, not once was it suggested to me that I should do something about my drinking. I was labeled a 'Ned' - a violent criminal who deserved to be locked up for the rest of his life. However, the bravado, the swagger, the growl – my 'mask' – just hid the pain and fear. So, let me take you on a journey of how kindness, hope and compassion can save a dying man's life.

A lethal absence of hope

Chaos and violence were my life for a long time. A lethal absence of hope was taking me to a destination of either prison for the rest of my life or an early grave. I was a regular attender at the Glasgow Sheriff Court and the Glasgow Royal Infirmary. The destination did not matter; the perception was much the same. If I was wheeled into the emergency department of the Royal Infirmary with another knife injury, the perception of the police would be, "*Aye, but what did you do to deserve this? Just another Ned in another gang fight.*" If I was led off the back of a G4S van into the dungeons of the Sheriff court, the narrative would be similar, "*Just another Ned who deserves to be locked up for good.*" No one recognized the boy who was diagnosed with PTSD at 17 years of age and was self-medicating with alcohol and drugs. When you grow up in an environment that has high levels of crime and criminality, it is a difficult place to thrive and be the best version of yourself. I felt for a long time I was on the margins of society looking in. I was written off by society as someone who was never going to change.

On January 28th 2017, I was violently assaulted and stabbed 9 times. I thought that was it; my life was over. I was going to die like so many young men do in a pool of their own blood in The East End of Glasgow. I was rushed into A&E in the back of an ambulance. That had been done so many times in my life; but this time I was beat, mentally and emotionally and now physically. I was 26, a father of 2 and a partner. I had everything to live for, but that right there was the problem. I did not know how to live. My problem was trauma, poor life skills, addiction, broken relationships. Dealing with life was my problem. Going from prison to community often brought me fear, anxiety and worry, as I knew I had to try again at the game called life, without the required tools. Ultimately, I would fail. Truth is, I had a desire to stop offending and change my life – I just did not know how to.

I arrived in resus and the amazing doctors and nurses worked on me for hours to keep me alive. Horror came over me when I realised I had survived and would be returning to the madness. Outside, there were a few police officers waiting for the go ahead to try to take a statement so they could go catch the "bad guys." Inside, there were loads of medical staff attaching me to drips and other lifesaving equipment and a guy in a pink t-shirt. He made his way through and knelt down beside my bed. He had a lanyard around his neck with some photo ID on it. I knew by his distinctive pink t-shirt that he was not a police officer, nurse or a doctor. He crouched down beside my bed and introduced himself as Alan. He was a Navigator from the Violence Reduction Unit (VRU). He asked if there was anything he could help me with. I asked him for some water, and he grabbed me some. When he returned, it amazed me. He didn't ask anything about my injuries. He explained a wee bit about what the Navigators are: a hospital-based intervention team who engage with people who are caught up in a cycle of violence. They worked to help navigate them to a more positive destination.

Where hope has an address

Alan treated me as a human being; he never saw the gang member or the violent offender. He saw Callum. He sat with me for hours sharing his own lived experience with me. He told me he was 7 years sober and had completely transformed his life, and more importantly, he told me how he'd done it. He gave me a huge injection of hope. I trusted the Navigators as I never felt judged by them. I felt like all they wanted to do was help me. That night I admitted to myself but also to another human being, for the first time, that I was an alcoholic. Alan told me that there was a place I could go to get sober. He navigated me into 12-step recovery. The mask was gone and the bravado replaced with desperation and a willingness to stay alive and change.

At 90 days sober, I could see life through a new set of eyes. I could also see the pain I had caused my loved ones. I knew I had to give my kids a role model, someone they could be proud of. But when you have lived a life of violence, hospital and prison most of your days, it's not an easy task. I thought about possibly doing some voluntary work because I believed I was unemployable. I discussed this with Alan the Navigator and he began to tell me more about the VRU. He told me about another programme they facilitated called Street and Arrow. Street and Arrow is an employability programme for people with an offending background; people whose previous convictions are a barrier for them to gain employment.

It is so much more than that though. It is where hope has an address for people like me, because I do not think anyone would have taken a chance on me at that point in my life.

Street and Arrow understand that a job on its own isn't the solution; there will be challenges along the way for trainees who are on the programme and they recognise the significant amounts of trauma that individuals carry. An offender who gets a job may offend again. However, a 'healed offender' will never offend again! Street & Arrow don't just offer their trainees 12 months employment (in one of their social enterprise cafes) where trainees learn a vocational practice, they also offer mentors with lived experience who trainees can access 24/7, as well as counselling sessions once a week and therapeutic group work.

This appealed to me massively. I didn't know anywhere where having a criminal record could actually be an advantage. It was time for Alan to drop the bombshell. He told me that if I was interested I would need to go for an interview with an inspector of Police Scotland, as the VRU is a Police Scotland unit.

Now, the belief system I grew up with – which was learned behavior – was that all cops were the enemy. They didn't want to help people like me, they wanted to lock me up for life and throw away the key. Alan explained to me that these police officers were not like that and they wanted to help guys like me. The belief system that I grew up with was being challenged. Truth was I didn't have a list of people who were willing to help me, so I went and met this Police Inspector. He welcomed me and spoke about why he was so passionate about the approach of the VRU and Street and Arrow. He asked me about my life and I gave him an honest account of how my life had been up until that point. He said to me, '*Callum, that's your past. I'm not interested in that. That can go in the bin, as far as I'm concerned. I'm interested in your future. What does that look like?*' I said, '*I want to be a sober responsible father who has some peace in his life*'. He told me I could start on Monday. I left that meeting feeling very emotional. I felt for the first time in my life that someone believed in me, even when I didn't believe in myself. He knew my past and never judged me for it. He saw the potential in me, he saw that I was far more than the worst thing I had ever done.

Finding my true self

I went through the Street and Arrow programme, an abstinence-based programme, for 12 months. The programme was life changing for me: I was sober and I used it as another form of support to my recovery.

Street and Arrow also pays trainees the living wage (approximately £16,000 a year). This allowed me to provide for my family legitimately and I was contributing to society by paying taxes. Whilst £16,000 per year may sound like a lot of money, in truth it costs the taxpayer approximately £40,000 to keep a prisoner in prison for 12 months. I was able to find my true self at Street and Arrow. I found I had a skill set that I never knew I had before. Street and Arrow's goal is to help move trainees on to full time employment, at the end of the 12 months, having engaged with the support on offer during their traineeship and addressed the causes and conditions of their offending. I realised I wanted to help people like me to get off the path of chaos and violence and navigate them towards the exit ramp. I had this discussion with the Inspector who was the project lead. He recognised I had a skill for this and said he wanted to keep me on as a mentor. I graduated the Street and Arrow programme to become the first trainee to become a full-time mentor. I mentored the new trainees on the programme, providing them with hope of what could be achieved if they gave themselves to the programme. I case managed them and supported their wellbeing throughout their traineeship.

Alan the Navigator joined Street and Arrow when I was a mentor and 18 months after showing me the way out of a chaotic life – we were colleagues, working alongside each other providing hope for others. I became the lead mentor on the Street and Arrow programme, teaching best practice to other mentors who joined us. In 2019, I won a Community Champion award for the work I did with people who have convictions as well as my work to develop intervention programmes for young people on the cusp of the criminal justice system. I now work to redirect them to a more positive destination using my lived experience. Most of all, I'm getting them to believe they are so much more than the worst thing they have ever done. I'm now a Development Officer for the VRU, developing services that work with individuals society deems hard to reach. I say they are not hard to reach at all - they are easy to lock up and ignore. We reach these individuals by showing them compassion, kindness and a huge injection of hope – exactly how I was helped.

If I could look back and give advice to my 16-year-old self, based on what I know now, I would tell him: *It is ok to be scared. Not everything that happened to you was your fault. You are so much better than the worst thing you have ever done. I understand you may not see the light and the end of the tunnel yet but it's coming. One day all the stuff that didn't make sense is going to make sense and it will become one of your best assets. You will use it to help others find the exit ramp to hope.*

KINDNESS, HOPE AND COMPASSION: A MATTER OF LIFE AND DEATH FOR THOSE IN PRISON

Brenda Birungi

To answer this question I had to first ask myself another question. Can there be or is there kindness, hope and compassion in the criminal justice system, and if so where is it?

I think the women and men who live behind those walls with no names create a space for kindness, hope and compassion in the criminal justice system. The hearts that can only love from afar, the eyes that see the things no one else wants to see, the souls of broken promises, unheard screams and secret tears that can only be felt or relived from behind those walls.

When I first arrived in prison I was afraid of everyone, especially those who seemed too kind. How could I fear kindness? I knew from TV shows, fake news and articles that in prison kindness comes at a cost. I feared what I would have to do to repay that kindness.

What I found was that most women just wanted to be heard and seen. The older women would naturally take on the mothering role to all the younger women, I was only twenty one years old when I was sent to prison. I'm not going to lie to you and say everyone is nice to you from the very start, but once one person brings you in, everyone else starts to be drawn to you.

After I got over my fear of being in prison and stopped hating myself for messing up my life, I started to have compassion for myself and the many women I had now become friends with. I started to be more understanding of other people's pain and suffering – something that I once thought I would never understand. All these feelings and emotions made me question life after prison and if any of us would ever get the chance to live it. That's when hope for the future was born deep within me. That hope came from the women I met in prison, the friends I made there that had been released and not returned and the ones who had managed to find work and would write to me about how they did it. But the women who gave me the most hope were:

- The women who still lived with me in prison;
- The women who couldn't see their kids but still checked in on other women to make sure they were okay;
- The ones whose appeals had been turned down but still pushed me to have faith;
- The women who after living in the UK made one mistake that landed them in prison, which resulted in them being served deportation paperwork, but somehow still found the strength to support others going through it.

The men and women who live behind those walls with no names mostly take on the role for kindness, hope and compassion in the criminal justice system. However I think every single person who walks through those gates should take on that role, prison staff, volunteers, outside organisations, everyone. In fact, I think before they are even allowed to work behind those gates, they should prove how they meet these qualities, after all, as inmates before we can be released we have to prove or display how we have changed our way of thinking. Therefore, I think anyone working within the criminal justice system should show they deserve to work with us, because working within the criminal justice system with those qualities is rewarding.

It's simple really, let's solve this problem:

You are a prison officer and it's time for bang up. One inmate is refusing to go behind their door. She says she just needs to make a quick phone call, she seems very distressed, tearing up and is starting to shout. What do you do?

1. Lock her behind her door first to teach her a lesson?

2. Tell her to quickly try to go and make the call as you lockup everyone else?

Some officers may say if they allow that inmate to make that call it would make them look weak to other inmates. I say it would make them look like they have a heart. I repaid every officer who showed me kindness with respect. Inmates share information just like officers do.

What if I told you that if you say no to that lady and locked her up first to teach her a lesson, it could be the last lesson she will learn, because she may not be alive by the next roll check. If you allow her to make that call, you may just be saving her life, and giving her hope in at least one officer.

So, what is the role for kindness, hope and compassion in the criminal justice system? I say it's a matter of life or death.

A KIND PRISON

Nick Moss

Introduction

As an ex-prisoner, I baulked at first at this question. Apart from wanting to simply give an answer parodying Mahatma Gandhi's apocryphal response when asked his thoughts on Western civilization ("I think it would be a good idea"); I was initially convinced that kindness as an act was an exchange between individuals. As such, it was not something that could be applied as a standard in relation to institutions. Institutions should be judged on the extent to which they uphold and respect the rights incorporated into law of those who come into contact with them. Kindness is meaningless in this context. Having started from that point, though, I became less convinced that I was correct.

The Collins Online Dictionary defines "Kindness" as the quality of being gentle, caring, and helpful. The Macmillan online dictionary gives its etymology as coming from the Old English word 'kyndnes' meaning 'nation' or 'produce, increase'. The word is further derived from the Middle English word 'kindenes' meaning 'noble deeds' or 'courtesy'. Let 's try then to conceive of a starting point for the question that draws all of this together – that kindness can be the act of a nation, or, logically, an institution within and of a nation, which constitutes a "noble deed". A gentle, caring and helpful act. Let that be our definition – a caring, gentle and noble act carried out by an institution.

I want this to be the starting point because any other would be banal. Any prisoner can recall the kindness of other cons. The things added onto someone else's canteen sheet out of friendship, the coffee shared, the door open for a sit down and a talk when the outside world crashes in with some bad news over which you have no control. We can all remember that acts of solidarity carry more risk and involve having to take on an institution that, in the end, can always resort to force, and out-violence its challengers. We will remember too that within the institutional context of prison life there are staff who go out of their way to acknowledge that prisoners are human beings, not chattel; who will pass a joke, ask if someone's ok, give you a cheery "Mornin" during free flow, listen when someone's in meltdown. Jail is not always a battleground between cons and staff. But unless prison as an institution has a "noble" intent then the "gentle and caring acts" which may take place within its walls necessarily lose value.

A current example: The coronavirus crisis

As an extreme example of prisons demonstrating a complete lack of kindness, let's take the government response to the coronavirus outbreak. In March 2020 the Iranian judiciary said it had so far released 85,000 prisoners in response to the coronavirus pandemic. This was in marked contrast to the UK Ministry of Justice, which had at that point refused to consider any such measures. Prisons Minister Lucy Frazer said that prisons were (of course) acting "based on the very latest scientific and medical advice" and plans were in place to enable prisoners to be given single cells to self-isolate where necessary.[1] Where these single cells would appear from in already overcrowded prisons, where prisoners are warehoused 2–3 in a cell, was left unclear. Of those perhaps asymptomatic already – in shared cells – nothing was said.

Andrea Albutt, President of the Prison Governors Association has said, "In prisons we don't completely mirror society with our demographic of prisoners, so we do have a higher number of people in the vulnerable groups, so they will be ill and there will be deaths."[2] These comments were not reported by the majority of the news media. Prisons are overcrowded and unhygienic, with poor healthcare regimes. The Secretary of State has publicly accepted that the prison population will need to be reduced and a substantial number of prisoners will need to be released in order to save lives in response to the Covid-19 pandemic. The Ministry of Justice accepted that that on present accommodation levels, between 10,000 and 15,000 would have to be released to achieve single cell occupancy. As of 14 April 2020, according to figures from the Howard League, just 18 people had been released under the COVID-related accelerated release scheme (0.02% of the prison population).[3] The refusal to adopt early release as a response to the impact of coronavirus on UK prisons is as far removed from "kindness" as is conceivable. It goes alongside a denial of visits and information to prisoners and families that leaves the UK government trailing in the wake of regimes like Turkey and Iran (regimes condemned by Amnesty International as "inhumane.") When Priti Patel said she wanted offenders to "feel terror", perhaps this callous neglect is what she envisaged.

We have, then, a clear example of what an institution operating without "noble intent" might look like. It is not a unique example in the history of the prison estate in England and Wales. Lord Justice Woolf's 1991 Report into the Strangeways revolt can serve as a useful source of reference.[4] In the period immediately prior to the Strangeways revolt, one wing at Strangeways was found to require integral sanitation. The certified normal level of accommodation was 970. On 1 April the population was 1,647. Lord Justice Woolf noted an inadequate regime, poor standards of hygiene, and repeated prisoner complaints of arbitrary and oppressive behaviour on the part of some officers. "Over-taut staffing levels would make it difficult to provide a consistent and constructive regime which would have helped to alleviate the dehumanizing effects of the insanitary and unsatisfactory conditions within the prison."[5]

Lord Justice Woolf concluded that there was a common theme in prisoners' evidence (of a lack of justice) particularly in relation to transfers, and conditions. He also noted that the "need to maintain security and control needs to be balanced against the danger that an excessive emphasis on them can have the opposite effect." Alternatively, to put it more plainly than Lord Woolf's careful phrasing, if you treat people like animals, eventually they'll bite back.

There was nothing surprising in Lord Woolf's report, beyond his particular frankness about the failings he encountered. There were prison revolts in 1969, 1972, 1976, 1978, 1979, 1983, 1986 (across 40 prisons), 1988 and 1989. The same issues – overcrowding, oppression, lack of sanitation, limited time out of cell – always arose. The same recommendations were always made and never implemented. Post Woolf, some of the detail of the report was implemented – albeit haphazardly (sentence planning) and primarily as a means of control (the IEP scheme). What was significant about the Woolf Report though was that it gave significant thought to, and articulated, what might be described as the "conditions of kindness" necessary for a well-run prison estate. (I accept for the purpose of developing the theme of "kindness" that this is not the place to debate issues around abolition – the question put is being engaged with on the presumption that the prison estate exists whether we wish it to or not.) Lord Justice Wolf states that prisoners should be treated with respect if they are to treat others, both staff and prisoners, with respect. He notes that the Prison Service Statement of Purpose does not refer to treating prisoners with justice. We should ourselves then note that some 30 years on; justice still gets no mention in the updated statement. Crucially, he also states that one of the purposes of prison should be to minimise the harm done by imprisonment.

Thus, in examining the causes of the 1990 disturbances, Lord Woolf concluded that the prison environment was a) unjust and b) harmful. Subsequently, others drawn from the establishment to consider the experience of prison have expressed similar views. In a speech to the Legal Action Group, in November 2008, Lord Ramsbotham, former Chief Inspector of Prisons, commented on the Prison Service's statement of purpose:

"[Some people think prison]...should provide retribution or be a deterrent. I do not think there is any evidence that prison works as a deterrent...I have always thought that it is better to look at a more practical view of what prisons should do and I found the solution was actually there staring at us in the statement of purpose given to the Prison Service... It is our duty to help those committed by the courts to live useful and law-abiding lives in prison and on release, with the qualification that they must not be allowed to escape and they must be treated with humanity. I suggest that if the aim had been put in that way, security would have its proper place and not be considered the number one priority, as opposed to doing things with and for prisoners which is what I believe prisons ought to do."[6]

Let us put it this way. A "kind prison" would be one that seeks to remedy the harm done by the fact of imprisonment, through treating prisoners justly. This would involve, as per Lord Ramsbotham, doing things for prisoners, to help them lead useful and law-abiding lives on release. (Again, I'll postpone the necessary debates about obedience to bad laws...) There is, I think, a tension then thrown up between the Prison Rules 1999 r3 "The purpose of the training and treatment of convicted prisoners shall be to encourage and assist them to lead a good and useful life" and the idea of a "useful and law abiding-life." And it is this tension we need to push further if we want to identify the core of what a "kind" prison might be.

A "useful and law abiding life" suggests that the duty of "usefulness" is owed to society. I do not want to suggest that individuals do not owe duties – of care, respect, kindness – to those around them. This is all of a piece with functioning ethically within any society. But, surprisingly, the Prison Rules 1999 appear to hint (almost certainly unintentionally) at a wider conception of life as a "good and useful life." If a useful life is one lived with awareness of duty towards others, then a good life is one lived, in terms defined by Aristotle, in a way which is good for oneself. So to take this further, what – in the Aristotelian conception of the good life -is required to ensure this living well "for oneself"? To live well, we need, he tells us, three types of good:-

1. Bodily goods – health, vitality, vigour, and pleasure;

2. External goods – food, drink, shelter, clothing, and sleep; and

3. Goods of the soul – knowledge, skill, love, friendship, aesthetic enjoyment, self-esteem and honour.

And here's the catch. Access to bodily goods and external goods require an equal distribution of such goods within society, and equal availability of means to produce them. They are socially produced and socially distributed. Equally, "goods of the soul" cannot be developed if bodily goods and external goods are beyond reach.

So, if the kind prison is one which seeks to remedy the harm done by imprisonment, is it not also the case that it must enable prisoners to lead a "good" life by seeking to repair the damage done to prisoners by society? If prisoners are to be enabled to lead a "good life" as an objective for themselves, then it follows that prior to imprisonment there were societal obstacles to them doing so – and that they will be unable to lead a "good life" on release unless these obstacles are removed. If we release prisoners to an environment without food, clothes and shelter, they will not be able to lead a good/useful/law-abiding life and will return to prison, harmed yet further. If we slash prison education budgets and drug rehabilitation schemes, then we also deny access to the possibility of goods of the soul - knowledge, skill, love, friendship, aesthetic enjoyment, self-esteem and honour. There are always individual success stories – prisoners who can't read learning to read and prisoners who left school at 16 doing PhDs. The issue is whether such achievements are valued;

1. by the prison regime

2. by the governments who determine policy and funding.

All of the above, clearly, is no more than philosophical play. We can envisage what a "kind" prison might be like, to a point. However, there will always be that fundamental contradiction. If part of the purpose of imprisonment, as per Lord Woolf, has to be to minimise the harm done by imprisonment, what is the point of an institution that causes harm and thereby can only damage further those it is called on to help? How can an institution that does harm be kind? How likely are we to develop institutions of confinement that can undo damage caused by inequality, abuse, brutality?

At least, though, by attempting to conceive an idealised "kind" prison, we can see how far we are from such kindness and "noble purpose" today. Because today we have a prison service which is happy to release prisoners to street homelessness in the middle of a pandemic. A prison regime that, in conjunction with Public Health England has paid lip service to early release but in fact has simply implemented a restricted regime. This stopped all social visits, all education, training and employment activities (except for essential workers), all access to gyms, religious association and general association, and introduced restrictions on numbers of people unlocked, numbers of people in exercise yards at any one time.. In other words, the response to COVID-19 was simply to make prison life yet more restrictive and thereby worse, while allowing only a trickle of early releases.

To conclude, it is certainly possible to conceive of prisons run with kinder aims and objectives, and with kindness as a core aim. It is my contention though that this will never be enough to "minimise the harm done by imprisonment" and that the current practice of HM Prison Service is as far from any form of kindness as this ex-con has seen.

My Hidden Hero

ANONYMOUS, COURTESY OF THE KOESTLER TRUST

This inspiring lady
Goes by the name of Cilla
She gains the women's
Trust and respect
Being so relatable
You won't meet an officer more realer

Someone who will always listen
Supporting ladies on their journey
Here at Bronzefield Prison
Working Together
You have assisted us in recreating our own vision
Providing us with the tools we need for the future
In making a better life decision

A big helping hand
During the Covid-19 Pain
Contributing her special qualities to the job role
It's recognised by staff and residents
That all you do
Is given with your heart of gold

Acts of kindness
Should never go unnoticed
That's why I chose you as
My hidden hero
As Cilla, you truly deserve to
Be the main focus

Only hope and kindness can save us

AMANDA VISCONTI

Knots in your gut, you're on the sweatbox to hell
Inside the confinements of your temporary cell
No-one to talk to, no-one to care
Don't even know if anyone's there
Night-time arrivals are always the worst
End of the line and you're dying from thirst
Searches and questions and given a number
Supplied with a plastic plate and a tumbler

Hurried along, wishing you had died
Open the door and shut you inside
Praying the morning will bring some relief
Enough of this now, can't take any more grief

Continual banging, shouting and crying
Officers oblivious and not even trying
Misery surrounds you and seeps into your soul
Programmed to break you, so you'll never feel whole
Archaic laws that decree it's the only way to stop crime
Society believes rehabilitation is achieved by serving your time
So called 'justice' is corrupt because it's all about the money
Incarceration a means to fund the land of milk and honey
Only hope can save us and our kindness to each other
Never forget we're either a wife, sister, daughter or mother

THE NURSERIES OF CRIME – FINDING KINDNESS, HOPE AND COMPASSION

Malcolm Carter

A Worthy Investment?

The aims of the criminal justice system in England and Wales are to protect the public, administer justice and facilitate the reintegration of reformed offenders. If the delivery of justice is measured by finding those who appear before the court guilty, then justice is indeed being served, as around 84% of those who appear are convicted as charged.

On reflection, this does suggest that the system rather favours crime control through imprisonment. Furthermore, in a system that seems to be based, in praxis, on securing conviction, one has to question whether it is indeed just. It is worth noting that the system is presented as operating under an evidence-based and objective ethos, underpinned by the principle of 'due process', which is by definition a requirement to guarantee an individual's legal rights. I believe that, in the majority of cases, due process is observed. It is for that reason I feel there is no place for kindness, hope and compassion at the point of sentencing. The law and sentencing guidelines make provision for all that need judging, with leniency available at the judge's discretion, depending on mitigating circumstances. Those mitigating circumstances negate the need for kindness, hope and compassion at this point in the offender's journey through the criminal justice system. However, I am not suggesting that they have no part to play. I believe they are essential with the prison system.

The prison population of England and Wales is approximately 86,000 – double the numbers in the early 1990's. This dramatic increase has resulted from a rise in the use of custodial sentences and an increase in the average sentence served by prisoners. The cost of having to clothe, feed and provide adequate living conditions – including security, prison staff and maintenance of Victorian era buildings – is absorbed by the taxpayer, at approximately £3 billion per annum. One has to question if the taxpayer is getting value for money, when recidivism amongst those serving sentences of one year or less is currently around 60%; and access to meaningful education, training or those ever elusive rehabilitation programmes is generally poor.

For some offenders, a prison is no more than a place of incarceration, a warehouse steeped in gloom, despondency and sorrow. A production line ejecting broken and joyless individuals back into society, ready to repeat the cycle of offending. I believe that the very build (or structure) and environment of a prison – coupled with a myriad of draconian rules and forced compliance - strips a man of his dignity, individuality and autonomy; forcing him to question his self efficacy and value. It is no wonder that levels of self harm and suicide in prison continue to rise year on year and exceed comparative numbers in the wider community. Figures collated by the Prison Reform Trust (2017) suggest that 25% of women and 15% of men in prison purported symptoms of psychosis – compared to a rate of just 4% amongst the 'outside' community.[1] Self-inflicted deaths are around 8.6 times more likely in prison.[2]

Hope and Humanity: frontline officers 'make time'

There is no doubt that prisons are, on the whole, violent austere institutions, not fit for the demands of a population with complex issues and problems. 70% of people who die in prison from self-inflicted death have already been identified as having pre-existing mental health needs.[3] One has to question if the prison environment is adequately supporting not only the wellbeing of the residents, but also their mental health needs. These rather bleak figures suggest that they are not.

Few get to see what goes on behind the walls of our prisons. Even though they don't know whether residents are simply marking time or working hard to turn their lives around, we should all care; because – with a few exceptions – everyone who spends time in one of Her Majesty's Prisons will, one day, return to the community.

The picture so far looks rather bleak for our residents, but I can assure you that there are moments of joy, moments when kindness and compassion are shown – when a veil is lifted and light shines like a beacon of hope. It is those moments that I want to share with you now.

The task of prison staff is to implement the wishes of the court regarding the sentence, in a decent and humane manner. This is not as simple as it sounds.

Staffing levels vary in prisons and it's not always possible for staff to have meaningful one-to-one interactions with residents and focus on an individuals needs; but many frontline officers will make time for those who are struggling or are identified as particularly vulnerable. When I say 'make time', I mean go above the minimum required to meet those needs.

It would be erroneous to conclude that prisoners (the term is pejorative but serves us here) are a homogenous collection of nefarious men or women. They are not. They are individuals with personal experiences of life. Sadly, the expectations of hegemonic masculinity can often mean that men feel the need to be seen as coping; asking for help or support is akin to an admission of weakness or failure. A consequence of this being that many suffer in silence, exacerbating existing and already concerning issues.

Christmas Inside – One Man's Story

For those residents feeling isolated and unable to cope, there are mechanisms that will provide them with additional support. Some are staff-led and another is peer-supported, underpinned by the Samaritans

– this is called the Listener Scheme. Conversations with a Listener are confidential and I believe provide an invaluable service within prisons. I was a Listener for a number of years and would like to think that men who had the intention of taking their own lives changed their minds, after sharing their problems.

I once sat with and listened to a man throughout the duration of Christmas. He was inconsolable and wept for 2 days. The staff did all they could to alleviate his stress, as they understood that Christmas is a very emotive period for most prisoners. For the young man in question, he had only been in prison for a few weeks and this was the first time he had ever been separated from his young family. He had exhausted his telephone credit, so was unable to share his distress with his family; and because of the Christmas holidays, the finance department was closed. So no emergency pin credit could be added. The staff can use their discretion in matters such as these (with the use of the office telephone) and did allow him to call his family. They also reassured them that all was being done to keep him safe and provide the support he needed. This particular occasion and the memory of it has stayed with me; because in one way, it was so normal, but in another so abnormal.

A man missing his family is a normal and understandable event, but when that experience occurs in the confines of a prison, it manifests itself with an altogether more visceral intensity. I have sadly witnessed that level of despair on many occasions, with men trying to get through each day. I have seen men punctuating the hours with horrific acts of self harm - pools of blood seeping under the cell door, flooding onto the landing. It is on occasions like these – which sadly occur on a daily basis in prisons up and down the land – that the compassion, empathy and professionalism of the staff shines through. Coaxing a man to hand over whatever sharp instrument that he has decided to mutilate himself with – before they can administer first aid. Sometimes, having to wait until the patient becomes drowsy and weak with blood-loss before entering the cell; if he refuses to hand over his destructive – yet seemingly restorative – tool. I have seen those staff return day after day to repair wounds, opened up hours after they've departed, never flinching. Always calm and professional.

My own story – hope amidst hostility

The uniformed staff (or prison officers) play a huge role in the daily running and maintaining of the regime. Theirs is the first face you see in the morning and the last at night. These are the frontline staff – all questions and queries start with them. I am aware that not all residents of HMP have a positive experience when dealing with the staff or adjusting to the regime. It is for them to relate their stories and regale you with their anecdotes, as I can only tell you mine.

Early in my sentence, I decided adding to my skills and enhancing my qualifications would be a positive and valuable use of my time. This requires a great deal of interaction and assistance from not only uniformed staff, but also civilian staff, working in the provision of education. Prison education is a provision of adult education. This is done by colleagues who have successfully tendered for the privilege. The purpose of the system being that the college submitting the lowest bid gets the contract. This suggests that the provision of education is under-funded and not a priority. And sadly, I would have to agree with that. I digress.

After a poor experience with a member of staff, who neglected my application for an Open University course for 6 months; I was fortunate enough to be assisted by one of her colleagues, whilst she was on leave. This man was indeed a principled and dedicated pedagogue. His actions on our first encounter set me on a journey of learning and enlightenment that has not only boosted my self-esteem, efficacy and confidence, but given me the opportunity to study in a subject that interested and excited me.

I was fortunate that I had the tenacity to pursue my goals in that hostile environment and I will be forever grateful for that man's intervention and support. I have encountered many hard-working and dedicated teaching staff during my time and would say their role is not an easy one. Level 1 and Level 2 functional skills (numeracy and literacy) are compulsory in prisons, but not always popular with those adults being forced to return to the classroom. Prisoners receive a wage for their endeavours and education is the poorest paid of all activities. Little wonder then that there are inmates leaving prison gaining no skills or qualifications, because they needed to earn the maximum wage to pay for phone credit and basic toiletries. There is no real incentive to attend education, beyond that of the individual seeking to better himself. So when you consider that many learners have previously experienced poor teaching or educational experiences – such as being excluded from school, truancy or poor peer and scholarly relationships – it will always be a struggle to recruit learners.

For those uninterested in more traditional measures of education or struggling with the curriculum, there is some vocational training available. I was able to retrain as a chef, working and learning in a training kitchen/staff mess. My tutor was a professional from the hospitality industry and it was a joy to partake in the learning process. I completed my course and had the privilege of having the renowned chef Tom Kerridge present at my graduation. He gave a rousing speech and presented us with our certificates. That now feels like a long time ago but for me, it will remain an eventful occasion for a number of reasons. Primarily because Tom spoke to us not as convicts but as chefs. He asked me where my passions lay in the kitchen - fish meat, maybe patisserie - and encouraged me to pursue my dreams. He inspired me to continue cooking and baking and to believe that I don't have to be defined by my crime. I walked a little bit taller that day and felt that maybe I could have an equal chance when seeking employment in the future.

It is essential that we reflect on our past mistakes, but we need not dwell constantly upon them. There comes a time when a man must start looking forward and planning for his future. I have met many inspirational men and women during my sentence and each of them has given me a little bit of courage and a little hope.

I want to finish this essay with a statement from the past. In 1819, the social reformer Elizabeth Fry returned from a tour of violent and squalid prisons in England and Wales and branded them *"the nurseries of crime"*.

"The better the actual state of our prisons is known and understood" she wrote, *"the more clearly will all men see the necessity of these arrangements by which they may be rendered schools of industry and virtue"*.

Her words echo through the generations and remain all too relevant today.

KINDNESS, HOPE AND COMPASSION IN THE CRIMINAL JUSTICE SYSTEM: IS IT WORTH IT?

Alan Jermey

What is prison for?

I started to write this piece in February, before the start of the Covid-19 crisis. Little has changed for us inside, we're still doing 23 hours locked behind a steel door.

It's Tuesday 4th February 2020. Here I am sitting down in my cell waiting for the door to be unlocked for 45 minutes of association before another full-day lockdown on what staff call a "training day."

Piers Morgan is hosting a debate on Good Morning Britain on the recent Streatham stabbing incident. They're discussing whether prisoners should be released if they are not rehabilitated. Chris Atkins, a former prisoner promoting his recently released book *"A bit of a stretch"* is stating that the prison system is broken while Carol Maloney, a journalist argues that prison is for punishment.

As a graduate with a BSc in Criminology and Psychological Studies, it was interesting to observe the debate in which Carol was not demonstrating any form of kindness, hope or compassion for prisoners; while Chris was putting across a reasonable argument for the problems in giving people no hope for the future in a flawed and failing system.

Having spent 12 years incarcerated, inmates, the rules and staff have changed, and not for the better. I remember my first night on remand. Who can I trust? How am I going to survive? What hope is there for me? There is a disconnect between what the media portray the prison system to be – a holiday camp in which every prisoner lazes around playing xbox all day long – and the true reality of prison life.

Data from the Bromley Briefings of Summer 2019 states that nearly half of all adults (48%) are reconvicted within one year of release.[1] This is despite sentences being increased. The average sentence now is 58.3 months. The minimum terms of life sentences have also increased from an average of 12.5 years in 2003 to 21.3 years in 2016.

The data tells us that prison does not work as a deterrent or as a form of punishment. In the same report, "fewer than one in 10 people surveyed said that having more people in prison was the most effective way to deal with crime.[2]

Covid-19 lockdown: Spare a thought for us 'locked in'

Then came 23 March 2020, the UK was put into lockdown due to the coronavirus pandemic. Many people were complaining about feeling imprisoned within their own homes, how dreadful it was and how it affected their physical and mental health. Now spare a thought and some compassion for those of us locked in a ten-metre by six-metre cell for more than 23 hours a day without running water and a toilet.

During the first weeks, some were confined to their cells for more than 20 hours without access to a toilet and had to resort to urinating in a bottle and laying stools in a bin. That is the truth about prison life that never seems to be told. Where is the compassion?

Is it because knowing that somebody else is worse off than you makes you feel better about your own state? When the government announced an early release scheme in April to ease the burden of overcrowding and sharing of cells, the media reported that murderers and rapists would be released. Yet when one looks at the detail it was for those with low risk. Currently only 418 have been released. Compare that with the 85,000 prisoners released from the Iranian prison system.

What does that say about the ways in which the 2 countries view their prisoners and the compassion with which they approach them?

With such negativity directed towards prisoners, it feels as though there is little kindness offered to those struggling to keep hold of hope until their release. It feels as though the belief of 'once a prisoner, always a prisoner' is being fuelled by the risk averse society we live in today. The fear of something that may happen far outweighs the opportunity of giving someone a second chance.

There are many reasons why people find themselves incarcerated: making a mistake or an error of judgement, social circumstances, lack of opportunity, mental health, economic reasons or worse being innocent are but a few.

However, before anyone makes a judgement, they should take a long hard look at their own lives first. Who hasn't broken the speed limit, been over the drinking limit, taken a pen home from work or told a lie? You are just lucky that you have not been caught or you may be in a cell next to me. Let's not forget about the corruption within the police. George Floyd demonstrates what is happening all the time. Don't throw stones when you live in a glass house yourself.

So how do you think you would survive having a steel door slammed behind you and not being able to get out? Not knowing when is the next time you are going to see another human being? There is plenty of noise, bass from speakers, screams from those suffering from mental ill health and self-harming, then there are the "window warriors" shouting out all night long. Do you think there should be some kindness extended to those in prison?

Mental ill-health in prison - treatment or exploitation

Mental ill-health is an issue that is becoming more socially acceptable to talk about and admit to suffering from. 26% of women and 16% of men said they received treatment for a mental health problem in the year before custody.

Those suffering from mental ill-health often keep quiet for fear of ridicule, abuse, and lack of support.

Often, spending time with somebody who has the compassion or kindness just to listen to how somebody feels is all that is needed. But who can you trust? Will opening up leave you open to exploitation? Outside, there are many beacons of hope. Yet, inside do you really want to get referred to mental health? The answer is often medication, but will this then slow down progression? More courses, more appointments with psychologists who ask you, "Was this why you committed the crime you were convicted of or is it just because you were feeling a bit low and need a break from the testosterone fuelled environment of my biceps are bigger than yours?"

(il)literacy as a barrier

Now try to imagine all of this while not being able to read and write. Statistics show that over half of prisoners were assessed on reception as having English and Maths abilities of a primary school pupil.[3] We as prisoners have access to a canteen sheet once a week where we are able to purchase additional items not supplied by the prison: cans of tuna, sweets, crisps, capes, shower gel and we can't forget protein powder. Money comes from wages earned within the prison or money sent in from families and friends. Now if your reading is not the best how can you get what you want? Who can you trust to fill in your sheet for you? Who is kind enough to do it for nothing?

Treating us like animals – Prison makes people worse

Moving back to the original subject of this essay: kindness, hope and compassion in the criminal justice system, we all have hope that one day we will be released. But for some that day will never come. They will die in prison. Where is the compassion in that? Arguably, there are a few that should never be released as they are a danger to themselves as much as to anybody else.

But what is missing is that prison makes people worse, whether this is due to resentment, unfairness or that prison makes you a better criminal. The regime you become conditioned to can change at any time due to staff restrictions. It is always easier to lock prisoners up behind their doors than to work towards a progressive alternative. The hours and days are lost because staff can't count and report too few or many prisoners. It is laughable but also so frustrating.

Yet if you treat people like animals then they will behave like animals. Have you seen the large animals in zoos confined to small spaces that end up going round in circles in a confused manner? That is what happens in prisons. This is not compassionate and it reinforces the belief that there is no point in rehabilitation. If we are the ones that have to change, society should have the compassion to welcome the rehabilitated back into the community with open arms and treat us with kindness and care. Yes it will be tough, mistakes will be made, the rough edges and conditioning we have experienced in prison won't be easy to discard nor will the label of being an ex-offender.

All we get is a £46 discharge, a black holdall to carry our worldly possessions and a sarcastic comment about not coming back. What next? Benefits don't kick in for 2 weeks. What will £46 get you? One night in a Travelodge maybe.

It was reported last year that some women prisoners who were released without an address to go to were issued a tent. Is this how a civilised society treats vulnerable people? Where is the kindness and compassion? What hope do we have?

Are we teaching men to fish?

So we have served our sentence, became rehabilitated, been given £46, what next? Only half of employers would consider employing an ex-offender...Is it such a surprise that 48% of us are reconvicted within a year of release? Do you think there is much hope for ex-offenders when all you see is negativity, failure and resentment at a time when you are hoping for a fresh start; when what you need is some kindness and support to get you back on your feet.

After years of being told what to do, when to do it and by how much, a person is left 'punch drunk.' Now you have to get up on your own, feed yourself, and find work to pay your bills. Instead of having to shout at officers to get their attention, you must learn to become polite and ask in a more articulate manner. What's the worst that can happen in prison? You row with an officer, get into an altercation, get wrapped up, taken to the seg, where you may get punished by loss of privileges or get extra days in segregation. In society, you lose your job, don't get paid and lose your home. This leads to desperation.

I don't have a magic brush that will make everything better but I ask the question. If it costs approximately £40,000 per annum to keep us behind bars, why isn't some of the money to keep us secure, invested in our future upon release. There are many of us wanting to learn a new skill or trade in prison so that we start a new career upon release. Most youngsters these days don't want to get their hands dirty, yet all the lads that I know would love to learn a trade: bricklaying, plumbing or plastering to name a few. Learning a trade and perfecting it inside would give every prisoner hope that they have a chance upon release. Yes it would need a bit of front-end investment but as the saying goes, "Teach a man to fish and he can eat for the rest of his life."

Just to add a bit of truth, these courses are available at open prisons but why not teach people these skills before they get there? They could then work using those skills when they are on day release, start paying tax and contribute towards the victim charter while also saving money so that when they are released, they aren't leaving prison with just £46. It's a no brainer I know, but I am a mere prisoner.

The system fails us – inside and out

Prison is a very lonely place. Arguably, it is not fit for purpose and fails those inside and out. Kindness, hope and compassion within this system are rather lacking due to the confrontational environment created within the prison system. Each individual grasps on to shreds, real or perceived, offered by their nearest and dearest. Realistically, everybody you can access is what gives each person hope they can grasp and find solace in. Kindness and compassion needs to come from outside. What can you offer? The ball is in your court.

Everyone Needs Good Neighbours, HM Prison Northumberland

Image courtesy of Koestler Arts

'HOPE – ABOVE ALL, GIVE US HOPE'

Graham Johnson

I am a mandatory lifer who has served 27 years in prison across the custodial estate from Young Offenders Institution, High Security, Category B and C prisons as well as a therapeutic prison and an open prison. Given this experience, I do not believe I would still be here or become the person I am without kindness, compassion and hope.

Kindness, you need. To know that not everyone is a hater or hating on you for what you may or may not have done. You're quite capable of doing this yourself.

In all my years, I have experienced some wonderful members of staff, but, sadly, I have also experienced ones who are not so good at the other extreme.

I have to say that I have witnessed some very disruptive prisoners respond so much better to kindness. Normally from the type of officer who takes the time to listen, to help if they can, instead of immediately resorting to the discipline process of adjudication or the Incentive and Earned Privileges scheme when a little bit of kindness or human compassion is needed.

On the other side, I've seen officers go in like a bull in a china shop which usually only escalates a situation causing more upset, possible injury and a more resentful individual likely to meet fire with fire. A lot of us only know how to respond in this kind of manner and have never necessarily had the nurturing needed, when growing up.

Often witnessing violence as a child becomes a learned behaviour as an adult and becomes an automatic response. When we're not approached in a compassionate, caring way – our automatic negative reaction continues.

Unfortunately, there will be a minority of individuals who will not respond well no matter the approach. However, generally, the lads will respond much more favourably to a positive approach and I can think of many occasions when I myself responded much more positively to a kinder and compassionate approach.

Luckily, for me, I have learned over the years to be much more patient and tolerant so as not to react negatively to those who simply should not be in the job at all. Every jail has them unfortunately.

Hope: How would I be now without hope? I most probably wouldn't be! I most certainly wouldn't be worried about the potential consequences of acting a certain way without hope.

Having hope has got me through some very low times in all the years I've served. Now being in an open prison, expecting numerous home leaves, and nearing release, I can honestly say without some kind of hope or light at the end of the tunnel I would not be here now.

I always hoped I'd get to this stage but back in closed prisons it can be very negative – not so much hope exists – in fact the total opposite. I believe fellow prisoners who are doing well in open prisons and have now been released could help those still in closed conditions with no or very little hope. It seems rare for those who have done well or are doing well to be given the opportunity to feedback to the lads still in closed prisons, who are feeling despondent.

I've said lots of times that there are many of us who would be prepared to go back and share our story, to try and give others hope, so they can achieve similar outcomes. It's amazing how well others respond to someone who has been there and experienced what they are experiencing. This in turn reiterates – there is hope!

I still feel like pinching myself whenever I remember that I am now in the position I am in, having felt I would never get to this stage. Yet, here I am, writing this with compassion to fellow prisoners who are still where I was. I hope I am giving them the hope to be where I am now!

This is the importance of the role that kindness, hope and compassion play in the criminal justice system.

TALKING ABOUT LISTENING

Simon Kenny

For 2 years during my time in prison, I was a Listener. Let me talk to you about Listeners: their role and how that relates to hope, compassion and kindness within the criminal justice sector.

Introduction

The principal aim of Listeners is to reduce the risk to prisoners of suicide and self-harm.

Prisoners have problems that can happen to any of us: depression, suicidal thoughts self-harming, domestic issues and the like. Problems not only seem worse, but often are worse for someone deprived of their liberty. They can often feel they have little or no control or opportunity to resolve problems and few people they feel they can talk to about issues confronting them. It is all too easy to lose perspective when incarcerated. We have to spend a large part of each day confined to a cell with limited opportunities for contact with family, loved ones, friends and our usual support networks. Experience shows that risks of suicide and self-harming are greater when first entering prison, and when moving from prison to prison.

Listeners are prisoners trained by the Samaritans to provide a service to fellow inmates. Our primary function is to do what the label says: we listen to other prisoners. We do not judge or comment. Our role is to provide someone who understands what prisoners may be going through. Therefore, generally speaking, we do not offer advice, although we can. We simply signpost callers towards avenues of help or advice.

The first Listeners scheme was set up in HMP Swansea in 1991 and now there is a scheme in nearly every prison in England, Wales, and Scotland, as well as schemes in many prisons in Northern Ireland and Eire. Like Samaritans, we refer to those who contact us as callers, although our contact with them is always face to face.

Confidentiality

Listeners offer a confidential service. Prison Officers are not present when we talk to prisoners. We do not discuss their concerns with officers, or with other inmates. There are two rare exceptions to this. The first is that we are governed by safeguarding principles and therefore do have to talk to officers if the prisoner is actually attempting suicide or is threatening to attack another prisoner or a member of the prison staff. This is in practice very rare. The second is that sometimes a prisoner will ask us to raise a concern with staff. If so, we try to do this with the caller present.

Experience shows that the confidential aspect is something prisoners value. It is often a help to them to be able to talk through a problem with someone who is not in authority, is not going to judge them and who has empathy with their issues. Knowing that the service is confidential encourages prisoners to feel that they can ask for help and talk about what is worrying them.

Sadly, a lot of prisoners have, or acquire, mental illness or difficulties. This can range from worry and depression through to self-harming and even attempts to take their own lives. This can be gruelling to deal with. Listeners often cope with quite disturbed callers at night when health care provision is very limited. One good aspect of the Listeners is that we meet regularly for a debrief (again without officers present) and it was my experience that this was extremely useful. Listeners work together, sharing experiences and ways of dealing with particular issues.

Selection and Training

An exceptional part of the scheme is the training and support we receive from Samaritans, who come into the prison and give their time to meet with us regularly. Before beginning service, we have the benefit of extremely good, well thought out and intensive training. The level of support and commitment from the Samaritans who work with Listeners is outstanding.

One essential aspect, to my mind, was understanding that our approach is one of showing *empathy* to a caller's concerns. This means showing that we understand his concerns. This is different from *sympathy*, which entails agreeing with the other's point of view. By appreciating this difference, Listeners are able to fulfil their role even where the attitudes to say violence, self-harming and even suicide might be different from our own.

Our role is not to advise or actively persuade callers: we do not push them, for example, away from considering suicide. We respect each person's right to self-determination. It is the fact that we listen that can sometimes have a positive impact.

It is also my experience that the skills and experiences obtained as a Listener are ones you can take into life after prison and in particular are a great help with the adjustment process after leaving prison.

Callouts

After training, new Listeners undertake call outs with an experienced Listener before going solo. Listeners then normally have a rota, with a Listener (and a backup) covering each 24-hour period. Listeners wear a distinctive green shirt so are recognisable to both prison officers and inmates. This helps to promote the scheme and make us approachable.

There are two types of call-out: those organised by Prison Staff and informal calls when prisoners contact a Listener direct (or a Listener will stop and chat to someone who appears distressed or worried). Signs and leaflets are displayed advertising the service, and the availability of Listeners is usually part of any induction process. Prisoners can use their cell bell at any time of the day or night to request a Listener. Many prisoners prefer a call out after other prisoners are locked up so that fellow inmates are not aware that there has been a callout: this is particularly useful in instances of bullying or violence.

Once the Prison Staff arrange the call-out, including escorting where necessary, they take no further part in the process. The writer's experience is that the very great majority of prison officers, both Wing and Senior Staff, support Listeners and accept and value their contribution towards resolving what are often difficult situations. They understand the confidential nature of the scheme and know not to ask about any particular conversation.

Many calls are therefore at night or are to prisoners held in the segregation unit ("the Block"). Due to this, most schemes have provision for two Listeners on each call outside the core day or where the prisoner is volatile. My experience as a Listener in closed conditions was that a significant proportion of our call outs were to prisoners in the block where prisoners often felt isolated, as well as anxious or angry about their removal to the block. This was often in addition to any other worries or issues they may be facing. In those circumstances, the callers would welcome a non-judgmental visitor who was prepared to listen and let them talk without fear of reprisal. Quite often, a call would end with the prisoner smiling perhaps for the first time in days or weeks.

Listeners in Open Prisons

Like almost all Listeners, I trained in a closed prison, which happened to be a C category. Some of my fellow Listeners had trained in B Category prisons. I met one fantastic Listener, a lifer, who despite his own issues, had been a Listener from a Category A prison right through to open prison.

There is perhaps a misconception about the need for Listeners in open conditions. Prisoners in open prison are reaching the end of their sentence and are of course considered to be of low risk. Yet even these prisoners have concerns. They may be worried about adjusting to life after prison; they may have domestic issues, particularly where a relationship with their spouse or partner is struggling as a result of the separation. In these circumstances, prisoners need someone they can talk to on a confidential basis, particularly as it can have an adverse effect on ROTL (home leave) if raised with prison staff. This is yet another example of where Listeners act as a release valve and help prisoners complete their sentence intact.

Impact of Listeners

It is not possible to quantify the impact of the Listeners scheme. It is difficult to quantify in any empirical way the impact Listeners have in terms of reducing suicides or self- harming. What can be said in general terms is that the number of callouts demonstrates both the value and the need for Listeners.

At HMP Maidstone, where I trained, there was not a single death in custody for over 5 years, and I know that the Listeners played their part in this. I can think of 2 or 3 callers who might well have taken their own life if we were not there to listen.

More dramatic perhaps, in my experience, was the reduction in self-harming. I recall a call out to a prisoner (an asylum seeking orphan from a war torn country who was also a victim of modern slavery) who had 150 cuts on his body. There is no doubt that his regular contact with Listeners played its part in reducing not only his self-harming but enabled him to survive yet another traumatic experience in his life. This is an example of quite a few individuals who reduced their self-harming due, at least in part, to having someone to talk to who did not judge, or even comment adversely. What Listeners could do is to structure the conversation to enable the caller to explore how they feel and to articulate their concerns. This alone often helped callers to begin to cope better.

Listeners usually have input into the monthly meetings of the Safer Custody Team meetings in prison. We attend the first part of the meeting to provide data as to numbers of call-outs. We can highlight types of issues of particular concern to inmates within the prison. For example, at HMP Maidstone, a prison for foreign national offenders, there were additional issues concerning possible deportation and separation from families and loved ones. This feedback could and did help inform the Safer Custody Team with their planning, but without breaching our duty of confidentiality.

So, what was the impact on me as a Listener? Having gone to prison at the age of 60 with no previous convictions, I did not find it easy. Becoming a Listener took me out of my own misery and ended my self-pity. I developed a sense of self-worth, became more involved in the community aspects of prison life, chairing the Prison Council and becoming a Peer Support Worker. A very positive aspect of being a Listener was the involvement with the Listener team, sharing our experiences, and working together for the benefit of others.

Having left prison in January 2020, I feel the skills I developed as a Listener have had practical benefits in rebuilding my life. I am more tolerant and (often) more understanding of others.

Conclusion

So what role do kindness, hope and compassion play in the criminal justice system? As Listeners, I feel that we all must have a quality of compassion first to take on the role, complete the training and then to be available to fellow prisoners. One outcome of our work is, in many cases, to provide a degree of hope to our fellow prisoners. Possibly kindness again is a by-product rather than our primary aim.

It is my view that most prisoners do want to improve their position and change their lives. Listeners, who are fellow prisoners, can help with this. They are one example of ways in which prisoners can contribute in a positive and helpful way. Other examples are the various Peer Support Worker roles running in most prisons: this is an underused resource.

Finally, I would like to pay tribute to the many Samaritans and Listeners who give their time, training, and experience to try to ameliorate the often tragic effects of being sent to prison. I have no doubt that this does reduce both suicide and self-harming. They are a good example within the Criminal Justice Sector where compassion and kindness can lead to hope.

SHINING A LIGHT ON GOOD PRACTICE

John Dodd

Introduction

Many people within the criminal justice system will have differing views regarding the question at hand depending on their personal experiences. My experiences have overall, been positive and I will outline in the coming paragraphs times when I feel that I have experienced kindness, hope and compassion through my journey as a serving prisoner in a UK prison.

Areas I will look at include:

- Innovative solutions to assist prisoners to prepare for their release;
- Staff who, despite facing rude and aggressive prisoners, are respectful and compassionate;
- The hard work of those working to reform the prison system by ensuring that prisoners have access to information and conditions are safe;
- How COVID-19 has impacted the hopes of those in the justice system;
- Finally, how legislation and archaic policies can lead to a toxic environment within prisons despite the hard work of those working to reform prisons.

The essay will conclude that in spite of evidence to the contrary, kindness, hope and compassion play a key role in the current criminal justice system. In fact, with a strong emphasis on rehabilitation, all are achievable. Without these key elements in our prisons, however, no one incarcerated would aspire to live a pro-social life, as it would seem too out of reach.

Not all experiences are the same

From the opening of the first penal institution to the present day, there have always existed those with the "us and them" mentality. This can be seen in the portrayal of prisons in varying fictional television programmes and true-life documentaries where the notion is used and witnessed on many occasions. This however, is not always the case. During my time as a serving prisoner, I have never had any reason to agree with the statement and have countless examples to the contrary.

Having said that, there will always be those who have a negative opinion of the current criminal justice system and this may be for a variety of reasons such as:

- Being convicted following a false accusation;
- Previous experiences of prison
- Having family members who were mistreated by the system to name but a few.

The opinions of these people should never be forgotten as, the same as in life, all of our journeys through prison will be different. In prisons today, you will come across many who will thrive on causing disruption and not all of these people will be serving a sentence. Some will be wearing a uniform. Although this is not my opinion based on my experience, I thought it relevant to highlight that there would be many who do not experience any kindness, hope or compassion whilst on their journey.

Preparing prisoners for release

One of the most common disappointments within the UK prison system is the assistance prisoners receive in preparation for their ultimate release from custody. Employment searches are hard to organise, curtailments on the provisions of release on temporary license (ROTL) make it hard to prepare for release. And with prison wages averaging £10.00 per week, it is very difficult to save any money to use towards housing upon release. This leads to a high proportion of prisoners relying on the state for support when they leave custody.

However, there are examples where prisons are excelling in this area with innovative ideas that could easily be repeated across the prison estate.

HMP Ashfield in Bristol, a Category C male prison housing exclusively males convicted of sexual offences, created though a prisoner led focus group an idea many thought was too "out of the box." The 'Resettlements Savings Scheme' is now in place and assisting prisoners on a weekly basis. The scheme encourages prisoners to save for release and rewards those who do. The scheme includes a prisoner agreeing to save £3 per week from the prison wages towards their release. In reward for committing such a large percentage of their weekly income towards their release, the prison matches the saving with a further payment of £3 into their account. There are many who would have left prison with no money but, due to the creation of this innovative scheme, these men can now afford housing upon their release. This is a very clear example of kindness within the prison system and although only available in one prison, this could easily be rolled out across the estate with the cost not coming close to the bill for housing those released from custody homeless.

Prison staff: The greatest purveyors of kindness

In the same way that everyone has a unique journey, so are their experiences of staff within prisons. It is true there are some working within prisons that do the job simply for the steady income and that have no interest in those they are tasked to look after. However, there are staff in prisons who will go out of their way to help and assist. I have met many officers who, whenever they identify when someone is having a bad day, open the doors to their offices and take time out of their day to comfort people or just listen to them rant in their office (as I have done on many occasions) about frustrations related to appeals or individual sentence plans. Everyone within the UK prison system should be able to name at least one officer to whom they can turn. I have been lucky to meet a couple of officers who I have the utmost respect for as, despite facing rude and aggressive prisoners, they can still be professional and show kindness and compassion regardless of how they are treated.

The best officers will quickly deduce exactly how to best treat you, such as the officer who playfully clipped me around the ear when I was cheeky to them, knowing that this reaction is the best way of dealing with me. Without officers such as these, there would be no hope for those of us within prison walls; and all those officers doing the job to simply earn a wage need to learn from the decent staff who treat us all as humans and not prisoners. They need to see that by showing kindness and compassion we will have hope for a better future.

Charities: The change makers

Working alongside the prison service and holding them to account are the many prison reform charities, pressure groups and resettlement/ legal advice groups whose sole job is to assist those in custody. Until recently, prisons were horrible places to live with appalling conditions. It took various actions of prisoners through many protests (some peaceful, some not) to start changing the living conditions within prisons. An example of this is the installation of in-cell toilets in place of buckets.

However, not all of the fights have been won and the mantle now falls to the sectors that work tirelessly to ensure prisoners' rights are enforced, living conditions improve and prisons become places of rehabilitation and not simply farms to house the worst in society as they were in years gone by. In 2018, the Prison Reform Trust (PRT) took this to the next level with the launch of the Prisoner Policy Network

(PPN) giving those held in our prisons a chance to have a say on the policies governing the institutions housing them. This is something that the PRT did not need to do, but giving prisoners a say in how the rules are applied gives us all hope that change is possible. Access to information in prison is a major obstacle but again, charities such as the PRT and Prisoners' Advice Service offer up-to-date information across a range of subjects to all prisons. Through publications such as the PRT's 'Bromley Briefings', prisoners are able to access information surrounding elements such as reconviction rates, deaths in custody and the current make-up of the prison population. In times gone by, access to information such as this would not have readily been available and prisoners would have been questioned regarding their motives for requesting such statistics. Without the many charities and companies working on behalf of prisoners, there would be no hope in our prisons and we would return to the conditions seen prior to the riots at HMP Strangeways and the subsequent Woolf report in which there was no kindness, no hope and no compassion.

Kindness and compassion even in the darkest times

Prisons, along with the rest of the world, are facing an incredibly difficult time because of the COVID-19 pandemic. Stress levels are high, people are ill and dying and with all of that burdening us, we are locked away for 23 hours a day with limited access to the outside world. Visits have been cancelled (but are now slowly returning) and life is not the same as it was prior to the pandemic.

Yet, in spite of the darkness in the world now, I have witnessed some truly inspirational acts of kindness amongst my peers in custody. Be it ensuring that someone gets a card on their birthday or has a treat on canteen day whilst they are on restricted wages, we have all pulled together as a community and despite tensions flaring on the odd occasion, we are all staying strong for each other. The world will be different when we come out of lockdown but, knowing that there can be kindness and compassion even in the darkest of places such as in custody, gives me hope that when I finally walk free from prison, there will be a community waiting to stand by me, just as there has been throughout this difficult year. If we all stick together and show a little kindness, there will be hope for all of us however the world may change.

There is still work to be done to make an archaic system fit for purpose. It is only right, before concluding that we explore some times in which there is no kindness, hope or compassion within the justice sector. Despite the hard work of the many charities mentioned earlier such as the PRT and the work of those working in prisons with the desire to effect change, there remains key pieces of legislation which make hope an impossibility. Prisons in the UK are still governed by a 68-year-old act: the archaic 'Prisons Act 1952'. Couple this with the rules laid out in the Prison Rules 1999, which limit everyday tasks, members of the public take for granted. Could you survive on only one shower a week, 30 minutes in the open air or wages set at £4 a week? Surely it is impossible for any reasonable person to agree to such impositions but these are the principles that prisons (should they choose to) can apply to all. Imagine only being allowed to see your loved ones for 30 minutes, twice a month and then ask yourself – do you have hope? There are thousands in prison who experience these restrictions on a daily basis and can only hope that times change one day. In times like these, there is no hope for those in prison, as the 68-year-old rulebook does not give allowances for kindness or compassion. If these two are not present then hope cannot exist.

Conclusion

In conclusion, kindness, hope and compassion play, in my opinion, a significant role in the criminal justice system. Without these elements, those incarcerated would have no desire to change their behaviour and prisons would slowly start to decline to the days gone by, with rooftop protests and mass disruption becoming the norm. The majority of prisons today are set up to encourage rehabilitation; and it is through

the compassion shown by those working within the justice system that gives all involved the hope that this will be their last experiences of the custodial estate. There are changes that need to be introduced to assist in the increase of hope for those feeling let down by the system, with step one being the release of an update to the archaic Prisons Act bringing the governance of our prisons into the 21st century. More investment is required to reduce injustices and the wrongful imprisonment of the innocent. Prisoners must, at present, accept the finding of guilt imposed by the court; but if more time was spent investigating a small proportion of crimes, those unlucky enough to suffer a miscarriage of justice would have hope in the system, whereas currently many resent the justice system in its entirety. To finish, with kindness, hope and compassion we can overcome any obstacle life will throw at us. Pandemics, the imprisonment of the innocent, long sentences in custody and more. Together we are strong, together we have hope. So try to be kind and compassionate, as you may be giving someone else hope during their journey through the justice system.

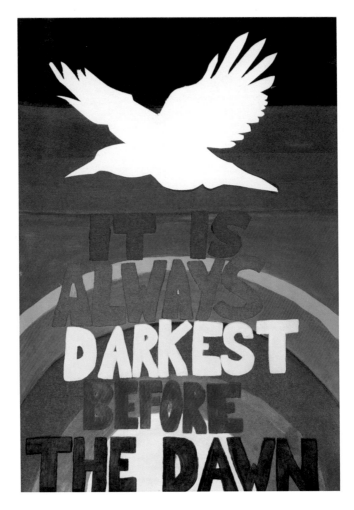

It is always darkest before the dawn, HM Prison Wandsworth

Image courtesy of Koestler Arts

SECTION 2

EXAMINING THE SYSTEM

A parallel universe a mutated imitation of normal
ANONYMOUS

"Being inside the criminal justice system is to be in
a parallel universe, a place where one's perception
of what would be considered part of a normal world
has been moulded into a mutated imitation of it.
Yet this is a place where I have experienced kindness
and compassion from both prisoners and prison
staff. The goodness in humanity comes to the fore
here. The hope I have is deeply rooted within my
faith, and that develops within one's self."

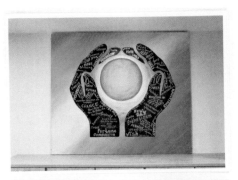

Home is Where You Are, Low Newton

Image courtesy of Koestler Arts

CASTING OFF THE GILDED BLINDFOLD: THE ROLE OF JUDGES IN CREATING A FAIRER, MORE REHABILITATIVE, JUSTICE SYSTEM

His Honour John Samuels QC

The traditional view of the judge or magistrate is that they must, like the figure of justice perched in its gilded glory atop the Old Bailey, be blind to human sentiment, and must deliver even-handed justice to all with whom they deal. The theme of this contribution is that this detachment, while theoretically productive of abstract "justice", is of itself incapable of producing the reform and rehabilitation of those who have come into conflict with the criminal justice system.

I have explained elsewhere how my involvement with the criminal justice system, like that of so many others caught up in its tentacles, occurred by accident. However as a Crown Court judge, both full-time and part-time, for some 27 years, followed by a maximum 10 year term as a judicial member of the Parole Board, I acquired more than an onlooker's experience of citizens who end up as unwilling participants in the sector.

My initial answer to the question may strike the reader as counter-intuitive: it is that those who sentence, whether as lay magistrates or judges of the Crown Court, must cast off the gilded blindfold. They can only do so if they routinely engage with those whom they have sentenced, albeit in a light-touch and over-arching way, throughout the sentence that they have imposed. That sentence (the grammatical one, rather than the court-inspired sentence) may need a second reading for its full sense to sink in. Sentencing should not be a "*snapshot moment*", with the implementation of whatever was the primary objective of the sentencer delegated to whatever the prison officer or probation officer

Humane Justice

may from time to time identify. If the initial sentencer, or a representative of the sentencing court, retains a responsibility periodically to review the progress being made by those to whom the warrant of imprisonment or the community order relates, not only would that of itself encourage the person primarily so affected to aspire to achieve the rehabilitation which is one of the statutory purposes of sentencing, but it would provide the judicial monitor with practical oversight of the prisoner's release and risk management plans.

That continuing oversight might facilitate a closer awareness on the part of sentencers of what in practice was available, both in the community and, of even greater importance, within the custodial environment, to achieve the rehabilitative outcome which has to be a critical aspiration. The reduction of offending is not a mere philosophical benefit. Statisticians tell us that the cost of reoffending is in excess of £18 billion annually, quite apart from its impact on victims and the economy as a whole. If particular kinds of sentences are more likely to produce outcomes which objectively reduce recourse to future criminal behaviour, those are the sentences which should be promoted: not those which in all probability are not only going to achieve nothing, but by exposing those who receive such purposeless sentences to other more sophisticated criminals, will encourage the development of entrenched criminogenic behaviour. In a phrase: "*short sentences make bad people worse.*"

Judges as problem-solvers

By an adventitious route I have discovered that involvement in judicial monitoring, providing increasing familiarity with what on a daily basis is being experienced both within our prisons and in the probation service in the community, has enabled me to relate to and empathise with the practical issues being routinely faced. It is for others to say whether this experience amounts to compassion; but it certainly promotes a more thorough understanding of what is the daily experience of those who work at, or are impacted by, the coal face.

76

Some explanation for this Damascene conversion is overdue. In my case it was the arrival of the Drug Treatment and Testing Order which, for the first time in 2000, authorised sentencers to review the progress being made of those under such an order. I found this a revelation. Inevitably there was no training offered to the judiciary in relation to how to conduct such periodic reviews; and the pragmatic experience of parenthood was pressed into service.

While inevitably not every such order was successful, the positive advantage which it bestowed on both the sentencer and the offender was that a supportive relationship developed. The judge was keen to see the offender break away from their addiction; and the offender, responding to the active interest in their progress being displayed by the judge, did not want *"to let my judge down."*

This new approach was initially dubbed the *"problem-solving approach"*; and it has led internationally to the creation of many specialist courts, all of which are underpinned by the positive and supportive ongoing relationship which develops between the judge and those whom they have sentenced. Critical to this relationship is the routine review, by the same informed and engaged judicial supervisor. Sadly within this jurisdiction, apart from the few family drug and alcohol courts, we lag a long way behind other courts abroad.

We can, however, learn much from the way in which the reviewing role is undertaken internationally. At its heart is the concept of procedural fairness. As I once wrote: *"Fairness has a wider meaning than ensuring just outcomes and upholding due legal process. The concept of 'procedural fairness'– that the process by which decisions are made needs to feel fair to people coming to court – takes the conversation a step further. It promotes the idea that how an individual is treated has a profound effect on the perception of the process and the ongoing likelihood of complying with court orders and the law generally."*

That comment has a wider relevance than merely dealing with individuals in a court setting. It is a truism that those who are on the receiving end of the sanctions applied within the criminal justice system have an acute sense of what is or is not fair: and to the extent that they are treated fairly by authority figures – fairness in this context including, of course, being treated with kindness, with courtesy and with understanding – their response to that treatment is likely to be equally positive.

The benefits of localised justice

A corresponding benefit from the existence of this judicial reviewing role is that the judge who regularly engages with those community programmes provided to those sentenced to non-custodial orders will become that much more familiar with what is on offer locally. Similarly the judge who attends the prisons where those sentenced or held on remand by the court at which that judge routinely sits may in non-specific ways enhance the rehabilitation prospects of those so sentenced (or remanded) by overseeing the conditions in which they are detained; by becoming more sensitively aware of the practical problems experienced by such establishments in terms of staff shortages, prisoner assaults, escalating use of new psychoactive substances; and by generally responding to any deterioration in what should be identified as a public service. In short, the judge who engages in "judicial monitoring" may actively enhance the rehabilitation prospects of those so sentenced by ensuring, so far as is practicable, that arrangements are in place for their effective supervision once they emerge from the prison gates.

A further benefit from this continued engagement of the judicial sentencer is that it promotes "*intelligent sentencing*". Unless you, as the sentencer, have an informed appreciation of what is likely to happen to those whom you have sentenced, you are unlikely to achieve one of the express statutory purposes of sentencing, namely "*to achieve the reform and rehabilitation of the offender.*"

It would be wrong to assume that the benefits of judicial monitoring should be restricted to the judicial officer, whether judge or magistrate.

A similar role could well be undertaken by members of Independent Monitoring Boards ("IMBs"). It is a commonplace that committed members of the IMB, particularly if they have come to that role as serving or retired magistrates, may feel a sense of personal frustration that they cannot do more to secure the successful rehabilitation of prisoners with whom they have routine contact during their duties. While the general duties of the IMB include "*directing the attention of the governor to any matter which calls for his attention*", what these general duties manifestly do not do is to give IMBs the power and responsibility to oversee the rehabilitation of the prisoner, and to plan for their reintegration into the community to which almost inevitably they will return.

Green shoots of change

If the reader has followed my argument thus far, you may well be asking: "*Well, what have you done about implementing these proposals?*" The short answer is: it is a work in progress. However there are a few green shoots in what would otherwise be a desert of unbroken sand.

First, early in 2019 the then Justice Secretary acknowledged, in a far-ranging speech, that we have far too many prisoners in our prisons, serving sentences which rise inexorably in length at a time when overall crime rates are falling. The principal questions identified in the same speech were these:

• Does current sentencing policy, particularly that involving the short prison sentence, actually reduce crime?

• Are our prisons run in a way which maximises offenders' chances of turning their lives around, leading to gainful employment, and rejoining society as a responsible citizen?

• Should we not be seeking opportunities to find better and alternative ways of punishing as well as rehabilitating offenders?

Building on those themes, by July 2019 a Green Paper was poised for publication, which would have outlawed the imposition of any sentence of 6 months or less; and made it very difficult in practice to impose a sentence of less than 12 months. Regrettably the change of Conservative Leader led to the removal of the Justice Secretary; and these obviously sound proposals await implementation by others.

Second, we are promised a Royal Commission on Criminal Justice. While this is no more than a political promise, and the membership and terms of reference of the Commission are as yet unknown, it would be extraordinary if the obvious shortcomings of the present system were not appropriately addressed.

Third, the proliferation of television programmes about prison life, as well as a smattering of widely-read books about their recent prison experience, written by articulate former prisoners, and more particularly the presenting problems of those who find themselves incarcerated, have increased a general awareness in the public at large that prisons are not holiday camps; and that it is in the interests of all of us, taxpayers, potential victims and the wider community, to address the problems which so many, particularly serving prisoners, must face. Programmes such as Gareth Malone's Choir in HMYOI Aylesbury have reached out to a broadly far more sympathetic audience than the tabloid press previously portrayed.

Fourth, despite the fact that access to justice was not an election issue in the General Election of 2019, there has objectively been a growing and widespread appreciation of the fact that the courts are in crisis. The programme of court closures has come on top of cuts to legal aid which have left wide areas of civil law inaccessible to those without means; and inadequate funding of criminal legal aid has created an incoming tide of potentially unsafe convictions. Couple this with the decimation of the Probation Service in 2015, as a result of what the government now accepts to have been the ill-considered *"reforms"* of the Offender Rehabilitation Act 2014, the inevitable rise in litigants in person, and the falling morale in the full-time judiciary and its staff, and you have a potential tsunami gathering on the horizon, even before the impact on the Court Service of the damage yet to be wreaked by Covid-19.

Thus far I have looked at a broad landscape; but, closer to home, I feel real grounds for optimism. Once again I acknowledge my debt to serendipity: what I have personally experienced has happened to me largely by accident. It was fortuitous that I first became involved as a trustee (later as Chair, and now President) of Prisoners' Education Trust; and discovered how far the availability of distance learning courses to prisoners was literally transformative. Similarly fortuitous was my growing friendship with leading members of the International Association of Treatment Courts, and my visits to drug and other problem-solving courts in a variety of jurisdictions; and the cross-fertilisation of ideas which flowed from that. Involvement within the Prisoner Learning Alliance, an offshoot of Prisoners' Education Trust which I am proud to have developed with the invaluable support of the Monument Trust, led to my routine involvement as an *ad hoc* discussion group leader in two Surrey prisons; and being privileged to act as mentors to some of the alumni whom I have met under those auspices after their release.

On 29 November 2019 I was in conversation at Fishmongers' Hall, now notorious for the murders of two outstanding members of the Learning Together team, when Usman Khan developed his rampage; and was so bravely confronted by three of those who have become my personal mentees. I cannot begin to describe my pride in their selfless conduct, save to say not only that I salute them; but I take quiet satisfaction in the fact that public opinion generally instantly recognises their heroism, despite what would otherwise have been the persistent shadow on their reputations as "murderers".

Most recently, and to my immense pleasure, I have experienced what gives me real grounds for optimism. In conversation with an Open University lecturer at a recent Prisoner Learning Alliance event, I was expounding on the virtues of judicial monitoring; and to my surprise received the response "*I would love to meet the judge who sentenced me*". "*Who was it?*" I asked. The answer was not only a judge whom I know well, but a judge who actively supports many of my enthusiasms.

I have introduced them, to their mutual pleasure; and I now plan to facilitate a conversation between them, to an audience of sentencers, as well as the wider public.

Conclusion

That this has been a snapshot response to the title to this piece is self-evident. However I close on two observations which have underpinned my approach to judicial monitoring over the years. First, it needs emphasis that those who are being punished by the criminal justice system are not outlaws, namely outside the law: they remain citizens, for whom the law prescribes appropriate punishment, in the knowledge that those so punished will return as members of the community. As such, key aspects of their potential return must remain the twin targets of **hope** and **normality**. Whether the offender is serving the punishment imposed by the court in custody or in the community, if the individual is throughout that sentence being treated as a citizen who will ultimately regain a valued place in the society from which they have been temporarily excluded, the twin objectives of hope and normality will be fostered by the judicial monitoring which I have attempted to describe. Whether that judicial monitoring includes the elements of compassion and kindness as well will be up to the individual judicial monitor to develop; and, with appropriate luck and skill, to demonstrate.

BINDING OUR WOUNDS: COMPASSION AND HOPE IN TACKLING RACIAL DISPARITY

Phil Bowen

The unlawful killing of George Floyd in Minneapolis in May 2020 shocked the world, while at the same time confirming a far too common truth about the experiences of people of colour in the USA. That his murder would lead to the drowning of a slaver's statue in Bristol in England came as a surprise to some people— people who have clearly not been paying attention to the reality of racial injustice in the UK. But even if the previous protests about the UK's justice system and fury at individual injustices in our police cells, our prisons and courts had not made it to particular British breakfast tables, the warning was there for all to see, and it was there in the careful language of Government.

Almost three years ago, David Lammy's review of the criminal justice system brought together the abundant evidence that clearly demonstrates that BAME individuals are over-represented in the criminal justice system of England and Wales.[1] The Lammy review went into painstaking detail about the full breadth of the wounding racial disparities in our justice system. The Lammy review, of course, recognised that many of the causes of BAME overrepresentation "start long before a young man or woman ever enters a plea decision, goes before a magistrate or serves a prison sentence." Yet the review was clear that the complex web of institutions, laws, and people that form our criminal justice system, have biases which themselves deepen these pre-existing disparities. Take, for example, how we police, prosecute and sentence cannabis offences. Despite surveys showing that there is no racial disparity in the prevalence of cannabis use, it is clear that the policing of it, and the subsequent convictions and sentencing of it, treats BAME individuals much more harshly than similar white individuals.[2]

For our own part at the Centre, our focus on tackling racial disparity in the criminal justice system has primarily been to strengthen and expand the use of pre-court diversion for low level offences, a key recommendation of the Lammy review. Pre-dating the Lammy review, we saw that helping police forces, youth offending services and other agencies implement effective pre-court diversion schemes, which seek to de-escalate individual's contact with the criminal justice system, had a role to play in ameliorating unmerited disparities and delivering better outcomes. Our assistance to the Government's Choice to Change diversion pilots and our much wider work has played an important role in ensuring that 33 police forces have a pre-court diversion scheme for adults and that the vast majority of local authority areas have one for under 18s. Moreover, we have been looking at improvements that can be made to the youth courts, an area which the Lammy Review labelled as possibly the biggest concern in England and Wales.

There is clearly more we can do. We know that disparities that start accumulate into larger disparities downstream. This is why we are undertaking a research project to explore disproportionality in youth diversion. This will explore the impact of race and ethnicity on children and young people's access to, and engagement with, youth diversion. We continue to seek to work with practitioners to change how the system operates for all, under the hope that fairer hearings in youth court and more active diversion of cases from court will benefit everyone, but in particular BAME individuals.

Yet the Lammy review was always faced with an uphill struggle in turning its recommendations into fundamental reforms that picked up their own momentum. Our own research prior to the Lammy Review found that when Governments in different jurisdictions had commissioned reviews into racial disparity, these inquiries "succeeded in consciousness raising" but that "…(p)redictably, the government responses, and action plans that stem from these reviews, often attract criticism for failing to implement recommendations at all or as intended."[3]

And that is what we have seen. When looking at the Government's response to the Lammy review, the activity generated has clearly been subject to the type of bureaucratic compliance that comes when hard-pressed officials are asked to deliver defensible changes but not tasked with fundamental reform.[4] This is not, in retrospect, surprising. The Lammy review was Cameron's review, and he was out of office before it reported. Despite Theresa May's stated commitment to "tackle burning injustices", her domestic agenda was swallowed whole by Brexit. And the current administration was no sooner in office than Covid-19 came round the corner.

So, it may well be that the moment provided by the Black Lives Matter demonstrations is just the time to gather a new head of steam to heal the injuries of racial injustice. But the crucial question is - what reforms do we need? And that's the hardest question of all. And it's one where international borrowing becomes fraught. Solutions for the American situation are not necessarily solutions for ours, as our institutions and practices have their own culture, their own history and their own sensibilities. It's clear, for example, that the recommendations of the 2015 Obama Policing taskforce that "Law enforcement culture should embrace a guardian—rather than a warrior— mind-set to build trust and legitimacy" is a response to the disgraceful over-militarisation of police, which is itself a response to a uniquely American addiction to guns. In 2016, *the Guardian* estimated there were 1,011 people killed in police shootings in the US. In that same year, the number of fatal police shootings in England and Wales was 4. According to the Economist, between 2000 and 2014, 2,445 US police officers were killed on active duty, compared to just 25 in the UK. The reckless over-armament of both the people and the police in the US has little to inform the British experience.

But nonetheless there are ways to build trust in our justice institutions which apply across jurisdictions. And we can do so only if we ensure that compassion for one another, and hope about building a better society, are at the forefront of our reforms. For, though the wounds are deep, they can be healed.

For example, the Government's own research,[5] following the Lammy review, points to the need to humanise our justice system, in order to build trust – "Efforts by staff to humanise themselves make it easier for people to connect with them... Admitting fault and saying 'sorry' where it is applicable – for example, when nothing has been found after a 'Stop & Search'." We know people will trust a process if it uses clear, accessible and understandable language about what it has done, what it will do and what the options for citizens are. This means explaining in simple terms what is happening, why, and what to expect next.

But, as hard as adopting these more human centred approaches might be for justice professionals - working as they do in environments which tend towards the impersonal and administrative - we also need to recognise that institutional reform involves larger political choices. For example, rethinking our attitude to the prohibition of drugs requires political will. The experiments internationally with de-criminalising marijuana suggest that it's no panacea but, nonetheless, it has the potential to change what we choose to police and criminalise, which itself has ramifications for racial disparity.

Rethinking the orientation of the criminal justice system - away from a catch, convict and sentence mentality - requires rethinking and new experimentation in public health models of law enforcement and prevention. This includes models of policing which are more situated within a wider web of social service provision, in which a wider social compassion for the impact that pre-existing inequalities have for individual and communal opportunities, guides the justice's system's response. It requires hope in how we adopt new models of 'court'. Where the focus is on a more problem-solving approach involving restorative, and transformative justice responses, rather than purely a focus on case disposals, in which there is hope that people can change.

Placing hope and compassion as a systemic context, also requires us to re-orientate how justice institutions view individuals. People enmeshed in the justice system are often assessed for risk, and for good reason given the duty to protect communities from harm. However, an exclusive focus on risk makes people feel misunderstood and untrusted. We know the value of relational practice in which trust is conferred on those justice professionals who take the time to get to know an individual, their background and specific needs and vulnerabilities. For example, we know that having a consistent caseworker or legal representative throughout enables more in-depth understanding of an individual's circumstances. People and organisations able to demonstrate real insight into different communities are more trustworthy for the same reason.

The Black Lives Matters protests ask us all to challenge what seems settled about the way we 'do' justice in the UK. It challenges us all not just to critique and argue, but to actually work together to change things. A communal commitment to change is the key to binding up the wounds of racial injustice. Real solutions are never likely to be found in reviews, research and programmes of work, if there is a wider absence of compassion and hope. It will only be when we have inculcated what Bobby Kennedy called a "leadership of humane purpose" in our own hearts, and in the hearts of our institutions, that we will succeed. The challenge is whether we can take this moment to have the political will, the common purpose and the moral fortitude to work harder to bind and heal the wounds among us.

KINDNESS AND ACCOUNTABILITY: LESSONS FROM THE CITY COLLEGE BASKETBALL SCANDAL IN NEW YORK

Greg Berman

The City Game by Matthew Goodman is a book about basketball in New York City that should be required reading for anyone interested in thinking about the meaning of justice. The setting may be grounded in a specific historical time and place, but the questions the book raises are universal: How should government respond when important social values are transgressed? To what extent does context explain, and even dictate, behavior? Or are we ultimately responsible for our own misdeeds as individuals?

In 1950, City College of New York (CCNY) were the national champions of college basketball in the United States. This was an exceptional achievement: City College was regarded as a prestigious academic institution, not an athletic powerhouse. Charging no tuition to those who met its rigorous entrance requirements, the school attracted many of the best low-income students in New York City. The CCNY basketball team was entirely comprised of Black and Jewish students – a rarity in an era of discriminatory Jim Crow laws and de facto quota systems that limited the enrollment of Jews at many universities.

Unfortunately, the CCNY basketball team is remembered today less for their prowess on the court and more for their involvement in scandal: the entire starting five were convicted of taking bribes from gamblers to influence the outcomes of their games.

The City Game tells this story in absorbing detail. It catalogs the shame and guilt experienced by the participating players, all of whom were young men from modest backgrounds. They clearly knew that what they were doing was wrong.

They were judged harshly in the court of public opinion. For example, their coach, Nat Holman, blamed the scandal on the players' moral deficiency: "the youngsters lacked the moral fiber to make a decision when they were faced with temptation, when those unscrupulous gamblers approached them."

On the other hand, the players' crimes were not isolated incidents: they were part of an endemic citywide problem. According to Goldman:

Cops were on the take everywhere in the neighborhoods in which the players had grown up, the crooked cop as much of a local fixture as the bookie taking bets in the pool hall...When the players got into trouble with the law, everyone understood that their strongest hopes lay not in an attorney who was legally astute but one was politically well connected... The corruption was not abstract: it was both intimate and pervasive, a rotten smell that seemed to hang in the air, seeping into all aspects of [the players'] lives, reminding them always that this was the way things were done in the city.

As Goodman describes, the players paid a high price for their crimes. After pleading guilty, all of them were effectively blackballed from playing in the National Basketball Association. All of them suffered public humiliation. Their lives were forever altered for the worse.

This was particularly true of Ed Warner, the only member of the CCNY team who ended up serving time behind bars. It is perhaps no coincidence that Warner was also African-American. Warner, who had engaged in minor misbehavior as a juvenile, served six months for his role in the CCNY scandal. Years later, he would serve still more time after pleading guilty to selling heroin.

Was justice served in the case of Ed Warner and the other CCNY players? Were their life trajectories improved by their engagement with the American justice system? *The City Game* suggests otherwise. The portrait the book paints is of a justice system focused on retribution at the expense of goals like rehabilitation and restoration.

In the years since the CCNY scandal, the politics of criminal justice in the US have taken several twists and turns. As crime rose in the 1960s, 1970s and 1980s, conservative voices were largely ascendant, arguing for stiffer penalties for criminal behavior. A massive increase in the use of incarceration followed.

More recently, as crime rates have decreased, liberal advocates have begun to dominate the public debate, focusing attention on the underlying causes of crime, including inequality and racism, and arguing for more lenient responses. Their arguments have been bolstered by a number of high-profile injustices perpetrated against African-Americans, including cases where individuals were killed by police officers in dubious circumstances.

The creative tension between the liberal and the conservative tradition is likely a permanent feature of the American criminal justice landscape – advocates of law and order will always compete with bleeding-heart liberals in the marketplace of ideas. But in recent years, there has been some movement in the US toward synthesizing the two traditions – to acknowledge that justice demands a combination of kindness and accountability.

Signs of this synthesis can be found in a number of different places. For example, a group of prominent Republicans has launched Right on Crime, a campaign to reduce American reliance on prisons that they view as expensive and ineffective. Another example is the US Department of Justice's effort to promote "evidence-based programs," which seeks to bring a level of rigor to the business of investing in rehabilitative programming.

Perhaps the most dynamic effort to synthesize the liberal and conservative traditions in American criminal justice has been the emergence of problem-solving courts across the country. These programs – which include drug courts, mental health courts, community courts, and others – seek to reduce the use of incarceration by expanding the use of alternatives like drug treatment, mental health counseling and community restitution. New York City has been at the forefront of problem-solving justice in the US, pioneering the community court model and, more recently, investing in the spread of opioid intervention courts.

New York has changed in many ways since the days of the CCNY basketball scandal. College basketball no longer dominates the sporting scene. The influence of organized crime is dramatically diminished. Perhaps most important, the justice system has undergone a cultural shift, moving away from the assembly-line and toward a more problem-solving brand of justice. It is too late for Ed Warner and his CCNY teammates, but thousands of New Yorkers are benefitting from this new approach to justice, which acknowledges the harms caused by criminal behavior without resorting to overly punitive responses, like incarceration, that can do long-term damage to individual defendants, their families and their communities.

HOPE, COMPASSION AND KINDNESS: REFLECTIONS FROM THE SCOTTISH VIOLENCE REDUCTION UNIT

Niven Rennie

Humble beginnings

'Violence is preventable, not inevitable.' So said Nelson Mandela and that statement has become the byword for the Scottish Violence Reduction Unit.

It doesn't sound so radical nowadays but it was in 2004/5 when Scotland was said to be amongst the most violent places to live in the developed world and when the City of Glasgow had the reputation of being the 'murder capital of Europe.' In the communities of Glasgow, young people were being maimed and were dying on the streets almost every day. For them, violence was merely a part of their constant struggle of everyday life. It had been thus for generations and many high profile policing campaigns, aimed at addressing the issue and reducing the carnage, had come and gone without much change resulting.

To believe in a different future, a better set of outcomes for those young people, amongst the darkness they were experiencing was truly radical. It was with that mindset, however, that the Violence Reduction Unit was born.

Initially the design of Strathclyde Police, its initial challenge was to find a different way of addressing violence from the usual 'stop and search' based police approach. It was recognised even then that the idea of addressing violence through enforcement was not sustainable, that it merely suppressed the problem temporarily before it re-emerged and more lives were needlessly lost or ruined. It was understood that 'You can't arrest your way out of the problem'.

From the start we adopted the 'Public Health Approach' to violence as recommended by the World Health Organisation, understanding that to truly address the issue we need to recognise that wider society has a role to play and not just law enforcement. That providing hope and opportunity for those with the most difficult start in life, better living conditions and health outcomes, higher educational attainment and more care and compassion for others will lead to a more stable society and thus a less violent one. In this teachers, social workers, doctors and health professionals have as much of a responsibility as police officers, lawyers and judges.

This fresh approach quickly gained political traction and the Liberal Democrat/Labour coalition government of the day provided partial funding to create a more ambitious 'Scottish Violence Reduction Unit' believing that the improvement designed for Glasgow could bring benefit across the country. Subsequent SNP led governments have invested further from 2008 and from 2013 have provided 100% funding for the VRU. Last year, a cross party debate in the Scottish Parliament produced a whole hearted political endorsement for the work of the SVRU.

Incorporating international best practice through hope – a 'reachable moment'

This is because Scotland has come a long way since those dark times of 2005 and the Scottish Violence Reduction Unit has doubtlessly played a part in that. We have walked beside an army of determined doctors, teachers, nurses, police officers, social workers and many more who do their duty every day – putting communities and the people who comprise them at the core of their daily work. Long term change can only be achieved if everyone pulls together with a message of prevention allied to mutual respect and understanding.

Since 2005, homicide rates in Scotland have dropped significantly from 137 to the 60 homicides recorded last year. Doubtlessly, the greatest decrease has been in Glasgow which accounts for over 50% of the reduction.

I believe that the basis for a significant proportion of that reduction was the VRU Community Initiative to Reduce Violence (CIRV) campaign which ran from 2008-2012 in the City of Glasgow and successfully addressed a long term problem of territorial gang violence. This was achieved by understanding why people are drawn into that lifestyle and offering gang members alternative options which would provide hope, opportunity and a longer life expectancy. This project was based on 'the Boston Ceasefire' which operated in the USA and has recently been successfully applied in Northampton, England.

Extremely highly evaluated independently by academics, we utilised a series of 'call ins' to deliver hard hitting messages about gang activity identifying that it normally led to early death or a long period of incarceration. We found that the majority of gang members lived their life in constant fear and were seeking an opportunity for change. One by one they took the opportunities we offered of supported education, mentored employment, rehousing etc and by such means the problem that blighted Glasgow for generations was eradicated.

Allied to that we embarked on a unique educational programme 'Mentors in Violence Prevention' which continues to this day and is now delivered by colleagues in Education Scotland. Across the whole country senior pupils discuss and explore issues around violence before delivering similar packages to their more junior fellow pupils. These lessons and the attitudes they implant remain with the students long after they leave school.

In 2006, we discovered the American study of 'Adverse Childhood Experiences' (ACES) and brought the authors to Scotland to influence thinking. They identified that the harder the start in life a child has the more likely they are to have poor outcomes. In other words, childhood trauma is more likely to lead to alcoholism, drug addiction, domestic violence, criminality, imprisonment and similar issues. That, for many children, life chances are dictated before birth.

That study has had a huge influence on the work of the VRU and since 2008 our focus has been on prevention, understanding and opportunity. It wasn't until we started to show the documentary film 'Resilience' in 2016, however, that the ACES work really took off in Scotland. Our national aim is now to be an 'ACE aware nation' with a wider public understanding of childhood trauma and the adoption of public policies which take account of this issue.

At the SVRU, we utilise 'trauma awareness' to search for intervention points, places where we can engage with people when they arrive at a 'reachable moment'. Along with our friends at the charity 'Medics Against Violence' we established the Navigator Programme in hospitals across the country. Through this we talk to people who have arrived at Accident and Emergency as victims or perpetrators of violence and assist them to embark on life changes which address these problems, problems that are very often recurring. The success of this programme has led to us establishing 'Navigator' projects in police custody suites and in our local community hubs.

We adopted another successful American Programme from Los Angeles, the Homeboy Industries Project, which takes former gang members and provides them with mentoring and employment, supporting them to integrate into wider society often for the first time. Our 'Street and Arrow' programme, based on the aims and design of Homeboy, takes former violent offenders in Scotland and replicates the training and mentoring programme preparing the trainees for employment elsewhere when the 1 year course is completed.

For many of our trainees, this experience is the first occasion in their lives where someone has believed in their ability or has provided an opportunity for them to grow and thrive as a person. The fact that this is a project run by police officers is, to them, eye opening.

Sustaining social change – trauma-informed at community level

All of our projects are unique and innovative in a Scottish context. The themes of hope and compassion are continuous threads. But we also seek to influence other organisations and wider public debate by repeating the mantras of understanding, hope and opportunity.

We seek to challenge wider public attitudes, ones you see replicated in our newspapers and quoted by politicians, often with no understanding of the issues that lie at the heart of the problem. We challenge the judgemental nature of society, we explain that many of the issues that face us today are entwined, drug addiction or alcoholism, homelessness and violence are often prevalent in the same individual and tackling them in isolation is unlikely to bring about change. We stress most loudly that building more prisons and throwing away the key will not bring an answer to our problems, if it did America would be the safest country in the world.

The journey that Scotland has undertaken has been identified by many as 'good practice' and thus 'Violence Reduction Units' are now appearing elsewhere. Whilst it is nice to see our initiatives being recognised, I always stress to those who look for advice that our work is not yet done. We may have reduced homicide by more than half since 2005 but Scotland remains a relatively violent country. 60 homicides in the last year pays testament to that fact. Too many lives still scarred by violence and too many lives lost in tragic circumstances. We may have seen significant and undeniable progress but there has been a levelling off in terms of reduction and the big drops we once saw are now harder to achieve. Further reduction will require social change.

We know that it is in some of our poorer communities that violence remains a daily normality. If you are poor in Scotland you are still more likely to become a victim of violence. That is unacceptable. Added to that we know that those living in our poorer communities are more likely to self-medicate with alcohol and drugs to blur the reality of their daily lives. Indeed, their children are more likely to grow up with significant childhood trauma and the likelihood of poor life chances with limited expectation. Thus, the cycle repeats.

In the last year, Scotland has recorded the highest number of drugs deaths in Europe per capita, our levels of suicide are a cause for concern and homelessness and foodbank usage appears to be on the rise. These issues are related and whilst a 'public health approach' is within the current lexicon of the public sector, we still appear to tackle each issue in isolation rather than addressing the underlying causes of poverty and inequality. I constantly reaffirm my belief that the structures of our public services were created for the problems of the 1950's and may no longer be suitable to address the challenges being presented to us in the 21st century. The arrival of COVID-19 has merely exacerbated problems that were already evident.

Many of the key services dealing with drug addiction, alcoholism and homelessness are delivered by the third sector for low levels of remuneration and subject to constant competitive tendering where cost savings often appears to be the driver. A true 'public health approach' would recognise the importance of these vital services and prioritise them accordingly.

Added to that, our historic approach to drug and alcohol misuse have not addressed the problem. Perhaps there is a need to take a wholly fresh approach, one which addresses the chaotic needs of the individual rather than seeking to punish them for their shortcomings.

With this in mind, we are embarking on a new project this year, one that recognises that communities can suffer trauma and not just the individuals who live there. Indeed, in many respects our traditional approach neglects the problems of our communities. We tend to set national policies with a view to improving the country as whole and our services are aimed at supporting individuals or family groups. We tend to overlook the fact that it is communities that sustain and support these families and that these communities also require nourishment, compassion and the provision of hope.

And finally, follow the evidence – not the ideology

Clearly, a small unit like the VRU cannot bring about the sort of change required to support and develop communities that have suffered from numerous social problems for generations. We can bring our unique approach to these communities to help create a movement for change, to introduce fresh thinking and to assist in enabling third and public sector organisations to work more coherently. We aim to work from ground up and listen to the views of the community about their needs and aspirations rather than provide the services that we think they require. To do it' with them' and not 'to them'.

The arrival of COVID-19 has delayed the introduction of this project. It has provided greater opportunity for planning and for making essential connections in the community and with a vast variety of partner agencies. We have had staff working in foodbanks throughout the lockdown period observing the levels of poverty and desperation, which are common in towns and cities across the UK, and building confidence and relationships with numerous individuals with whom we plan to work in the coming months.

We have gained a significant knowledge of the cause and effect of violence over 15 years of operation. This knowledge has underlined the need to provide properly funded and sustained services if we are truly to address the impact of poverty and social exclusion in all its forms. I believe that employment offers the best solution to these issues but our young people require equality of opportunity and the removal of often unnecessary barriers if that is to be achieved. One such barrier is the difficulty to make a fresh start once an individual has been convicted of a criminal offence. As a society we need to become more understanding and forgiving, to allow people a 'second chance'.

In Scotland, the VRU will continue to work with partners to develop solutions to the violence that still infects us. Our strength has been in our ability to innovate without being held to the normal public sector demand to meet targets and produce outcomes.

We don't believe in quick fixes, it takes time to develop interventions that work. Soundbites are not solutions!

Determination, graft and a commitment to follow the evidence (not the ideology) have been the hallmarks of the SVRU approach. There can be no bystanders in addressing the issue of violence in our communities. There can be no excuses if we are to prove that violence is preventable and not inevitable.

I sincerely hope that the recently established regional VRU's in England and Wales provide such a vehicle for change elsewhere.

POLICE OFFICERS AS PEACE OFFICERS: THE ROLE OF KINDNESS IN POLICING

Dr Peter Neyroud CBE QPM PhD

During the lockdown phase of the Coronavirus pandemic in 2020, the primary role of the police portrayed in the media appeared to be that of strict enforcement. Police in the United Kingdom were shown challenging families in parks to justify compliance with crude "stay at home" restrictions. Police drones were flown over National Parks to deter walkers. Police issued several thousand Fixed Penalty notices to, mostly, young people, who had transgressed the restrictions to see their friends, or "gathered" in a group. Images from India showed police officers humiliating citizens breaking the curfew, and even beating them with lathis.

The Lockdown saw a level of state intrusion into our private lives that paralleled and, in some ways, exceeded the 1940s war-time regulations on rationing, fuel use and curfew. The encouragement to people to call out their neighbours on police websites, if they felt that restrictions were being breached, was even compared to life behind the Iron Curtain during the Cold War by some commentators.

Small acts of kindness – confident policing in a crisis

Yet, even in the midst of such restrictions, there were some extraordinary examples of the police in a completely different role. In Karnataka in India, a local Police Inspector converted the kitchen of his police station into a feeding station, to pack meals for homeless and unemployed citizens that his constables came upon whilst patrolling the streets. In the northern state of Haryana, when police came knocking at one elderly man's door, it was not to enforce restrictions. For, locked down on his own, with his family locked down in a neighbouring state, he was stunned and reduced to tears when he opened the door and the police officers sang *"Happy birthday to you!"* The police told him there was no need to feel lonely, because they were like his family too, before producing a birthday cake and lighting the candles.

These were by no means isolated examples of police kindness during Lockdown. Nor, indeed, is police kindness rare in more normal times. Whether it be that a police officer gives a homeless man shoes and clothes, and then directs him to a shelter where he can get food and a bed, or when another officer comforts a person after having to notify them of a loved one's death, there are many small acts of kindness by police officers. One might argue that they are trivial amidst the wider noise of enforcement and the traumatic worldwide images of acts of extreme "unkindness", such as the lethal force used by police officers that caused the death of George Floyd in Minneapolis. However, in the face of a wave of calls for police reform, defunding, or even abolition of the police, kindness matters even more; and the evidence for this goes well beyond mere hope and warm sentiments.

The emergence of community policing

At the beginning of the 1980's, after the clamour of the first great era of police reform in the 1960s had faded to a whisper, police leaders found themselves facing a deep crisis. Their operations were being driven by escalating demand from the telephone and a need to react to increasing crime loads, whilst their resources were restricted. Yet, the research on what works in policing had demonstrated that reactive investigation was ineffective. Responding faster and faster to more and more calls neither prevented crime nor satisfied victims; and police patrol tactics, based on random omnipresence, were largely akin to King Canute's well-known attempt to hold the tide back.

Instead of despair, what emerged was the development of Community Policing. This approach refocussed the police towards a "peace officer" role, trying to solve community problems with the community rather than through a law enforcement role, where law largely defined the problems, and enforcement and arrest dominated the solutions, as well as the measured outcomes. Community policing has had a roller-coaster ride over the four decades since its formal conception. For some politicians and police leaders, community policing conflicted with a Manichean view of crime and criminals, in which offenders constitute a distinct "other" deserving only of punishment and deterrent policing.

However, research has increasingly identified the benefits of a community policing approach. A Campbell Collaboration systematic review of the effectiveness of community policing found that, whilst the impact on crime numbers might not be that significant, the benefits – in confidence in policing and the legitimacy of the police – were substantial.

Central to this gain are the core elements of community policing. These are: the commitment of the police to listen to community concerns and the communities' definitions of the problems that they want prioritised; and a problem-solving approach that sees enforcement as only one of a wide range of possible interventions, and the police as part of a network of organisations that could provide them. Indeed, a careful reading of the literature promoted by the "defund the police" movement would support a model of policing that is recognisably community policing.

Finding the right balance: Rightful not 'lawful' – effectively preventing harm

Listening to the community and learning to stand in the shoes of those being policed is a critical first step to a kinder policing. Moreover, an increasingly important body of research on procedural justice and legitimacy is showing us that listening, a preparedness to change in response to concerns, and a careful respect for every citizen – be they victim, offender, protestor or just encountered in the street – is a key component of the legitimacy of the police. On the other hand, where police seek to justify their acts primarily by standing behind statute and regulation, they lose respect. Rightful policing, emphasising listening and respect, rather than just "lawful" policing, is more effective.

This becomes all the more important when we consider the challenges that we will face in the aftermath of COVID 19, and amidst the global depression that now seems inevitable. A central task of policing has always been policing the poorest and most desperate in our communities. Global depressions tend to tip many more in our communities into such a plight. Time after time over the last 200 years, since modern policing began, police leaders have faced the challenge of maintaining order and preventing crime in the midst of hard times. One dilemma that has constantly tested police leaders has been to find the right balance between over-policing by excess use of enforcement powers and street-stops of citizens in an attempt to control crime (often egged on by crude statements from politicians), and under-policing because police are either fearful of disorder, or simply unengaged with the community. Sir Robert Peel's acknowledgment that the task of British Police was to prevent harm, rather than repress the poor and needy, remains a fitting reminder for our times about the importance of the police as peace officers, and the need for kindness, rather than an over-eager reliance on the enforcement of the law.

A PRACTICAL REFLECTION ON GLOBAL PERSPECTIVES OF YOUTH JUSTICE – HOW KINDNESS, HOPE AND COMPASSION DELIVER EFFECTIVE YOUTH JUSTICE SYSTEMS

David McGuire

Isn't it sad that we ask ourselves this question? But it is sadder to know that some people would be thinking whether kindness should play any role in the criminal justice system at all. To be kind, hopeful and compassionate should be qualities of any human being, the lack of these being one of the reasons we have a criminal justice system. And one of the reasons the criminal justice system fails, in terms of outcomes for offenders, is basically the lack of kindness, hope and compassion.

If we do a simplistic divide of the criminal justice system, we would have victims and perpetrators. No one would argue that victims deserve the qualities which would help them to heal from what they have gone through. No one would argue that these victims deserve to have well trained, highly qualified staff to help and support them through all the trauma caused. I do not dispute that for a second. I have been the victim of an offence, not once but several times. Most of the people I know have in one way or another, and it is easy to have empathy with victims – it is normal, it is human.

Humble beginnings ... 'fighting' with kindness

However, when I started to work in the youth criminal justice system, nobody prepared me for what I was going to face in my role as an educator. In fact, I had no idea what an educator was until way after I started work. It was my 23rd birthday and working in custodial settings was not something I grew up wanting to do, I studied to be a teacher. By chance, how most of the best things happen, I was recruited to work as an educator for Diagrama in Cordoba. Friends and family questioned more than once about how risky my job was going to be and wondered how I could even think of helping young offenders.

But it was in my first shift shadowing another educator when I discovered the exceptional humans that were there. It was quite remarkable. You could feel everybody's joy in the atmosphere, even when there was tension. Staff were positively supporting the young people (or young offenders – as I should have called them, not forgetting who they were). As that was my first interaction working with the other side of the system, I simply accepted everything as the norm.

I thought my organisation was nuts – they were paying me to have a good time with young people (I still think they are nuts paying me for the role I have now 19 years after).

I had my best and worst moments in life in that role. I cannot say that every second I spent there was perfect, far from it, but I can say that every second I learnt how to be a better person.

As you can imagine, I did not analyse what I was going through. I was a young man, I just did what I was shown. I watched as others failed to stay working there and I could not understand it. To me, it seemed the easiest job ever, but now I recognise this is not a job for everybody.

I quickly understood it was not my place to judge any of the kids placed in custody, for two very clear reasons. First, I was not a judge – my role was a different one. And second, I realised I could not honestly say that I would not commit the same crime as any of them had, in the same circumstances that they had been through.

I remember like it was yesterday, when I discovered this. It was when I was with friends and family watching news of a very serious crime committed by some young people. They questioned how I could work and spend a second working with this type of rubbish?

I knew the children in the news personally, and my response was only: Who knows what the hell they have gone through to do that? I was not justifying what they did, and I did empathise with the victims. But, why? Why did they do that? Would I do the same? I just remember answering... I cannot say that I would not have done the same.

I continued working, the years went by and I learned a lot, mainly by making mistakes myself.

Mistakes... it's a word that did make a great deal of sense for me and my development. It was my best tool for learning. Most of the time we all criticised ourselves for not doing enough when a young person failed. On the one hand, this was a positive thing because we were so focused on improving ourselves. On the other hand, we needed to understand that young people were responsible for their own acts, and we were not responsible for changing them. In fact, it is not our role. Our role is to guide them - but they do need to make decisions and understand the consequences.

Kindness played its part. I cannot count the times a young person made serious mistakes (acted aggressively, insulted staff). When the same educator – the target of these transgressions – said 'good morning' with a smile the following day, the young person's face was a picture. The young person had what I can only describe as like a short circuit. It was difficult for them to understand how – after they had behaved that way – we did not take anything personally, and we kept 'fighting' with kindness. It was foreign to them.

Global perspectives – different isn't always better

It wasn't until I went travelling a long time after, visiting youth justice systems worldwide, that I started to discover something was different. I did not recognise the practice I was seeing. It took me a while to analyse that, because I realised that I had worked in a bubble - and not all gardens are so green.

I have visited over 20 different youth criminal justice systems to date. Not all countries have got it wrong. I will not say who is who in this article, I will just highlight some differences.

The first difference I noticed between systems was the vision itself. There were countries that focused on punishment and others on rehabilitation. And countries that had changed their criminal justice objectives for the worse over time.

It was obvious where kindness was part of the approach in the most simplest things. How the staff smiled at the children, how they spoke to one another with respect, the food that was provided, their manners while they were eating, the contact between staff in the different activities. There are infinite examples to highlight. Every single interaction based on being kind.

Another very notable difference was the language used in the systems, which linked very closely to the vision for the service itself. For example, the use of UN rules and recommended language, how the perpetrators were named (young offenders, young people...), how workers were named (prison officers, custody officers, educators)... I can go on and on.

Some systems follow a person-centred approach and others a money-centred approach. We all live in a society where the finances drive pretty much everything. We live in a liberal economy where much of the time money has become not just important but central in decision making.

Providers are also diverse in different countries. Some are just pure public sector, others are private sector. These could be separated by for profit and non-for-profit private sector. I am very public sector driven, but I have to say I have been disappointed by them, mostly because their focus is wrong.

Finally, there is great disparity in the members of staff delivering the service in the youth justice system. I am not going to say that in any of the systems the majority of staff were bad people. But as was the same for me, they normalised to the system they entered into. I was just lucky enough to be modelled in a certain way, by an organisation which had a clear vision of how to work in this field.

Kindness – the best training I ever had

All these variances are on different levels of the spectrum, nothing is black or white. There is an amalgam of colours in each of them. But in Diagrama's system kindness, hope and compassion played a key role for the perpetrator.

What Diagrama showed my colleagues and myself was simply kindness, hope and compassion – just that – and it was done in a way that we were parenting without even knowing we were parenting. Isn't that nice? That's the beauty of simplifying the complex – making easy something that appears so difficult. It is the best training we received.

Being kind helped us to break down the barriers the children came with, when they arrived in custody. They really understood that we cared. It was maybe the first time someone cared about them, and it was not just a job we were doing. The children understood that being kind made them achieve more in all circumstances. And they learnt how being kind to each other would make them progress in life. An obvious measure we can apply in this approach is the amount and type of incidents in the centre. Children understood how to resolve problems in different ways and to avoid those behaviours which landed them in custody.

And so we can understand parenting as the process of promoting and supporting the physical, emotional, social, and intellectual development of a child from infancy to adulthood.

And guess what? Which systems would you say had better outcomes? The one with, or without, kindness, hope and compassion?

My observation and analysis confirms that those without will find more violence, more harm, more trauma, more reoffending. I have noticed that countries which include kindness in their legislation and in their objectives tend to involve kindness in their implementation. When the training is based more around kindness, the staff who deliver the service are kind. And ultimately the incidents are less. The children learn how to become kind citizens and the reoffending rates are lower than those countries for whom punishment is the basis of the system. The contrary happens within those systems without these characteristics of kindness.

So to put it bluntly, kindness, hope and compassion are simply and basically the key to the success of the criminal justice system.

Window of Opportunity, HM Prison Isle of Wight (Albany)
Image courtesy of Koestler Arts

The Butterfly Effect

Mr Gee

You can never predict the precise moment when someone realises their need to change.
To accept a song of sympathy,
To partake in that alluring elixir of "perhaps",
Which allows them to perceive that which must,
And close their eyes forevermore to that which can't,

Change usually offers no hand of comfort,
It provides no promise of peace,
And rarely relents its secrets easily,
It's like that first gear considered to get your first car moving,
It makes a whole heap of noise,
And barely takes you from your parked position without stalling,
But finally, that engine gets put to work,

Maybe that's why we fear it so,
For it requires duty from our thoughts,
A determined decision,
So much effort,
So little gain,
And amidst the coughing and spluttering of our natural aversion to shift,
Strains whisper in our ear,
A creaking challenge to our vain thoughts of understanding,
Cranking against every secure idea of our nostalgic emotion,

Poets often use the cliché of a caterpillar to signify change,
And sadly my friend; I am no different,
Consider even the most cantankerous caterpillar,
One that remarkably crawls day-by-day

Until a gear-shift occurs, prompting a decision to re-emerge,
As a magnificent butterfly,
Still cantankerous; probably more so.
But with flight!
Please stop me if you've heard this one before,

Yet a butterfly cannot perceive its own beauty,
The spectrum of its wings fall far outside its gaze.

It enjoys the freedom of first flight but cannot see itself
At best, it can only appreciate its aesthetics via the kindness of others,
Who admire such change and offer encouragement,
With an applause of compassion,
How else would it ever know to emerge from its stagnant echo?

I once gave a speech about the "role of a poet"
during a workshop in Brixton prison, I spoke of the power of
poetry to cultivate the idea of self-love,
And how this would instigate change,
I rambled on about how the greatest choice that we have to make,
Is the decision to love ourselves,
And how all positive change will stem from that,

But this was Brixton,
And my own poetry needed searching,
I was soon stopped to fit the description,
Someone had indeed heard it all before,
One of the inmates gave me wise caution and said:
"Bruv. Living is easy, it's loving that's hard".
"Look around Poet-Man and show me where those
hopeful wings dwell."

I looked into the eyes of the other inmates,
I couldn't see them,

I surveyed the stern visage of the Officers,
The maintenance staff, the nurses,
The Governor,
I couldn't see them,

I even recalled coming in, as I got off the bus,
At that familiar stop,
And crossed the familiar road to walk up the familiar path,
Of a black man entering prison,

I caught a reflection of my own self,
Within the darkened window of a frustrated car,

Engine screaming yet stuck in traffic,

Almost devoid of purpose,
Yet it held my image well
And I still couldn't see them,

Was I really walking around this prison with
No butterfly wings?

No Love?
No hope?
No compassion?
Had I forsaken my role before I had even arrived?
Something needed to change

WE ARE DOING THE BEST WE CAN WITH A VERY BAD SYSTEM

Marianne Moore

A system contrary to hope

When Elizabeth Fry was told in February 1813, of the 300 women of Newgate gaol – of the sick women laying on a bare stone floor, clutching naked crying children, enduring the bitter winter, predatory visits from the male prisoners and turnkeys, and in an environment of dirt, menstrual and afterbirth blood and — it was compassion that compelled her to see for herself. Mr Newman, Newgate's Governor, had to be persuaded to allow Elizabeth and her friend Anna in. Once overcome, the women then met another barrier: the turnkey refused to open the cell door because he said the women were evil and vicious animals who could not be trusted. Yet in the face of the stiff, 'this is not how things are done', coldness of the prison infrastructure, Elizbeth Fry pushed on, until she was through the gate and together with the prisoners. Face to face with the women inside Newgate prison she recorded that, in their eyes, she saw a terrible hopelessness.[1]

The criminal justice structure was built to control and contain. It seeks to do little more than that because it has never been equipped to do more. Its rigid hierarchy allows only compliance and assimilation. There is little room for movement, for kindness, or for doing things differently.

Kindness and compassion are not embedded in the system – they show themselves despite the system. They come from outside, and they seep in between the cracks. Kindness shows up in the enthusiasm and hope of the new recruit, the benevolence of the volunteer, and the hard work of those who truly see and respect those who are trapped within the structure. Yet seep through it does, because at our core, people would rather love than fear.

That freezing first day in 1813, Elizabeth and Anna clothed the babies in the flannel, cuddled them, and reached out to their mothers with friendly touch and words of kindness. Connections were made and bridges were built between two wealthy, privileged women and those who had 'othered', disdained, and committed to the walls of that prison. Interrupted by giving birth to her ninth child, Elizabeth didn't return until Christmas 1816, when – alarmed by the children living alongside their mothers in the squalid conditions – she hatched a plan to educate them. The Governor, Dr Cotton, its chaplain, and two of London's sheriffs (the precursors to the police) rejected Elizabeth's plan because they said that educating the prisoners' children could only lead to disorder and possibly violence, and that all they were interested in was idleness gambling and drinking. With their prejudices and desire for the status quo butting up against Elizbeth's determination, they deferred a decision and suggested another meeting. When this meeting was held an excuse was settled upon – they couldn't allow any education because there was no space for it. This excuse covered up their underlying apprehension and hopelessness – they felt that her labours would be fruitless.

Elizabeth left the men in the governor room and went to discuss the matter with the prisoners. They agreed to make a cell available for the school, and they chose a representative, Mary Connor, to be their teacher. In the face of a united front, and with no more excuses, the men capitulated. The next day, with 30 children – many who had been born in prison, others having been convicted – the first school in British Prison history was established in early 1817.[2]

Kindness and compassion founded the school. The glimmer of hope it gave the women to see their children educated led them to petition for themselves. They asked to be taught to read and to sew, so that they might be able to make money for themselves in the prison and afterwards. Elizabeth wanted to help by setting up a workshop, but again met male resistance. Even her fellow prison reformers Fowell Buxton and Sam Hoare rejected her idea, insisting that the women were unteachable; the materials would be stolen, and then scissors and needles would become weapons. Disappointed but undeterred, Elizabeth turned to her female Quaker acquaintances, and eleven of them set up an exclusively female society called the *Association for the Improvement of the Female Prisoner*s in Newgate in April 1817. On the first day of the workshop Elizabeth and her colleagues asked the consent of the women to instigate certain rules of organisation and behaviour; all hands rose in unanimous agreement.[3] As Governor Newman watched on, 'to his surprise' he was deeply moved by the initiative, Elizabeth's faith, 'and by the expressions of earnest attention and hope that sat so poignantly on the ravaged faces before her.' [4] This outside hope made it more possible to see it from the inside.

Challenging through compassion

Elizabeth Fry struggled with depression. Struck down, by what is now known as post-natal depression on the birth of her first (of eleven) children, a tendency for depression stayed with her for much of her adult life, and she was often scared that she might descend into madness. These, "trials of a nervous imagination," she knew, "no one knows but those who have felt them."[5]

Her experience as a woman, and particularly one prone to depression was at the route of her empathy and compassion for prisoners. When he accompanied her on prison visits her brother was struck by her special concern for 'lunatics', noting that her manner was so tender and loving towards them that he sensed she shared an affinity with them.[6] Her affinity with the female prisoners she sought to help, was clear in her appeals to her fellow ladies to help themselves. She believed that, 'no persons appear to me to possess so strong a claim on their [women's] compassion, and on their pious exertions, as the helpless, the ignorant, the afflicted, or the depraved, of *their own sex*.'[7] The compassion that

Elizabeth felt, and urged in her fellow middle-class ladies, was based on her ability to empathise with the women in the way that the men in the justice system, could not, or sought not.

Five years after her first visit to Newgate, in February 1818, Elizabeth was invited to talk to a House of Commons Select Committee on prisons. Her evidence centred on three major points: the importance of religious instruction; the need to separate prisoners according to crime and criminal history; and the value to them of income-producing employment of which the earnings should be kept for their release.[8]

Confronted by a justice system that was exclusively designed and run by men, and speaking to an all-male Select Committee, Elizabeth Fry, as a woman, was an anomaly. In the strict social code of the day women's proper place was considered the home, and they were deliberately excluded from public life. As an active prison reformer, Elizabeth was not living the life dictated for ladies at the time. Yet she saw women's prescribed role as a 'most important check,' on 'a variety of abuses, which are far too apt to creep into the management of these establishments.'[9] Indeed, whilst she acknowledged the importance of a woman's role as daughter, sister, wife, and mother, yet stated, 'it is a dangerous error to suppose that the duties of females end here'.[10]

Female prisoners, derided as aberrations of what a woman was supposed to be, had the least respect of everyone. They were barely considered at all by the men who ran Parliament, and were considered as fair game for sexual desires by the turnkeys who ran the prisons. Elizabeth, as one of the few women who managed to get the ear of the government, did her best to use her position to advocate for them. Radically in 1818, Elizabeth suggested to the Select Committee that female prisoners should be kept in prisons that were exclusively for women, staffed by female prison officers and inspected by visiting Ladies Committees. The Committee did not act on her suggestions, but they sowed the seeds for later reform.

It was in Robert Peel, the famous instigator of the modern police force, who became Home Secretary in 1822, that Elizabeth was able to find the most willing ear. Keen to hear from experts he met with Elizabeth and Fowell Buxton, who was now an MP, and was in sympathy with at least some of Elizabeth's suggestions to the 1818 Select Committee.[11] His 1923 Prisons Act put a stop to governors charging private fees and instead prison warders became salaried employees of the state, prisoners were to be classified, and men and women housed in separate areas of the prison, and, a triumph for Elizabeth, to be supervised entirely by female wardens. The prison system was to be one of reformation, and the use of irons and solitary confinement was prohibited... for now.

By 1830, the country was gripped with rates of crime and offending that seemed to be endlessly increasing, and the transportation system, where prisoners were taken to the colonies as their punishment, was increasingly seen as little deterrent and a huge financial drain. Elizabeth was again called to a Select Committee, this time investigating what forms of punishment would most effectively bring about the reduction of crime. The 'silent and separate' system, popular in the USA and based on the model at the Eastern Penitentiary at Cherry Hill, Pennsylvania, was one of the key punishments investigated. In this model prisoners spent their entire sentence in solitary confinement, exercising alone in individual compounds. Another model – the human treadmill – was also widely endorsed. This was the idea that the prisoner should not spend their time in idleness but that their labour should still be pointless.

Elizabeth knew from her experience at Millbank prison that solitary confinement led to depression, the loss of mental faculties, and did nothing to "prepare for a return to social life." She told the Select Committee that the treadmill was downright injurious to woman's health and stressed continually that education and employment should be the priority rather than either of these two proposed methods.[12] Again, they did not listen. Instead, both the silent and separate system, and the treadmill were introduced into British prisons as part of a massive prison building project.

By the time Elizabeth was asked to a third Select Committee in 1835 at the House of Lords, Elizbeth's exasperation with what was happening to the prison estate was clear. She highlighted the abuses in the new system - prisoners who broke the silent regime were punished by a reduction in their already meagre diet, men were forced to pointlessly tread the wheel for up to ten hours a day. "I think there is more cruelty in the goals than I have ever seen before," she despaired.[13]

The resulting Prisons Act of 1835 did not put an end to the system, but began central government control, with the Home Secretary receiving the power to create and enforce new prison regulations. He also was given the power to create what the reformers had long asked for: a paid, professional prison inspectorate whose duty was to visit every place kept for the confinement of prisoners. One of the new inspectors was William Crawford, the enthusiastic advocate for the American separate system.[14] Elizabeth had clearly managed to make some policy improvements, but she was battling against a rigid commitment to a system where the goal was deterrence, punishment and control, rather than reformation.

Elizabeth continued to give as much kindness and support to female prisoners, and others, as all around her, the prison system became a more modern and strict machine. In 1841, she saw first-hand a young woman who had a mental breakdown straight after being kept in a solitary cell at Millbank, and had to watch the new prison at Pentonville – the model of the chilling silent and separate system – being built and applauded. Yet she deemed its dark cells and the thick window glass that obliterated the sky as unchristian and uncivilised. Too easily, she knew, did the darkness give rise to a gloom which eventually led to depression, and she was clear by this point that solitary confinement caused physical and mental deterioration, and a 'despairing and stupefied state'.[15]

Sadly, it would take another sixty years for government to hear her wisdom and abolish the damaging system in 1902. It is the structure of these prisons and culture of control which lives on in the system today.

Yet our system houses people, and people at their heart prefer kindness to coldness, and people need hope; it is the last thing to die.

On 17th February 1818, the same month that Elizabeth attended her first Select Committee, she received a letter from Charlotte Newman, a female prisoner waiting alone in the condemned cell. In the letter Charlotte expresses her "most grateful thanks," to Elizabeth for, "your very great attention to the care of my poor soul." She noted that despite her plight, "I have much to be thankful for. I feel such serenity of mind and fortitude," and she prayed that, "God, of His infinite mercy, grant I may feel as I do in the last moments," before she was taken by Newgate's chaplain to the scaffold.[16]

That, by her kindness and compassion, Elizabeth was able to bring some hope to Charlotte in her last moments, shows that whatever shards of light that can be let in, are the Justice systems biggest salvation. One can only hope that Elizabeth could be proud of this when she herself passed away on 13th October 1845 at the age of 65.

COMPASSIONATE CUSTODY?

Dave Nicholson

Back to the future?

We need to re-think custody and return to its origins of kindness, hope and compassion. So says criminologist and Christian theologian Andrew Skotnicki. And he's not alone. Nearly 100 years ago secular Fabian Socialists, Sidney and Beatrice Webb argued that even their ideal socialist state was unlikely to provide the compassionate treatment required for the reformation of serious offenders.[1] They suggested instead that religious charities should run selected prisons, because they would be more likely to offer the kindness, hope and compassion required to reform and bring out the better nature of serious offenders. Many contemporary Conservatives like Guy Opperman MP agree and argue that religious organisations are better placed to provide the compassion required to 'turn around' the lives of prisoners:-

> 'Why can't you have a Charity running a Prison or a Church/ Community coming together to take charge and turn around low-grade prisoners?'[2]

Skotnicki goes further and traces the origins of the modern prison itself to the religious quest *'to create the conditions for a conversion as a means of reclaiming one's inherent and virtually limitless reservoir of compassion.'*[3] For Skotnicki, the modern prison originated in the search for a compassionate form of custody that would create an environment that enabled conversion – the release of the prisoner's own innate compassion which would 'correct' their future behaviour.

Compassionate custody is based on the conviction that such a conversion is possible, regardless of the specific offence, without any need to inflict suffering, or to use the act of punishment as a warning or deterrent to potential offenders, or even without any need to make interventions into the lives of the incarcerated in order to 'rehabilitate' them.

Conversion to the 'Perennial Philosophy'

While this conversion is more likely to be found in a religious context, Skotnicki claims it is not necessarily conversion in a strictly religious sense. The purpose of compassionate custody should be to engender contemplation and introspection, leading the prisoner to see beyond their empirical self and convert to a larger conception of life and moral accountability. Such contemplation is not necessarily a purely religious practice:-

> 'Contemplation here means a compassionate openness to the moment without judgement or analysis, both in the flow of daily events and in regular periods of silence and solitude. Such practices are not only for those self-defined as religious or spiritual.'[4]

Nor is it conversion to any particular religious or secular creed. Rather it is conversion to a 'perennial philosophy' of compassion and civility that Huxley and many others claim underlies all the major world religions as well as many modern secular philosophies. It is a conversion that helps everyone 'find out who they really are' whatever their religious beliefs or lack of belief. For prisoners this enables them to turn their lives round and gain acceptance back into the law-abiding community.[6]

Conversion and Desistance

Skotnicki points out that this is also what many scholars of desistance recognise when they talk of the substantial character change required for successful desistance - desistance as 'coming from within...freeing *one's 'real me' from...external constraints.'*[7] Similarly, Giordano[8] and colleagues talk of the 'cognitive transformation' involved in desistance and Braithwaite[9] states, *'The cultural assumption of basic goodness and belief in each individual's capacity for eventual self-correction means that 'nurturant acceptance' is the appropriate response to deviance.'*[10]

A prison regime of such 'nurturant acceptance' would be a compassionate form of custody that engenders the conversion and self-correction that lead to on-going desistance from future offending. Skotnicki claims it was the early Christian monastic communities who first developed this methodology for self-correction through conversion. It was based on the unprecedented belief that time in custody, with the aid and encouragement of the community was sufficient in and of itself to bring about cognitive transformation and full acceptance back into the community.

Skotnicki sees Benedictine monastic practice as the fullest expression of this, creating what might today be called a *'psychologically informed planned environment,'*[11] to enable the offender to find his way back to his true self and rightful place within the community. Benedict devotes much attention in his rule to 'medicines' for the soul to enable this to happen by treating the erring brother with isolation in his cell, fasting, reflection on his life in contemplative introspection, meaningful work, and doing penance.

However, without the support of the community of brothers in enabling the offender to take these medicines, they won't work. *'The community is central to guiding and sustaining the life of the convert.'*[12] Many modern secular scholars again recognise this need for a compassionate, supportive and sustaining community within the unsupportive environment of the modern prison.

Irving Goffman speaks of the need of *'islands of civility'* in 'total institutions' like the prison to provide a supportive community.[13] Toch similarly speaks of *'niches'* or *'oases'* that perform the same function.[14]

Compassionate Custody Today

Whilst still maintaining that compassionate custody doesn't necessarily require a specifically religious community, Skotnicki nevertheless quotes modern faith-based custodial initiatives as contemporary expressions of the nurturant acceptance seen in Benedictine practice. The Humaita Prison in Brazil was handed over by the state in the 1970s to be run entirely by religious groups. Skotnicki sees Humaita as embodying fully the conversion model of compassionate custody without succumbing to an over-emphasis on proselytising which can result in an often superficial conversion to a particular religious creed. As Giordano (2008) puts it:-

> '*It is important to distinguish between fleeting situational use of spirituality in some trying circumstances from spiritual transformations that seem to have long term impact on offenders' lifestyles.*'[15]

Humaita is run as a specifically democratic supportive custodial community by staff (many of whom are also former inmates) and an elected inmate council. It is based on the philosophy that what nearly all prisoners lack is community participation and unconditional love and compassion. The former is provided by practical skills training and co-operative employment, while the latter is provided by a system of godparenting by outside mentors, many of whom are also former inmates themselves.[16] The nurturant acceptance of this custodial community manages to engender a progressive intellectual, moral and spiritual transformation without imposing any particular religious denomination or metaphysical system of belief, unlike some faith-based aspiring imitators in other parts of the world.[17] As such it approaches Skotnicki's ideal compassionate correctional facility which '*...would be organised to foster the progressive expansion of intellectual, moral and spiritual vision, but...would favour no specific secular or religious point of view.*'[18] It would be an '*enabling environment*'[19] for desistance-supporting cognitive transformation rather than a proselytising institution for forced conversion to a particular secular or religious ideology.

Humaita's supportive community and the work it provides for its inmates is organised on democratic lines because giving offenders joint responsibility for their own progressive expansion of intellectual, moral and spiritual vision is seen as essential to changing their understanding of themselves, revising their belief systems and changing their lifestyle. The same co-production of desistance can also be seen in Italian prison-based Social Co-operatives, which provide employment and mutual support for prisoners in custody and through the prison gate on release in the community.[20]

There are other faith-based compassionate islands of civility in the modern prison system, which nevertheless also conform to Skotnicki's ideal of favouring no specific secular or religious point of view in the pursuit of the progressive expansion of prisoners' intellectual, moral and spiritual vision. Some of these are Offender Behaviour Programmes and interventions fully accredited by the Ministry of Justice in England and Wales and all aim to change the thinking, attitudes and behaviours, which may lead people to reoffend.

'*Belief in Change*' for example[21] focuses on the 'prolific career criminal', males generally in their 30s, who have maintained a steady rate of criminality since age 15 with increasing breadth and severity of offending. The programme is suitable for all prisoners notwithstanding faith or spiritual affiliation or beliefs, although willingness to explore issues from a faith, spiritual, humanistic/philosophical perspective is seen as important for participants to gain maximum benefit.

Similarly, the Kainos Community[22] is a faith-based registered charity delivering a full time, twenty-four week, therapeutic community based programme, '*Challenge to Change*,' targeted at medium to high-risk offenders with criminogenic needs that match those targeted by the programme. It uses a hybrid model – combining elements of cognitive behavioural programmes provided in four main intervention module with learning, and delivered through a therapeutic community approach.

There are also increasing numbers of secular equivalents, including Democratic Therapeutic Communities and Psychologically Informed Planned Environment (PIPE) units in prisons and in probation-approved premises in the community. They are similarly designed as *'enabling environments'*[23] to engender and sustain what Giordano calls the *'replacement self'* and Skotnicki and the perennial philosophy would term the *'true self'* of serious offenders.

> '...offender rehabilitation in therapeutic communities involves a process of purposive and agentic reconstruction of identity and narrative reframing, so that a 'new' and 'better' person emerges whose attitudes and behaviours cohere with long-term desistance from crime. This is possible because the prison-based therapeutic community, with its commitment to a radically 'different' culture and mode of rehabilitation, socially enables, produces and reinforces the emergence of someone 'different.'[24]

Units like these help engender the conversion and long-term desistance-supporting communities for which Skotnicki calls. Crucially, they are also a compassionate form of custody functioning as islands of civility in an otherwise hostile and unsupportive prison environment:-

> 'Compassion is not a word I've heard a lot in prisons but it came up again and again when staff at the Democratic Therapeutic Community at HMP Send spoke about their work with the women in the Community.'[25]

Having said that, what they place less emphasis on is the contribution of work to conversion and radical identity change seen in the Benedictine model and in the specifically co-operative ways of working seen at Humaita and in the Italian Social Co-operatives.

Nevertheless, this idea of conversion as radical change engendered by compassionate custody is of particular interest and importance when considering more serious offenders and particularly those prisoners whose conversion has led to 'radicalisation'.

Conversion and Radicalisation

Radicalisation can itself be seen as a form of conversion:-

'...the notion of radical change remains the core of all conceptions of conversion, whether theological or social scientific.'[26]

Prison Reform International amongst others suggest that prisons can play a critical role in both triggering and reinforcing the radicalisation process which it defines as:

'a dynamic process whereby an individual increasingly accepts and supports violent extremism. The reasons behind this process can be ideological, political, religious, social, economic or personal.'[27]

And violent extremism as:

'promoting, supporting or committing acts which may lead to terrorism and which are aimed at defending an ideology advocating racial, national, ethnic or religious supremacy and opposing the core democratic principles and values.'[28]

But they stress that radicalisation is not concerned with the adoption of radical religious or political opinions, but with the undemocratic adoption, promotion and support of violent means to obtain demands.

Consideration of what to do with such radicalised prisoners has centred on whether to disperse those deemed to be at risk of radicalising other prisoners within the general prison population or to hold them separately. Some emphasise that holding prisoners in isolation from others is damaging to physical and psychological health and well-being and likely to prevent rehabilitation.[29]

But isolation within a supportive community in the form of compassionate custody discussed above suggests otherwise and could form the sort of programme called for by the PRI that is specifically tailored to the unique needs and challenges of radicalised prisoners; a programme which might include

> '...religious counselling and support with stigmatisation arising from being classified as a terrorist offender. A wide variety of different rehabilitation measures...including counselling, dialogue, religious teaching and disengagement.'[30]

The sort of custody run by religious groups called for by the Webbs and Opperman could well provide this, as exemplified by Skotnicki's compassionate custody and the existing faith-based and non-faith-based units already running in prisons. Belief in Change, Kainos Community, Democratic Therapeutic Communities and PIPE's may have different theoretical and philosophical underpinnings, but all aim to engender what Skotnicki would call conversion and self-correction through the nurturant acceptance found in compassionate custody.

"We must meet terrorism with democratic openness."[31]

The democratic openness seen in the compassionate custody and co-operative working at Humaita Prison potentially provides a model of how compassionate custody can engender the conversion and self-correction of radicalised prisoners at the prison-level in the same way as Belief in Change, Kainos, Democratic Therapeutic Communities and PIPEs can do at the prison-unit level.

Compassionate Custody: an 'enabling environment' for conversion and desistance

Such compassionate custody and co-operative working in PIPES and other specialist units in the modern prison system thus provides an 'enabling environment' for desistance and the sort of 'nurturant acceptance' that engenders conversion – the release of the prisoner's own innate compassion enabling them to 'correct' their own future behaviour with the help of a supportive and compassionate custodial community.

What's more, history shows this can work for all prisoners – even the most dangerous and radicalised.

A BRIGHTER FUTURE: THE ROLE OF HOPE IN WOMEN'S REHABILITATION

Olivia Dehnavi

'Curing the negatives does not produce the positives.'
MARTIN SELIGMAN

The scope of rehabilitation

In the last 30 years, the number of women in prison in England and Wales has doubled.[1] We lock up more of our citizens than any country in Western Europe despite the fact that there is no link between prison population and levels of crime.[2] In 2019, the government reiterated its commitment to creating 10,000 new prison places. Instead of making space for more, there is an argument for massively reducing the number of people – especially women – in prison, arguably to zero.

Zero women in prison is an appropriate goal: it would mean aiming for a society in which harm is prevented in the community; where those who do cause harm are able to engage in effective rehabilitation.

Rehabilitation is a term almost inapplicable to our criminal justice system. The prevailing dialogue on rehabilitation assumes that a person sent to prison begins from a place of pro-social stability: that national institutions successfully 'integrate' people into society, that some of those people go morally and legally astray, that the system must simply put them back on track. But this is not the case for most people who are incarcerated, and especially not for women.

Desistance theory acknowledges that the bond between the individual and society can persist only so long as the individual has an emotional attachment to societal goals that they believe are worthy.[3] Yet evidence shows that large numbers of women who end up in prison face multiple disadvantage before being incarcerated, mostly due to social exclusion. They are even more likely than men to face complex challenges such as, to name a few, experience of the care system, domestic violence, drug or alcohol dependency, poverty or mental health issues. The failure of the state addressing these forms of primary disadvantage often propels women into contact with the criminal justice system.[4] Plus, we know that black, Asian and minority ethnic communities are disproportionately criminalised, while care leavers and those excluded from school are vastly overrepresented in the prison estate.[5] How can we as a nation begin the task of reintegrating these groups, when we have not built a society that integrates them in the first place?

Women who commit crime are submitted to the neat package of prison and probation, which is not working. This is demonstrated by the fact that 58% of women are reconvicted within one year of leaving prison.[6] The failure is rooted in two uncomfortable truths: people tend to end up in prison because they have had difficult lives, and solving their problems requires long-term systemic reform both within and outside of the criminal justice system. As a starting point, the government must ensure that everyone enjoys the benefits of functioning systems that do not discriminate. This would require serious investment in education, health, and social work. It would mean not giving up on people.

A new model – from helplessness to hopefulness

On the journey to wide scale systemic change, we must look at the criminal justice system and ask how we can reform rehabilitation for the better. At the moment we know that in prisons some entitlements, such as Release on Temporary Licence (ROTL), are a crucial gateway to family contact or work experience, both proven to aid rehabilitation. But the prison system positions ROTL as a privilege, only accessible if women label themselves as guilty. They might be asked to do this in victim awareness handbooks, or as part of offending behaviour programmes. These interventions encourage women to take blame for their actions and forensically dissect where they went wrong, with little assessment of the social context that may have driven them to the actions that resulted in a conviction.

The most effective rehabilitative models bring about meaning and accomplishment through positive interventions, rather than merely seeking to identify and quash negative behaviour.[7] To take one example, Working Chance[8] is a charity that supports women with convictions to find employment. It delivers holistic care that encompasses mental health support, confidence boosting, and employability skills. In supporting women into work, Working Chance delivers a programme that goes beyond interview and CV skills. In response to the fact that many women with convictions describe having low self-worth, self-esteem is central to the agenda. The charity therefore works closely with partner organisations to deliver support that is far-reaching and unconditional.

Rehabilitation begins with an internal transformation. Martin Seligman, proponent of positive psychology, maintains that 'the way we think about this realm of life can actually diminish or enlarge the control we have over it.'[9] To illustrate this point, he uses a simple example: if you think that you are powerless to change your situation, you may start to think that nothing you do matters. This can cause helplessness: surrendering control to the external environment. When applying this teaching to the criminal justice system, it is hard not to think about prison, which diminishes the choices you have in day-to-day life and puts them in the hands of people who may not always be invested in your welfare. Other social realities that lead to learned helplessness, such as institutional racism, growing up in care, domestic violence or poverty, can themselves be gateways to a prison cell.

Thus, it is important in rehabilitative support to focus on the assets that women can use to their advantage (proving that they are not helpless) and that they can be proud of. Working Chance recognises that women with convictions may have been made to feel powerless. Many women report thinking they have no chance of getting a job after prison, and have little hope for their future. Working Chance works closely with women on an individual basis to identify their interests and talents, to see how these can identify a route to meaningful employment. In short, this is about making women feel good about themselves; motivation naturally follows. This process is trauma-informed, recognising the strengths and skills of the individual, building confidence, and re-educating by embedding new coping skills.[10]

One of the most apparent benefits of this approach is the considerably lower reoffending rates for women who engage with Working Chance's services. Labelling theory shows that being identified as 'criminal' by the criminal justice system leads to further involvement with the system as an individual becomes recognised as, and resigned to, the label they have been designated.[11] This is more likely to happen to people who are labelled on a community-wide scale, most obviously people from racialised communities and those from a deprived socio-economic background. Once a person is identified as deviant, it is extremely difficult for them to shift that label. Shame, stigma and marginalisation follow, and can be a driver towards reoffending.

Shame is an incredibly powerful force, and one that women experience disproportionately in a patriarchal society. Women, who face high expectations to conform to care-giving roles in their communities and families, face the stigma of having failed as a woman, a mother, a carer, once they are given a conviction. Women with lived experience of the criminal justice system report that, just as much as the sentence itself, the long-lasting shame of having been sent to prison is a punishment, and one that extends to their family members. Researcher Brené Brown defines shame as the fear of disconnection.[12] Much like prison, shame is invisibilised; it can make people believe that they aren't worthy of love and belonging. The rehabilitative process then, must necessarily focus on empowerment and inclusion.

Identity theory backs this up, observing that the way we behave is guided by our identity.[13] Labels become a self-fulfilling prophecy – the way that an individual gains status or security is connected to their identity, but that identity has been tied to offending behaviour by the state. However, this circular process can be disrupted. Working Chance works with women to foster an image of the 'desired self' as a psychological route away from negative labelling. The desired self is a positive image of what a woman would like to be, and really thinks that she can be.[14] The second part of that definition is important; the individual must believe that their desired self can become a reality.

The direct inverse and antidote to a pessimistic outlook is, of course, hope. Research shows that hopeful thinking can make a real difference to life outcomes. Hope has been identified as perhaps the single most important factor for an emotional trajectory of desistance, a powerful psychological construct for success.[15] Now we turn to the external element that is necessary for rehabilitation, because for an individual's mental transformation to manifest in material change, their vision of the future must be facilitated by their community. So we must ask, how can a community contribute to the rehabilitation of women?

Academic David Scott advocates for a process called 'interpretive generosity' in assessing the causes of crime; '*that is, a humanitarian and generous interpretation of events, troubles and problematic situations that can allow for alternative ways of reconstructing events and defining human responsibilities in relation to the behaviours reviewed.*'[16] This entails looking at the reasons why people commit certain acts with their background and social context in mind. A model based on interpretive generosity would necessarily lead to less marginalisation of certain communities, and work to address the root causes of harm.

At Working Chance, this generosity translates to holistic support that responds to the particular circumstances that leads each woman to the place she is in today. When you break down the reasons why women with convictions lack self-esteem, it often stems from past trauma and a belief that they don't belong. So it makes sense that women who have undergone positive personal transformation often put it down to the kindness and compassion of the people, sometimes just one person, who believed in them. This has been termed 'social buffering', and the importance of an 'emotionally available adult' to validate your experiences and guide you down the path to recovery has proved critical to helping individuals to process trauma.[17]

Having someone in your life who accepts you and takes your side sounds so simple, but it's true that even small instances of communal hope can change someone's psyche in a positive way and alleviate feelings of helplessness. Labelling works the other way, too. Positive labels can imbue a belief in yourself that is exponentially advantageous.

Hope: A collective responsibility

Hope is consistently the most influential factor in stories of rehabilitation, and the more that society fosters that hope, the more likely an individual is to succeed.[18] Repeatedly, we see women with experience of the criminal justice system turn a corner based on a simple premise: they can now see a brighter future ahead. But positive reinforcement must continue past the walls of charities to really make a difference. Individuals and charities can do their part, but only government can channel resources into the wider systemic change and transformation of public consciousness that can enable palpable, long-lasting benefits. Our leaders must invest in creating a society where justice is realised through a process of collective care and shared hope.

Organiser and educator Mariame Kaba has said that hope is a discipline.[19] It is something that we must practice on a regular basis, and put work into, based on the belief that another world is possible.

Belief in a brighter future, which is central to rehabilitation, requires the validation of a community. This year, we have seen that wide scale systemic change is possible, and that the needs of those most at risk are best met through cooperation founded on the hope that things will get better for all of us. It's time to apply that optimism to the criminal justice system.

We need a constructive rehabilitation model for women that is rooted in desistance theory and underpinned by collaborative hope. Cooperative care is the antidote to a discriminatory, punitive and individualistic criminal justice system.

UNDERSTANDING AND CHANGING THE NARRATIVE

Shola Apena Rogers

Narratives can take many different forms – romance, comedy, tragedy and irony[1] – and can signify how individuals look for meaning and spiritual depth in life. For many individuals convicted of offences, sometimes considered heinous and unforgivable, they narrate stories of 'shattered lives' within a criminal justice context. Narratives of individuals who offend not only offer insight into explanations and 'meaning-making' by the narrator;[2] they can also promote desistance from crime.[3] Cognitive transformation is central to an individual moving on from crime, with the creation of a new non-offending identity. Treatment and rehabilitation programmes are often catalysts for this transformation, by offering hope and compassion linked to the possibility of redemption. A criminal justice system that supports people as they begin to understand their criminal behaviour, as part of their wider life story and journey to embrace crime free lives, needs to create an environment in which forgiveness can occur. Adopting a more strengths-based, future focussed approach to instil hope, develop self-efficacy and to support individuals to develop a non-offending identity using narratives, can help our understanding of individuals and allow new positive identities to be formed.

Understanding individual pathways into the Criminal Justice System

Everyone has a story, narrated by a storyteller. But for those within the criminal justice system (CJS), their narratives are often met with suspicion about the degree of truthfulness being offered, especially when it is a perpetrator providing the narrative. Yet, understanding offender motivation and the 'why' individuals commit crime plays an important part in the CJS process. Lois Presser introduced an approach called narrative criminology[4], which focuses not just on the process of narratives in inspiring and motivating harmful behaviour, but also on how these stories assist in the sense-making of the harm caused. How individuals talk about their offences, what they say and what it communicates about the construction of their identities is key to the rehabilitation process. These stories, especially those containing tragedy and irony, all need a response that incorporates kindness, hope and compassion.

Like with any traditional story, there is always a beginning, a middle and an end. Many of the young people and adults within the CJS will have a storyline, which includes adverse childhood experiences (ACEs), or traumatic events in their early developmental years. There exists a substantial amount of research and evidence describing the negative impact of these experiences on physiological and psychological states of individuals, highlighting the increased likelihood of involvement within the CJS.[5,6] Still more can be learnt from how these vulnerabilities are woven into the fabric of the self-narratives of those who commit crime. When a child or young person has been referred to as "a mistake", emotionally abused, or has watched the prolonged illness of their mother result in her passing, the required response is compassion. Often this is not a response they get. The opportunity to relate to someone is missed and they are not able to make sense of what is really going on in their lives and the impact it is having.

The narrative path for an individual who has experienced ACEs has been linked to one that can encounter many negative outcomes, including increased risk of contact with the criminal justice system. Narrative identity is the core "story of the self" developed during this journey from adolescence – these are the stories we tell ourselves about ourselves, through many short stories over time. Each narrative will reveal a different journey, as to what led to an individual's offending behaviour. Going beyond the details of life histories, narratives expose what informed and guided actions in relation to offending, enabling insight as to how people understand their lives and the world around them. For individuals convicted of serious offences, that narrate stories of 'shattered lives' in the CJS, there may also be places within their narrative that are 'messy and hard to follow'.[7] Providing a safe environment within the various criminal justice institutions, can help an individual make sense of their experience and understand how it influences their decisions and subsequent behaviours.

Those navigating the CJS may present narratives that selectively sequence and organise events, as well as offering the multiple identities that feature within their lives. The significance of these contextual aspects is often overlooked for 'the facts' or 'the truth'. Notably, individuals narrating their story within the CJS are doing so from a subordinate position. Like most, those who are convicted of offences desire a 'normal life', which can prove difficult given how their actions have made it challenging to be viewed as normal by society and, indeed, to themselves. As the narrator/protagonist, they will tell stories in such a way as to promote their cause with the purpose of providing the 'moral' or 'valued endpoint' of the story. Narratives are there to arouse emotions within the audience, but arguably, they also do this within the individual themselves. The Police service, The Crown Prosecution Service, The Courts, and The Probation Service will become the audience at any given time, engaging with narratives of those who may or may not have transgressed. The challenge lies for actors in these different roles within the CJS to dispense with justice not just based on the illegal action, but on the complexity of harm caused.

Rehabilitation: When harm is met with compassion

Naturally, when focussing on the harm caused by a criminal offence, the victim experience should be central. There is still a considerable way to go in this area, with many criminal justice policies and procedures falling short of demonstrating the kindness and compassion victims deserve. Yet, there is also a need to rehabilitate, as well as punish, individuals who have caused harm. Rehabilitation can primarily be achieved by paying attention to narratives, which can start from the initial contact with the Police. When police officers apprehend a person on suspicion of an offence, there are different methods and approaches to investigative interviewing. Prior to the introduction of the Police and Criminal Evidence Act 1984 (PACE), the Reid interviewing technique was used which consisted of police officers using coercive, manipulative and persuasive techniques when questioning suspects.[8] This approach is now largely unused since the introduction of the PEACE model in 1993.[9] Interviewing officers are encouraged to adopt a non-accusatory stance, to enable an information-gathering approach to investigative interviewing, where building rapport is also a key feature. Not assuming that the suspect is guilty from the outset, improves the trustworthiness and transparency of the interaction.

Obtaining a suspect's account lends itself naturally to giving a narrative, albeit in the context of the criminal offence for which they are being charged. If officers are able to build rapport, this is most likely achieved through treating the individual with respect, despite their behaviour. At the very least, police officers can offer kindness in terms of considerations for the rights of individuals in their custody. An empathic approach by officers can result in a full confession or denial, however, the importance lies in allowing that individual to be heard and tell their story. This act of allowing insight into their behaviour and sense making can be developed and maintained as an individual progresses through the Courts process. Narratives, however, can be most significant when told in the prison and probation realms. Here, there is potentially greater time to listen to and unpick the motivation, values, attitudes and other contextual issues relating to why people persist or desist from a life of crime. Yet, the power hierarchy remains a challenge for practitioners trying to engage with these narratives with kindness, hope and compassion.

Viewing narratives within the context of criminal justice intervention, bare some similarity to the recovery narratives found in mental health rehabilitation services. A recovery narrative is one that describes an individual's personal reckoning with adversity, which the person has overcome and goes on to thrive despite their experience. Given the high prevalence of mental health problems within the offender population, utilising narratives can help as part of the healing process. A question often asked within mental health settings is "what are people recovering from/to?" An appropriate parallel question within the CJS is "what are people rehabilitating from/to?" By virtue of this question it encourages a narrative which embraces the notion that although an individual has a past, they will also have aspirations for the future. It is this dialogue that facilitates both understanding about the instigation of crime and desistance from it, providing the hope that is needed.

Case formulation is a prominent feature of clinical work in mental health settings, it is also a growing practice in specialist psychologically informed services within the CJS. A formulation-based approach understands a person's offending behaviour as a result of the interaction of biological (genetic) vulnerabilities, early experience with significant others, and social factors. Collaboration is a key process of formulation and is enmeshed with the qualities of kindness and compassion. Incorporating a person's narrative as to why they are in the CJS, is central to formulation and often reveals relevant background context, as well as certain cognitive distortions that fuel an individual's continued offending behaviour. Cognitive distortions may come in the shape of 'rationalisations' or 'justifications' for the wrongful behaviour, which allow individuals to maintain a positive sense of self. A practitioner's ability to show an understanding of how a person's narrative identity and the cognitive distortions are functional, but by not unchangeable can shape interventions as part of the rehabilitative process.

The division between the self and the self-concept is an important acknowledgement in relation to rehabilitation, as it permits practitioners to respond to the ideas of self-deception and self-knowledge. Taking the view that the self consists of a person's core commitments, aspirations and ideals, allows for the prospect that people make mistakes about what it is they need, what they stand for as a person, and what they really believe. Cultivating this environment can encourage and support cognitive transformation, which helps individuals change their thinking, choices and subsequently, their life direction. These changes in thinking can range from a simple recognition of harm caused by their actions, to the creation of a new non-offending identity and a desire never to return to prison. Thus, there is a strong argument for treatment plans for individuals convicted of offences to focus on what might best facilitate changing their self-narratives and enhance identity transformation. Empowering the individual to define their goals, identify their next steps and create a new narrative. This is in opposition to a sole focus on the deterrence component of the criminal desistence process, which is habitually the focus of the CJS.

A trauma-informed response: Creating hope and showing kindness

An intervention session which comprises of a person talking, sharing their narrative in a meaningful way and experiencing human interaction (in what often feels like an isolated, bleak environment) can be exceptionally powerful. Despite an individual's current offending behaviour, narratives can help them embrace and challenge rather than be in denial. Rationalisations, as a defence mechanism, protect an individual from internalising a deviant identity so that they do not become overwhelmed with shame, which diminishes feelings of self-worth. It requires practitioners, therefore, to work alongside the individual, to support them to engage with circumstances and to think honestly, without them feeling judged. This approach sides with trauma-informed care and is in direct opposition to overreliance on incentives and sanctions as the mechanisms of change and rehabilitation. In order to be true to a trauma-informed approach, practitioners will need vicarious resilience[10] to show each individual compassion when responding to the many narratives involving violence, trauma and abuse.

Ultimately, if kindness, hope and compassion are to play an effective role within the CJS, they will need to go beyond the individual level of analysis to be embedded at an organisational level. Buildings, locations, policies, procedures, leadership and communication need to be consistent with trauma-informed principles and rooted in a systemic and institutional approach to the rehabilitation of individuals. At the organisational level, balance means providing adequate supervision, managing the size and variety of client caseloads, ensuring staff members take their holiday, recognising achievements and ensuring feedback mechanisms for staff to contribute their ideas to the organisation's development and delivery. These actions contribute to supporting the self-care of criminal justice practitioners by shielding them from impact of vicarious trauma. There are also other societal factors which influence the degree to which the CJS can show kindness, hope and compassion. These are found in the narratives of society in relation to how individuals who encounter the CJS should be treated. Empathy affects how people think about crime and punishment in complex ways but can positively help to shape interactions between citizens and agents of the justice system.

An interaction exists between formal and informal social control and it can be difficult to isolate the effects. For example, when supervising individuals who have committed sexual offences, even though probation might not act as a deterrent it can start and maintain individuals' desistance from offending through the formal social control mechanism.[11] This is often achieved through supporting access to the right treatment when needed. More importantly, rehabilitation should include measures to support people as they begin to understand their deviant sexual behaviours and cognitively transform to embrace crime free lives. This suggests benefits aligned with current thinking around sex offender treatment programmes, with less focus on cognitive distortions, instead, adopting a more strengths-based, future focussed approach to instil hope for the future, develop self-efficacy and to support participants to develop a non-offending identity.

There is a strong argument for treatment plans for all individuals within the CJS to focus on what might best facilitate changing their self-narratives and enhance identity transformation. Thus, kindness, hope and compassion become the cornerstone of the rehabilitative process. Having time for narratives should not been seen as a luxury, but as a necessity throughout the CJS and a vital part of restorative approaches to intervention.

After A Mild Rebuke

It's funny how your criticism stung,
Gently chiding me to do much better,
And, though I smiled, the implication hung.
Long after I had put away your letter.
That day I'd read the speech that Heaney gave,
In Stockholm, back in 1995.

His thoughts on poetry were deep and grave,
Reflecting the importance of the prize.
It's true; I am not fit to tie his laces,
But reading him again re-lit my fire.

We both were schooled in knowing where our place is.
Yet that should not prevent us aiming higher.
By standing on the shoulders of the greats,
Like Seamus did, when he looked back to Yeats.

ENSURING RESTORATIVE JUSTICE GOES VIRAL – TIME FOR A SECOND SURGE?

Dr Belinda Hopkins

'The purpose of the Criminal Justice System... is to deliver justice for all, by convicting and punishing the guilty and helping them to stop offending, while protecting the innocent.'
WWW.CJSONLINE.GOV.UK

Introduction

As most of the world is experiencing the challenges of being forced to stay at home and keep our distance from all but close family the qualities of kindness, hope, and compassion have perhaps never been more important. They are vital to help us all get through these strange, stressful times. If there is one positive thing that this COVID-19 virus has done it is to show everyone that what we share is our humanity – in all its frailty and also in all its strength.

Humanity and how we can learn from the virus

When we consider the role kindness, hope and compassion play in the criminal justice system, we may decide to focus on the day-to-day working method of professionals like the police, the judiciary, staff in the Secure Estate and in services like the Youth Justice Service and Probation. Alternatively we might focus more on the role these qualities play for service users at every stage of the system – suspects, offenders, victims, family and friends. In this essay I begin with the latter but then consider the former.

My own perspective is that of someone who has had over 20 years of experience engaging with criminal justice professionals in my work as a trainer and consultant in the field of restorative justice. In this essay I describe how restorative justice[1] can act like a virus to spread kindness, hope and compassion throughout the whole system, infecting service users and professionals alike.[2]

Before talking about practice, it is important to explain that restorative justice is not simply about doing things differently. It actually starts from thinking differently.

A paradigm shift

The values, principles and, most importantly, the common paradigm that have influenced the criminal justice system for many years have influenced not simply how those within that system think and act. They have also had a significant influence on the way the whole of society thinks about 'wrong doing' (itself a contested term) and responses to it. It has impacted on the way parents, educators, social workers and indeed managers across the adult workforce respond to mistakes, rule-breaking and disruption in general. Within this traditional paradigm lies the view that there must be a consequence for wrongdoing – whether this is an error or a deliberate act of wrongdoing – and that this consequence is usually some kind of sanction or punitive response. This punitive response is given in the belief that the wrongdoer has in some way deserved it, will learn from it, and will be deterred from repeating the same mistake or misdeed. Another element of this belief is that the punishment will act as a deterrent to others, and thereby help to maintain standards in the institution or society at large. Within this paradigm those most impacted by the wrongdoing – the victims - are given very little attention and indeed may feel side-lined and disempowered, if not even re-victimised by the process. Perhaps the most insidious part of this traditional paradigm is the belief that punishment is in fact the just dessert of a wrongdoer – they should be made to suffer for what they have done. Revenge, an eye for an eye, is an intrinsic part of this punitive paradigm. This belief is played out not only in the criminal justice system, in the workplace and at home but also on the world stage.

The seductive nature of a paradigm is that it can be undetectable by all those within it. Like a fish in its fishbowl, like a character in The Matrix, the paradigm IS the reality. It took courage and vision to question the status quo of the criminal justice paradigm, and offer alternatives. In his edited book 'A Restorative Justice Reader'[3] Gerry Johnston pays homage to Barnett (1977) for first suggesting that the prevailing criminal justice system was predicated on a paradigm that was outmoded and needed re-thinking – the paradigm of punishment. Later Howard Zehr[4] developed this idea and contrasted this old paradigm with a new one, based on relationships and repair. The old paradigm emphasises law-breaking, identifying those guilty, relied on evidence and culminated in punishing perpetrators. The new one pays more attention to the human impact of a crime – looking at who has been affected and how, and to the ways that the harm could, to some extent at least, be repaired by those responsible for it. In the old paradigm the power and control lies with the criminal justice system and those professionals working within it. In the new paradigm power and control is more evenly shared – with ways forward being negotiated by those most directly impacted. This new restorative justice paradigm has been described as the 'empowerment model'.[5]

What writers and campaigners in the late 1980's and 90's argued was that there was a different way to 'do justice' – an approach based on a new set of values, with a new vision. The focus was on restoration and healing – helping both the victim and indeed also the perpetrator make sense of what had happened and restoring their sense of self; restoring the link between those responsible for causing harm and their place in their communities of care, (either long ago ruptured by their life experiences or perhaps only recently damaged by their actions). In essence, the focus was on hope.

A hopeful process

Restorative justice is often defined in terms of an encounter:

'Restorative justice brings those harmed by crime or conflict and those responsible for the harm into communication, enabling everyone affected by a particular incident to play a part in repairing the harm and finding a positive way forward.'[6]

The goal of repairing harm and of finding a positive way forward imply a sense of hope and of optimism. Hope will be what motivates people to take part – hope that the person responsible will be held to account and be deterred from repeating the offence, and that things will be better afterwards; the hope for some kind of reparation perhaps, and for closure. There may be other hopes too, almost too precious to name – for recognition; for a sincere apology; for understanding; for forgiveness. For the professionals involved there is hope too – that they themselves will have made a worthwhile difference in people's lives.

A kind and compassionate process

Every formal restorative intervention begins with individual meetings with those affected by what has happened. Participants report feeling better for being listened to in a non-judgemental way, being treated with respect and empathy. and being given a degree of agency in arranging the next steps (the when, where, what time etc).

Following initial preparation, a range of restorative face-to-face processes are available and all of them share key components. They all involve a facilitated encounter between people who have been impacted by harm or conflict – often somebody in this encounter will have been uniquely responsible for the harm, although this is not always the case. The facilitator either follows a structured framework or utilises a script but the process is essentially the same. All sides will have the opportunity to share their experience of what has happened and be encouraged to explain what they were thinking and feeling over the period before, during and since the event. Once the wider impact of the events have been considered by everyone they are invited to think about what they need to move forward. And finally, a mutually acceptable way forward is negotiated based on the shared needs.

Facilitating this process is a highly skilled job. The facilitator must remain non-judgemental and avoid partiality either by being impartial (taking no side) or multi-partial (taking all sides). He or she will show equal respect, empathy and genuine curiosity to all participants in the meeting, encouraging genuine dialogue between everyone once they have all had a chance to tell their own stories. I would argue that the quality of warmth is also important and can have a big influence on the participants. I suggest that another word for warmth is kindness, and another word for empathy is compassion.

I have also seen this kindness and compassion spread to participants, 'infected' perhaps, by the facilitator's own practice and the opportunities provided by the structure. By the time all sides have shared their stories, and the true extent of the damage has been acknowledged by those responsible, there is a real shift in the dynamic between all present. Not only do those responsible want to do something to make amends, but the people harmed, perhaps re-gaining a sense of power and control of their lives, are in a position to reach out and help. Whereas in the early stages of the meeting there can be genuine fear and hostility between people in the room, at a certain point these are replaced by recognition of a shared humanity, an understanding of what motivated the actions and a willingness to connect, or re-connect, as kind, caring individuals.

I have heard many kind, compassionate expressions of understanding and forgiveness from those harmed, and genuine expressions of remorse and compassion from those responsible. Examples include:

- victims and 'wrongdoer' hugging each other at the end of a restorative meeting;
- a victim of bullying invite the person responsible over to tea, recognising that she herself had been the victim of neglect in her own home;

- the victim of an attempted theft of his scooter offering to teach archery to the three youths responsible, acknowledging how boring it was growing up in their shared community.

The restorative process creates the framework for this extraordinary transformation and skilled, empathic, warm facilitation enables it to happen. Of course, there is much more to effective restorative facilitation than engaging these qualities. The process is about fairness, accountability, expressing remorse, taking responsibility and making amends. It can be a hard process to go through for all participants, with anger, distress, shame and hurt all playing their part. However, as described above, participants too can access their better selves by the end, with kindness and compassion spreading like a rash (to recall our virus analogy once again.)

Infecting the whole system

Restorative thinking has the potential to impact on the way the justice professionals think about wrongdoing – to change the paradigm mentioned earlier. This means that policies and procedures in the police, at court level, in the Secure Estate and at the rehabilitation stage can all be transformed when crime is viewed in terms of the impact on individuals (those responsible as well as those affected), and as harm to be repaired, rather than punished. Considering the impact of crime on individuals opens the door to kindness and compassion. Focussing on repair, and not on causing yet more pain, opens the door to hope. Therefore, merely by supporting and endorsing the use of restorative justice approaches at every stage in the criminal justice process, professionals can be impacted in a positive way.

Unfortunately, the restorative justice 'virus' still has work to do. In the UK we are still far from the situation where all victims of crime are offered a restorative process despite the work of charities like Why me?[7] and the Restorative Justice Council[8] that campaign for this to become the case. Not all police forces are as supportive of restorative justice as they could be. Police officers are not made aware of restorative justice nor trained as facilitators as a matter of course when they join up, and so the new paradigm described earlier has yet to transform policing nationwide. Whilst some attempts have been made to educate magistrates and judges to make space for restorative encounters pre-sentencing, this is still not widespread. If anything, in recent years, there is less support in the judiciary and in the Magistrates Courts; things have gone rather quiet on the matter.[9] Meanwhile, restorative practice in prisons varies from prison to prison. In some areas the opportunities for victims to meet with their offenders is facilitated by local restorative justice services. On the wings themselves some enlightened prison officers have introduced restorative ways to address conflicts and violence. So what more can be done? How can the infective power of restorative justice be introduced to more criminal justice professionals and 'go viral'?

Reducing immunity

One way is to introduce it deep within the system and demonstrate the power of restorative practice for the individuals themselves.[10] For that to gain traction however the virus needs to weaken the immunity that resistance to change provides.

Restorative practice encourages:
- Deep communication through the use of non-judgemental active listening
- Authentic connection by encouraging the expression of thoughts and feelings and appreciating that these are what motivates our behaviour
- Respect and empathy
- Attending to the unmet needs behind people's actions and encouraging awareness of our own and each other's needs in taking decisions
- Collaboration and shared problem-solving

Applied across an organisation or service amongst professionals themselves, these practices can be transformational and certainly create opportunities for kindness, hope and compassion to develop. Perhaps the way to infect the whole service is from within; once professionals can see how their own day-to-day relationships have improved they will be more ready to use the practices with their service users?

Conclusion

I would like to conclude with a story recently told me by someone who works with juveniles in the Estonian justice system. She related how a group of youths were referred to her colleagues for infringing the social distancing rules currently in place that forbid gatherings of more than two people. Instead of responding in a punitive way, these professionals, trained in restorative practice, facilitated an on-line circle. They invited the youths to talk about how lockdown was affecting them, how they were feeling and what they were missing. Having received empathy and understanding, kindness and compassion the youths were willing to accept that gathering in groups was putting lives at risk and agreed to stick to the rules from now on. They said how grateful they were to have been treated in that way and it made a deep impression on them. I would like to think that all sides emerged much more hopeful that the young people would keep their word.

In these curious times when there is so much fear and hardship, sadness and loss, it is natural to think of a virus as something to be avoided and overcome. However, there may be ways we can learn from the way a virus behaves and use the analogy to help inspire transformation. The virus works at its best when it can bring about exponential growth of infection. One infected person infects another. Then those two people each infect at least two more, and these each go on to infect at least two more and so on. We are all too aware of how fast the infection can spread unless controls on contact are put in place.

If restorative justice can act like a virus and infect the criminal justice system with kindness, hope and compassion then we each have our part to play. We are the vectors. If one person, convinced of the value of restorative justice, shares what they know with another (or demonstrates it by their own practice) then two are 'infected'. If these in turn spread the word and model the practice, the number of enthusiasts grows. Need I say more? It is by spreading our success stories and our good practice that we can all play our part in spreading this positive virus, and transform the way people think about and administer justice at all stages of the criminal justice system.

RESTORATIVE JUSTICE, PUTTING THE HEART INTO THE CRIMINAL JUSTICE SYSTEM

Pete Wallis

Temple of kindness

During a recent encounter with the NHS for surgery, I experienced kindness from many individuals. I felt held and embraced in institutional kindness at a time when I was brought low. I came to think of the hospital as a 'temple of kindness' which had meeting my needs – including for cups of tea and sticky pudding – as its prime concern.

Kindness involves an active interest in another's wellbeing. Both crime and criminal justice seem polar opposites of kindness. Crime involves harming others, while the traditional criminal justice response measures that harm in order to inflict a 'proportionate' punishment on the perpetrator. Could criminal justice, like the NHS, have kindness at its heart?

A restorative justice training exercise divides the participants into two groups, each with a sheet of flipchart paper. One group considers the needs of those who cause harm, the other the needs of those who've been harmed. The word kindness often features on one or both lists, and if not, is implied in words like support, understanding, a listening ear, apology and forgiveness. The exercise illustrates that the needs of harmed and harmer are similar. Identifying and addressing needs is a recurring theme in restorative justice, drawing on Marshall Rosenburg's understanding that conflict arises from unmet needs.

A good life

The youth justice system recently revised its national assessment framework, basing it on the Good Lives Model (GLM)[1]. Put simply, the premise is that everyone wants to feel good about themselves, to be content and fulfilled – basically to be happy. GLM identifies 11 basic human 'goods'. When someone offends, they're trying to feel more satisfied and complete by seeking a particular outcome relating to one of these 'goods'. Shortfalls within themselves or their circumstances mean they can't meet their needs in a prosocial way. Assessment based on GLM identifies those deficits which inform a plan enabling the young person to address what's lacking without resorting to offending.

The Lucy Faithfull Foundation and "Ward, T., Laws, D.R., & Hudson, S.M. (2004) (Eds.).
Sexual Deviance: Issues and Controversies. Thousand Oaks, CA: Sage.

Most young people dealt with by youth justice receive a caution, or if convicted, a short court order. Most aren't seen again. Youth Justice professionals recognise the teenage brain as a work in progress. Compared with adults, young people have a smaller capacity for making decisions and greater capacity for reckless behaviour. They're less likely to think before they act, more likely to be impulsive and irrational. Teenagers often misread social cues, misinterpret their own or other people's emotions, and think everything is about them. Dealing with lower-level crimes can feel like managing 'normal' teenage risk-taking and experimentation. Many adults, including criminal justice professionals, remember their own youthful brushes with the law, often considered a natural rite of passage.

For the minority who don't mature out of crime, who progress on up the criminal justice ladder, it's clear which 'goods' they lack. Deficits can be traced back to formative years featuring poverty, adverse childhood experiences (ACE's)[2] and cultural deprivation. Attachment disorders arise when a child doesn't experience kindness, without which they're less able to develop empathy and show kindness to others. Early experiences lay down core beliefs or scripts which congeal – 'I'm not wanted', 'Whatever I do will be wrong', 'I don't matter', 'I'm unlovable', 'I've nothing to offer'. These beliefs become the bedrock for an identity that feels dependable and familiar, and therefore 'good'. The child may act out these scripts unconsciously, with behaviour that seems baffling and counterproductive to us adults but stems from a strategy to confirm their identity, without which they have nothing. When I worked in a home for boys with emotional and behavioural difficulties, it proved hard to avoid taking disruptive behaviour personally, to respond kindly to the underlying needs being expressed rather than react angrily to their manifestation, remembering the behaviour was about the child, not about me.

Needs of those harmed

What about those harmed by crime? Their flipchart of needs is strikingly similar to the harmers. Victim services exist for more serious crimes, although it's a mistake to second-guess how someone is affected: the impact of crime is individual, and a seemingly minor offence can have a huge impact, whilst a grave offence sometimes creates few ripples. I recall visiting a woman whose car was vandalised by a youth, who thoughtlessly bent back the windscreen wipers. She was terminally ill, and would never leave her bedroom, let alone drive again. The incident felt deeply personal at a time when she was suffering, and she was devastated. Around the same time I met a man from Eastern Europe whose throat was slashed in a knifepoint robbery. He shrugged it off as 'just kids', saying in his country much worse things happen daily.

On the list of needs for those harmed, some look to the criminal justice system for safety, recognition or punishment. It would be interesting to have a third flipchart paper exploring the needs of the state. When rules are broken, when citizens are attacked, what does the state need?

Howard Zehr, the 'father' of restorative justice once created a table contrasting the restorative approach with what he called 'traditional' criminal justice of police, courts, prisons and probation, suggesting that restorative justice should replace the old 'punitive' system. Criminal justice bad, restorative justice good. In later writings Zehr recognised the legitimate role of the state: to hold people responsible, protect the public, to punish, to deter. Many people harmed by crime - a circle extending to anyone feeling less secure on receiving news of crimes occurring - appreciate a robust response from the police and courts.

The heart in the square

Criminal justice has the power to do things 'to' people, depriving them of liberty by directing where they are and what they can or can't do. I like the image of a heart in a square. There may be legitimate needs of the state to establish a firm boundary, hold people responsible for harmful actions, even box someone in if they

pose a threat to others' safety (though custody is hugely overused). Without the heart, the square is simply a sterile cage. The perpetrator is held responsible but may not feel responsible. The needs that led to and arise from the offence remain unaddressed and probably exacerbated, as more 'goods' are taken away from those who had the fewest in the first place. Criminal justice becomes a revolving door.

Parallel justice

'Parallel justice' considers justice in terms of what's 'just' for the harmed and harmer. Imagine the two rails of a railway track. The left-hand rail represents the journey of the harmer, the right-hand rail those harmed. Key milestones for the harmer include the events leading up to the offence, arrest, charge, conviction and sentence. Ideally, there follows a programme with interventions to address that individual's unmet needs and support them in achieving their good life, free of offending, tackling substance misuse, anger issues, mental health concerns, accommodation, family relationships and education or work, with offending behaviour programmes chipping away at denial and encouraging responsibility.

When I joined probation in 1991 those rails were well maintained, with attendance centres, specialist teams, group work programmes and throughcare for prisoners, providing a safety net to contain people who offended and support their rehabilitation. I worked in an inspirational day centre for the homeless. Recognising that homeless probation clients struggle to manage appointments, we provided a sanctuary where anyone could find warmth, food, showers, clothing, companionship - and kindness from the staff. Probation Officers met their clients whenever they happened to turn up, and people who might otherwise cause a nuisance in the town centre had somewhere to go. There was even a 'wet room' where people could find shelter and a comfortable chair if they were drunk (after handing over their booze at reception). Everyone entering the front door was made welcome.

Probation staff I meet now are still motivated by kindness, but changes to probation have been catastrophic, the service a shadow of its former self. The idea of probation running a homeless day centre, meeting universal needs to prevent offending is fantastical in these straightened times. I weep to hear of people clocking into a machine (with a button to press if they want to speak to an actual person), or supervision appointments made first thing, enabling staff with huge caseloads to catch up with other work, in the knowledge their clients won't show. I recently spoke to a man diligently turning up for community service each week only to be sent home because there's no room in the minibus. Inadequate funding limits the opportunity for workers to build relationships with clients, reducing their ability to express kindness to people who need it most.

Fortunately, there's always been additional support for criminal justice from charities, now left to bridge the widening gap left by shrinking statutory services. One fine example I worked with is the Prison Phoenix Trust (PPT), which takes yoga and meditation into prisons. The PPT recognises that the crisis of a spell inside offers a golden opportunity for spiritual growth. As prisoners learn to soften the jarring shouts and clanging doors by dropping into a deeper silence, taming negative thoughts and feelings with meditation, staff see reductions in depression and violence. Fear melts away and prisoners start being kinder to themselves and their fellow inmates. Hope and healing are found even in the darkest places.

The journey of those harmed

Running in parallel with the harmers' rail is the journey of those harmed. It's not only people who offend who have negative core beliefs and for some an experience of victimisation can confirm unconscious judgements carried over from childhood; 'I'm a victim', 'Bad things always happen to me', 'I don't matter', 'I'm to blame', 'I'm not supported.' A crime may compound other life challenges, feeling like the last straw – as it was for the woman with the bent windscreen wipers.

In a world where railways are properly funded these hurts will be met down the track with kindness from the police and courts, through hospital treatment if required, counselling and compensation for any loss. Unfortunately, those harmed by crime continue to be marginalised by a criminal justice system never designed to meet their individual needs. Some feel used and abused by the adversarial system of trial, others are left out altogether, sometimes only hearing the outcome of 'their' case in the news. The Victim Personal Statement read out in court potentially offers a voice, but this is one-way emotional traffic. Because defendants typically feel defensive, they're often perceived as unremorseful and uncaring, another blow for their victims. Courts look like temples, but for those attending they're unlikely to feel like temples of kindness.

Whilst most people who are offended against don't go on to commit crimes, research shows an overlap between the categories 'victim' and 'perpetrator'. Ask anyone in prison if they've been victimised themselves, and the answer is always "Yes". Hurt people hurt people. Added to these individual wounds is the criminal negligence of an unfair society that fails to address poverty, discrimination and injustice.

I sometimes wonder what would happen if the money spent on those who commit crimes (£17,000 for a jury trial, over £100 per day to keep someone in prison) was matched for those they harm. In reality, victim services are the poor relations in criminal justice, many people needing support falling into the gap between the rails. A society recognising the need for kindness would require a fundamental shift in how the state allocates public resources when an offence occurs, matching state funding for the punishment and risk management of perpetrators with services for restorative justice and therapeutic support, so that all parties truly experience kindness, and those causing harm have a better opportunity to feel and behave this way in the future.

The two parallel rails usually remain separate. The person who offended is probably keen to put their misdemeanour behind them, whilst for those harmed, with luck the crime fades slowly into a nasty memory. However, these rails are two sides of the same story. The space between represents the gap created by an incident that damaged relationships and separated people.

Immediately after the crime, those on all sides may naturally steer clear of one another. For understandable reasons the police or courts enforce the gap, telling those involved to avoid contact by setting bail conditions or, in serious cases remanding the perpetrator to custody. This cementing of the gap may meet both parties' need for safety, but looking back over the flipcharts there are needs it won't address. Answers to burning questions (Why? Why me? Will it happen again?), the transmission of an apology, redemption, forgiveness, reparation; these needs require communication between the people involved.

How restorative justice bridges the gap

The restorative practitioner is privileged in hearing both sides of the story, directly from those involved. As each person is invited to explore what might help them feel better, they may express needs that can only be met through what I call the 'hard conversation that has to happen'. Ideally, the idea arises from those involved, who direct and own the process, the practitioner's role simply to facilitate their dialogue, helping them bridge the gap like sleepers connecting two separate rails to make one track.

If people in conflict choose to meet, the facilitator creates a safe and open space, allowing each to hear and be heard. Remaining impartial and non-judgemental, they're like a mirror, keeping the focus on the participants. At the start of a restorative meeting everything is reflected to and from the facilitator, who uses skilful questions to encourage those present to share their perspectives as the narrative unfolds. As people process what happened, the harmer, confronted by the impact of his or her actions, may start taking responsibility, whilst the person harmed may gain insight into the suffering that led to the offence being committed. Struggles shared by both sides awaken empathy and kindness, each person unable to bear the sight of another's suffering and wishing for it to end.

Seeking ways forward, powerful words drop into the circle. The facilitator's question, 'What do you need to feel better?' frequently fills the space with beautiful expressions of apology, forgiveness, kindness and hope – concepts that can't be introduced by the facilitator but may be shared by those present, forming rocks that become stepping stones towards healing. Restorative practitioners speak of 'movement', a pull to connection like separate raindrops merging on a windowpane, and 'transition', when participants start speaking directly to one another, prompting the facilitator to stay very still to avoid disturbing the alchemy.

Rewriting the script

Crime and criminal justice often confirm the harmer's core beliefs: 'I'm bad', 'I've nothing to offer', 'I'm a loser'. It's a big step to dismantle an identity we've clung onto, change patterns of thought and behaviour that served us for better or worse since childhood. But people want to change, to feel good. Perhaps for someone locked into a life of crime, taking the brave step of meeting those they harmed can start to rewrite their script. This hard task, facing up to behaviour that was 'old me', showing up as 'new me' can bring out their nobler side, shifting the negative narrative to a more positive one; 'I have worth', 'I can be kind', 'There's hope for me'. Perhaps those harmed can also create a new story, reclaiming their power in the process: 'I'm not a victim', 'I'm not to blame', 'I have control of my life'.

The Dalai Lama asserts that happiness comes from looking outside oneself, from being kind to others. When suffering physical sickness the kindness of NHS staff helped my recovery and healing. In propelling people to think kindly of those they're in conflict with, restorative justice similarly offers a healing remedy for the wounds of disconnection within the self and with others.

It takes courage to face up to shame, fear and pain, and restorative justice is not for everyone. Criminally restorative justice is often unavailable to those who might gain most benefit. When it works well, it has the potential to nurture kindness – to awaken the heart – and transform lives even within the constraints of criminal justice.

SECTION 3

VIEW FROM THE FRONT LINE:
THE PRACTITIONER PERSPECTIVE

Grab the opportunities

IDRIS JAULIN

Hope is probably the most important principle.
To me, hope is having an opportunity.
Give me an opportunity and I will succeed.

In prison, there is the opportunity to learn musical instruments,
To play in chapel bands.
Opportunity to save money using the saving accounts provided,
To read books and develop business models.

If one takes these opportunities, one is developing hope.
Hope of being an independent fully functioning adult enjoying responsibility,
Making decisions and being far more inclined to being a valuable,
Contributing member of British society instead of a base criminal.

Opportunity is everything.
If prisoners want to thrive, they should grab the opportunities.

The Mask, HMP Dovegate
Image courtesy of Koestler Arts

CHARITY, KINDNESS, HOPE AND COMPASSION

Anne Fox

When I first heard this would be the question for this year's Monument Fellowship book, I immediately thought this would be easy for us to contribute to at Clinks as we support charities and this is what charities are for. In my view, bringing kindness, hope and compassion to people who need it is a huge part of what charities do.

The Oxford English Dictionary says that a charity is "an organisation set up to provide help and raise money for those in need". It also says that charity is "kindness and tolerance in judging others." So I wanted to think about how charities working with people in the criminal justice system and their families put that kindness and tolerance into practice, why it's needed and what change it might achieve.

I spend a lot of time listening and talking to leaders across the voluntary sector working in criminal justice in England and Wales. And earlier this year, I chaired a panel discussion on this very question with 3 charity leaders to get a sense of their perspectives on the role of kindness, compassion and hope and what charities bring in this regard.* This essay is my reflection on that discussion and others. I will use the terms charities as a proxy for the wider voluntary sector in criminal justice which also includes social enterprises throughout.

The need for kindness, hope and compassion

*"We need to be in a place to bring kindness, hope and compassion
and advocate for those that often are seen as less deserving, but
they are deserving because of their potential to make a difference
in this world."*
Dez Brown

There are an estimated 1750 charities in England and Wales established
specifically to work with people in the criminal justice system or with
their families. Of those the majority, which we work alongside at
Clinks, work specifically with people in the penal system: in prison,
under probation supervision, in the community or with a direct
experience of both. Turning again to the Oxford English dictionary,
it defines the term penal as "relating to, used for, or prescribing the
punishment of offenders under the legal system." And the informal
definition of "punishment" is "rough treatment or handling". It could
therefore be proposed that the penal system was not established and
nor does it exist to bring kindness, compassion and hope to people
who are subject to its penalties.

But given the complex needs of people who are in prison, have been to
prison and are subject to the penal system, there is an argument to be
made that, for those in this system, kindness and compassion in how
they're treated and hope that their lives and those round them can change
is essential if we are to improve outcomes and reduce reoffending.
A therapeutic approach to supporting people which subscribes to
desistance theory would almost require this of us. Understanding who
is subject to the penal system and what circumstances in their lives
have contributed to their being there is a very important aspect of the
work that we need to do if we are to succeed in supporting people to
turn their lives around and desist from crime.

For example, The Prison Reform Trust reports that 24% of adult
prisoners were taken into care as a child,[1] 29% experienced abuse as
a child 29%, and 41% "observed violence in the home as a child.[2]

These are all recognised Adverse Childhood experiences (ACEs), which evidence increasingly suggests, contribute to a range of poorer outcomes in later life including a higher likelihood of involvement in crime and experience of imprisonment.[3]

In the five years, that I have worked at Clinks and in criminal justice, what I have seen on a daily basis is organisations bringing hope, working in kind, and compassionate ways with people who often have never had kindness and compassion in sufficient amounts and who have little hope and little to hope for. I don't only believe that this approach to working with people in the criminal justice system is welcome, I believe it is essential for desistance.

"To help someone desist you can: convey a belief in them and a sense of hope and optimism about how they can live a better life and about their future".[4]

Operationalising kindness, compassion and hope

Above, I suggested that the penal system, by definition, does not allow much space for kindness, hope and compassion. When we do find kindness, hope and compassion in the penal system, they are often present in spite of, or exist outside of, the penal system.

In this respect, I believe charities have an essential role to play in desistance and in creating a kinder, more compassionate society towards people who have an experience of the penal system. They do this both through:

- What they do, with and for people who have lived experience of the criminal justice system;
- And in what they say about them, when representing their interests, to people who haven't had similar life experiences - whether that is the general public, statutory and non-statutory bodies or the people and institutions who operate within the criminal justice system.

My experience as the Chief Executive of an organisation that exists to support voluntary organisations has taught me that by virtue of both their definition and their operation, injecting kindness, hope and compassion into the criminal justice system is at the heart of what charities in this world do every day. I don't think voluntary organisations are unique in that way, but I think it is very much at the heart of why these organisations are often founded. They are founded to provide compassion and kindness and bring hope, when the opposite of those things is found in a certain situation.

> "It's not the system that brings hope, kindness and compassion, it's people".
> DEZ BROWN

Dez's reflection is an important one. It has been estimated that voluntary organisations in England and Wales employ or provide volunteering opportunities for more people than are employed by the statutory prison and probation services combined. Charities are resourced mainly with people and it is through the actions and behaviours of these people towards people subject to the penal system that they are able to spread kindness, hope and compassion. If these organisations are to facilitate desistance, the ability of these people to form and hold trusting relationships with those they support is essential. And to do this, training, development and ongoing support is an absolute must.

> "If we value people, we can show them their power to change and to be kind and compassionate to the needs of others is absolutely essential in this line of work."
> DAWN SIMPSON

Charities therefore must engage, train and develop people to work and volunteer for them; people who can impart a sense, to a person, of their potential for change and their worthiness of something better. Such work is complex and costly. Desistance happens over time and the professional or volunteering relationships required to support desistance take time. This work can be difficult to measure in hard outcomes and deliverables and so charities can face a real challenge in resourcing their work if it is to be therapeutic in the current funding environment of competitive contracts for service and often relatively short term charitable grants for projects and development.

Charities often also need to work in this way because the system itself can inflict harm. Many charities exist to ameliorate against that harm. Included here, are charities that connect people to the loved ones they are separated from in prison and charities that provide an outlet for the mental distress imprisonment can cause.

> "Our role is not to punish because that would be double punishment from the court in my opinion. And really, we need to be showing people compassion and kindness in the hope that that then brings them hope that they have the ability to change and, that they have the ability to cope with their sentence, that they have the ability to look inside themselves and live a crime free life".
>
> DAWN SIMPSON

Developing the case for change

We need not only to show kindness, hope and compassion to people in the criminal justice system as we work with them but also we need to encourage others to think and act compassionately, kindly and hopefully towards them in order to influence change in the penal system itself. In the 3rd book of this series "Crime and Consequence" Penelope Gibbs, Roma Hooper and I wrote of the need for and challenges in reframing the public narrative around crime and punishment.[5]

Public attitudes to people who commit crimes are affected by their beliefs and opinions, which are in turn affected by the narrative used in common and political discourse and in the media. If we wish for those people to be treated kindly, compassionately and to be instilled with hope for a better future, we must create an understanding across society of the role of trauma and disadvantage and of people's potential for change given the right opportunities.

Criminal justice charities have a valid role to play here in creating this understanding and the way in which they do it is important. I regularly read charities' websites, newsletters and impact reports and they are full of stories of how individuals are supported in kind and compassionate ways which allowed them to hope that life might be different in the future and to take the steps needed towards that future. Creating a space for people to tell their stories and to directly reach wider parts of the society from which they often feel separated is really important.

Charities in the criminal justice system also allow a perspective on a closed system which allows that hopefulness to pass through the impermeable gates and walls and many charities expressly work with their wider community to support a better understanding of people's situations and to engender compassion and kindness in audiences so that they may be more supportive of reform of the criminal justice system which would lead to more rehabilitative outcomes.

Tim Robertson, CEO of the Anne Frank Trust referred to the importance of allowing people to see themselves differently and be seen differently and gave the example from their model where people viewing the Anne Frank exhibition are guided through it by prisoners. *"What is very inspiring is to see how prison staff and managers will see prisoners differently when it is a prisoner who is acting as their guide to the Anne Frank exhibition"*.

Similarly, charities have a vital role to play in using the evidence they gather through their work to influence policy and practice in the criminal justice system. These activities should be carried out with compassion for the people they represent and advocate for, reflecting their hope for things to be different and what could happen as a result. This is often done through listening to and reflecting back service users' experiences. And these experiences are often shared in a context of a trusting relationship between practitioner and service user, charity and service user.

Imagining a different future – letting hope flourish

Charities operating in ways which are underpinned by desistance theory are by their nature bringers of hope. Desistance strikes me as a hopeful theoretical model. At its heart is that hope and optimism that things can be different.

There are many ways in which charities can bring that hope into their work and into the lives of the people they support. The very many charities who work through the arts for example do this daily. We regularly hear of people who transformed their lives following experiences of art and creativity in prison, imagining a different life in the future through creative expression. People who never believed they could do something like that - perform, draw, paint, sculpt, write.

> "*There is a relationship between the confinement of imprisonment and how it generates creativity that does mean that there is hope that comes out of that*".
> TIM ROBERTSON

Conclusion – the power of charity

This is my take on the reflections I have had on one panel discussion and other conversations. It is only mine. There were 130 other people listening on the day and there are thousands of people who work or volunteer their time in charities supporting people in the criminal justice system.

My view is we need to be kind and compassionate and hopeful about the potential of charities and social enterprises to harness the potential in people to change. We need to enable it, encourage people to be kind and compassionate and to hope for better. We can all work in different ways but there is so much power in us all being kind, compassionate and hopeful.

*Acknowledgements

I would like to thank Dez Brown- CEO Spark2Life, Dawn Simpson- Resettlement Coordinator NEPACS and Tim Robertson – CEO Anne Frank Trust for taking part in the panel discussion at Clinks' 2020 annual conference which this essay is a reflection on.

KINDNESS IN PRISONS

Gerard Lemos

In the world outside, empathy extends to family, friends and community. Built on these social foundations are kindness, compassion, charity and unselfish giving. All of these are also experiences and encounters in prison life – and they are all the wellsprings of building and re-building conscience, a pre-requisite on the road to rehabilitation. In prison, the residents, staff and the volunteers who visit prison, thrown together by fate, to some extent nevertheless come to represent a community themselves. Community life is characterised by customs, relationships and kindness. Laws and rules are always secondary, not least because they are hard to enforce practically however loud the threat, in prisons as elsewhere.

One of the most important aspects of community life is the role of charities and voluntary organisations. Their significance stems as much from emotion as from empirical evidence. Beyond family and neighbourhood, charities along with faith groups, are significant sinews that bind strangers together in communities. Without having to know each other first, people are drawn together magnetically to these groups by shared beliefs and values, cultural ties, social commitments, philanthropic instincts or just proximity. Charities are widely represented in prisons and their role in prison life is ubiquitous and essential. From the charities, the prisoner encounters activities and approaches that typically don't carry the stigma of offending behaviour of court requirements. They are not seen as part of the punishment.

Most of the people who come into prisons to help with charitable activities are volunteers. In a sense, activities run by volunteers are the best of all. Volunteers are people who have chosen to work at a prison and they do so for free. That altruistic commitment has an impact on the prisoners' reaction and feelings towards them. They treat these generous people with a special respect, attaching a special value to their time and commitment, different to that of the paid staff. Many of the volunteers are female, older and from an entirely different social background to the prisoners. These differences are important too. The fact that the volunteer may come from a rather more wealthy background confirms to the prisoner they have even more choices about how to spend their time and who to spend it with. That they have chosen to spend time with prisoners in prison in that context is even more remarkable. These generous commitments will have an effect on the prisoners, encouraging them to match their own commitment to the commitment of the volunteers and perhaps bringing the best out of them when a more routinised activity with a paid member of staff might not.

Both prison staff and prisoners know that these people are giving their time, skills and emotions without financial reward. They therefore feel a special kind of respect and gratitude to them. However skilled and beneficial the efforts of a professional member of staff, they are there at least in part because they get paid to be there. The act of generosity by a volunteer is more than kindness; it is a small statement of faith in that prisoner and his or her future. They deserve help, the volunteer's presence seems to say, and they will make good use of it. For a prisoner, often feeling alone and abandoned, the knowledge there are people in the world who are not bound to them by family or professional obligations who have not written them off is almost more powerful than anything else. The volunteer's presence is a silent statement that the unknown world which the prisoner can no longer see or feel has some faith in them and so they should have faith in themselves. For these reasons: the downplaying of stigma, the presence of benevolent altruism and the special respect and attachment that (invariably male) prisoners feel for (mostly female) volunteers, charities and voluntary groups have a unique and valued place in prison.

The staff too contribute to the quality and betterment of the prisoners' lives with small, often unrecognised acts of kindness, over and above the call of duty: locking and unlocking, canteen, searches and all the rest. I know one prison governor who is teaching a prisoner, a young man serving a very long sentence, to play the harmonica. This is not a requirement. Playing the harmonica is not on any action plan, nor will it be much help in a parole hearing, but the significance of this commitment they are both making stretches deep. This is a one-to-one repeated encounter in pursuit of an important shared purpose, at least to the two of them, and, moreover, a statement of commitment and trust by a very senior member of the prison hierarchy to the wellbeing of that resident, who will take note of that commitment with gratitude. When it comes to kindness, actions always speak louder than words.

I have now been involved in organising two large scale concerts by an orchestra of professional musicians from a world-renowned chamber orchestra, Britten Sinfonia, and the residents and staff of HMP Whitemoor, one of the most high security prisons in the UK. At the first concert, the newly formed orchestra played to an audience of more than 80 other residents. Clapping and whooping testified to the audience's enthusiasm for the performance of their peers and the rest of the band. The following year a new orchestra was formed which played a concert, not just for other residents who were as enthusiastic as ever, but also for more than 80 family members of the residents, including small children, visiting for a day of music-making. Family members were moved to pride and joy by the experience at the event, hardly knowing what their brothers, fathers and sons were capable of musically speaking. But the point I want to make here is not about the substantial benefits of creativity and music in prison life. I want to draw attention to the logistical and other requirements that are needed to make something like these events happen in a high security prison. The staff achieved that calmly and kindly, with no appearance of stress or tension. Both the manner and the matter of the staff contribution was extraordinary and extraordinarily kind, as I have noted, far beyond the call of duty.

Prisons by definition bring strangers into close proximity with one another, without friends or family. Quickly however friendships and reciprocal obligations are formed between prisoners, as well as rivalries, animosities and bad influences sometimes. Prisons can be dangerous and depressing places where many prisoners become deeply troubled and contemplate self-harm and suicide. The normal restraints and sources of assistance are inevitably not so easily available. Help is needed and the authorities may be difficult to approach, which is where the Listener scheme comes in, probably the biggest of many peer support activity in prisons, all of them valuable. It is a very important aspect of prison life. Empathy with other prisoners especially prisoners who are troubled, depressed or suicidal is a vital dimension of making prison life bearable for the more vulnerable prisoners. It is an opportunity for the volunteer helpers among the residents of the prison to strengthen their own sense of empathy and generosity while the troubled prisoner who has sought help learns collaterally something about kindness and generosity freely given.

The Listener scheme is a peer support scheme run by The Samaritans across all prisons. Established in HM Prison Swansea in 1991, the scheme is part of a concerted effort to reduce the number of suicides in prison.[1] The project has proven successful. By 1998 there were a hundred Listener schemes across England and Wales. Today nearly every prison in the UK is a member of the scheme.[2]

Central to the Listener scheme is its reliance on prisoner-to-prisoner listening, empathy and advice. Samaritans volunteers select prisoners that have expressed an interest in becoming involved with the scheme and have been cleared by the prison. These prisoner volunteers then attend intensive training. Listeners are easily identified: a sign reading 'A Listener Lives Here' is placed on their cell door, and 'Listener' t-shirts are worn around the wing. Each prison aims to have one listener for every 50 prisoners and a confidential listening rota is drawn up. Listeners are themselves supported by Samaritans volunteers.[3]

The strength of the project is that it is peer support. Prisoners approach one another on an equal footing, often with similar experiences and the ability therefore to connect and empathise with one another and so to develop a truer rapport. Prisoners are able to step outside of the usual norms and codes of communicating with one another and speak freely, openly and safe in the knowledge that they will not be judged for what they might say about what they are feeling.

Learning to listen properly is not easy, surprisingly uncommon and extremely valuable. Listeners acquire a genuine and deserved sense of achievement, as well as a skill that will benefit them and their loved ones well beyond incarceration. Listening to other people's profound difficulties without judgment or admonition is a hard tutorial in empathy, self-restraint, compassion and communication. These skills are fundamental not just for functioning social behaviour but also are the cornerstones of strong and empathetic relationships with others. Both parties take away the experience of measured and compassionate empathy and an awareness of a new and supportive means of communicating, dealing with problems or powerful emotions, and interacting with other people.

'*When you speak to the chap who informs you that he intends to die that night, you encourage him to think of alternatives. You take him directly to the pain, and not away from it. He needs to realise exactly what is causing his pain. You tell him that it is his life and his decision, but you will be there for him. "If you need me, I am here. So are all the Listeners," you say. The following morning, you anxiously look toward his cell, and then you see him step out. It is just like a birth! A new life!*'[4]

Many important, structured, evidence-based programmes and activities occur with offenders in prison and in the community. They are all important but alongside them sit the small acts of unstructured kindness and compassion between volunteers, staff, other residents and those serving the sentences, a few of which I have highlighted here. These informal contributions go unaccounted but without them the life of the sentenced individual in prison or in custody would be far worse, perhaps intolerable. We should not assume that what we cannot measure does not assume that what we cannot measure does not matter. Just the opposite in fact.

MEETING SHAME WITH KINDNESS, HOPE AND COMPASSION

Charlie Rigby

The threat of being shot is not a usual everyday occurrence for most people, but unfortunately for Steven this was his wake-up call. Steven, (not his real name) usually feels invincible: posting threats, making videos and mocking rivals were a regular part of his life. His parent, juggling Steven and his 2 younger siblings, had feared this is what would happen.

The threat was real. Despite some outward reluctance, denial, inwardly Steven was very aware that he had to step out of the world he was currently living in. His parent called The V.I.P not knowing where else to turn.

The Violence Intervention Project (V.I.P) aim to deliver therapeutic outreach to young people up to the age of 25 who are involved in or at risk of serious youth violence. Practical support is the vehicle to build strong, trusting relationships.

At the core of our work, is the understanding that shame is the catalyst for violence. I'd met Jonathan Asser, a Psychotherapist working in Wandsworth Prison at the time on his "Shame Violence Intervention (SVI)" and I was inspired. His work in turn had been inspired by the lifelong work of Dr James Gilligan, a psychiatrist in the United States Prison System for over 40 years. James is quoted as saying: *"My experience with violent offenders, is that they became violent because they felt overwhelmed by feelings of shame and humiliation"*.[1]

Jonathan would talk about shame as being the warning of the breakdown of social bonds and cited Professor Carl Schneider's quote: *"we experience shame when we feel we are being experienced outside of the context in which we wish to be experienced in"*.[2] That narrative of shame for young people nowadays sounds like: "they disrespected me", or "they violated me". This quickly turns into a fantasy of exacting revenge through violently shaming the other person (or their friends), re-establishing their own reputation and dominance.

It's important to point out that we all experience shame; excruciating moments where we want the ground to swallow us up or feel the need to lash out. Shame does this, and if there isn't an outlet for that emotion, we can end up making others feel small (physically or verbally) in order to make ourselves feel better.

In its simplest form, shame is that feeling of being made to feel small, worthless or insignificant – and the ability to shift the spotlight of shame onto someone else is a short-term way of dealing with it. And of course, it's a never-ending cycle of people being shamed, each time passing it on to the next.

Building trust through compassion and courage

The support that VIP provides, coupled with the drive to develop attuned relationships is an important part of building "epistemic trust", trust that is based in the young person's own knowledge. As an organisation we start from a culture of being available when people need us most – understanding that there is an ambivalence in the take up of support – rather than trying to force our support onto service users. To work from principles informed by the power of shame needs particular tools, structure and support. The team is AMBIT (Adaptive Mentalisation Based Integrative Treatment) trained, and we have clinical supervision on a weekly basis.

The cycle of shaming was an important aspect of our work with Steven – we had been involved with him since a referral from the police two years earlier and had periods of regular contact, followed by periods of not hearing from him again. Sometimes those periods could last several months. The same would apply to his parent, who would regularly reach out for support, often for Steven but also for themselves. Once a crisis was over, again there would be a period of non-contact. What made the difference this time for Steven, was that we had been there all along, picking up where we had left off from last time, without judgement or expectation.

Steven was stuck in this exact cycle. He certainly hadn't started it, but to say he was purely an innocent party would be slightly disingenuous, but either way he was left with a choice. He knew one route would lead to further violence, pain for his family and even possible death. The other option, however, was overshadowed by the fear of being branded a "pussy", or "moist" – the current pejorative language among many of the young men we work with. He could feel the mutterings already from his rivals – and without taking action against them, surely everyone would be saying the same?

In those dark moments, what we need most is a voice inside our head telling us: "you're going to be okay; you are loved". For some people we work with, they have never heard voices like that in their lives, so the voices in their own heads don't sound like that either. Instead, they've had judging, punitive voices, so what they hear during the tough times is... more shame. Shame can be all consuming making it hard to hold on to hope. Without hope what's the point? We may as well carry on doing what we're doing?

The third major influence on this area of work is Dr Brené Brown, a research professor who has spent the past two decades studying courage, vulnerability, shame, and empathy. She describes shame as "the intensely painful feeling or experience of believing that we are flawed and therefore unworthy of love and belonging". Brown also states, that "*Shame cannot survive being spoken.... And being met with empathy*".[3]

Without courage to be open and honest about our difficult feelings and emotions, none of us can truly make changes in our lives. For young people to manage feelings of shame they need to be met with kindness. When they communicate difficult emotions, they need to be met with compassion. If the adults in their lives cannot show them kindness and compassion, how can we ever expect them to?

An important reminder is the way "gangs" and serious youth violence groups operate using shame. Pride is the opposite of shame and if we can find positive, authentic sources of pride, these can counterbalance our feelings of shame. A great example of this is the sense of belonging you can get from a youth centre, sports group or even an individual. This harks back to Jonathan Asser's points on shame being an alarm bell for a break down in social bonds / connections – essentially something we have taken pride in, normally a relationship, is at risk of crumbling and being destroyed.

So, gangs exploit this by creating an alternative sense of pride, through the belonging to the group. Once that is in place, it's easy to control people through the risk of expulsion from the group or threat of being shamed by everyone else. If you are to refuse to take part in a group attack, seek revenge on a rival or take part in some other "group" activity, you risk being branded – as Steven was – a pussy, moist, or weak... All those things people don't want to be thought of as being.

Meeting honesty and vulnerability with kindness

As professionals, we need to be able to recognize that behaviours we may see as being challenging, are often a young person communicating they are at their most vulnerable. Without kindness and compassion in how we manage those interactions, we risk further shaming and ultimately disconnection. From their perspective, our inability to meet them in a compassionate way indicates we don't understand them – we aren't attuned, and epistemic trust is lost.

More importantly, when we are met with kindness, it encourages our own ability to be kind to ourselves. Compassion for ourselves can counter the shame and judgement placed on us from others. In a gang setting, it's easy to perpetuate the narrative of shame that – if I don't take part in this, or back someone in that – we are weak and unworthy of a place in the gang. Without a place in the gang we are weak and vulnerable. The step to breaking away from that life is having a voice inside telling you that you aren't weak for avoiding a planned revenge attack on a rival, and in fact it's the group that is not worthy of YOU – not the other way around.

As professionals, we may not always have direct conversations about the internal voices referred to above, but we always have the opportunity to choose the manner and method in which we respond. Kindness and compassion should always be the guiding narrative we follow. That may feel difficult sometimes, especially when we ourselves are feeling shamed by the person in question.

This reminds me of a situation years ago, when I was alerted that Tom (not his real name), a young person who I was trying to engage - had been beaten up and was in hospital with quite serious injuries. From all the professionals involved, it seemed that this was the moment where Tom could really benefit from an intervention. So, I headed down to the hospital, full of hope and excitement that this could be the breakthrough moment. It wasn't. I was told in no uncertain terms to leave and threatened albeit with a carton of juice – the only thing at Tom's disposal. I left feeling completely shamed. It was only when I brought the case up in clinical supervision that I could begin to understand how my attempt to help could have been interpreted as a completely shaming experience for Tom

Tom was very large for his young years – 13 years old, over 6-foot-tall and 14 stone, more or less all muscle. He could easily (and often wished to) present as an intimidating character. Laying on the hospital ward with his arm in a cast, battered and bruised, was far from how Tom would ever want to be seen by anyone. And in this vulnerable state, I burst in completely uninvited. The clinical supervision also helped me think about what to do next. In a criminal justice setting, the language he'd used could easily have resulted in a breach or at the very least a written warning. Instead, with the help of everyone in the clinical group, I came up with what felt like the most appropriate plan to move forward.

I met Tom in one of the council buildings unannounced and approached him. He seemed ready for some sort of rebuke from me for the behaviour in the hospital and had a stiff grimace on his face. I apologised. I immediately stated I had no right to impose myself on him at such a sensitive time. I asked how he was feeling now? I did my best to convey my genuine care for him and you could see from his face he didn't really know what to make of it. I reflect back on that time and feel that I responded with kindness and compassion – it would have been so easy to add in some sort of warning - something like, "*but, you really shouldn't speak to staff like that you know...*", but I didn't, and it proved to mark a turning point in our relationship.

As professionals WE also need emotional support. Without kindness, hope and compassion in our own lives it's a big ask to provide the same to the young people. At The V.I.P., we have a view that if we can't be vulnerable and honest about our own issues, we have no right asking young people to do the same. Through our clinical spaces we have that availability to be met with compassion and empathy as a team or on an individual basis. I like to think that this support to our team means we shouldn't be left in a hopeless situation professionally or personally.

But what of Steven? I'm afraid I'm going to leave that up to your imagination... Perhaps he's living outside of London, creating a life for himself away from the trappings that once underpinned his former life.

Life will always have challenges, but with kindness and compassion the journey is far less painful, and full of hope.

KINDNESS: A COMPELLING VIRTUE IN THE CRIMINAL JUSTICE AND DESISTANCE TRAJECTORY

Revd Dr Carver Anderson

Supporting friends and family members, in the aftermath of the untimely and violent death of a young person, is not unfamiliar to the Bringing Hope charity. Through our involvement with several of these families, we have had numerous opportunities to support them, whether through talking, offering emotional support, mediating in family conflicts, or officiating the funeral service of their loved ones. In effect, we have implemented what we call *the compelling virtue of kindness.*[1]

Over the past fifteen years or so, we have supported individuals in prisons and local communities, many of them categorised as "hard to reach", problematic, violent, gang-associated, socially excluded, difficult, and dangerous. Up to 90% of the individuals we work with, are black men and young men, with a combination of some or all the above labels. And behind this lies the evidence: black young men are disproportionately represented in negative criminal justice and mental health statistics, and black boys are excluded disproportionately from schools.[2] These are the people whose pained and harrowing stories we have heard repeatedly, especially in situations where we have been called in as the mediators, and where lives could have been lost if situations had been allowed to escalate. So here is where our kindness consciousness and its compelling virtues were applied.

Our aim is to engage and support young people, with their families, who are involved or at risk of involvement in activities, lifestyle-choices and behaviours that cause harm to themselves or others, or their local communities. Inevitably, this means that we need to address issues that arise in the form of criminality, serious violence, use of weapons and negative group or gang activities. It is in the context of all this that we have developed a praxis, drawing on faith for its basis, for implementation both within people's community and the prison context.[3]

Faith-based considerations in the desistance trajectory

As a Christian organisation, let me first say that, Bringing Hope is committed to inclusivity and respecting diversity. Consequently, we will work with people impacted by the issues highlighted of all faiths or no faith, provided they are willing to explore positive and sustainable approaches towards transformation, desistance and rehabilitation. Our programmes, activities and associated interventions are governed by a Christian ethos: they uphold principles of justice, love, compassion, kindness, integrity, humility, forgiveness, accountability, and anti-oppressive practice, and they enable us to understand people's spiritual, moral and ethical concerns, as well as their other needs, holistically.

As the late John Lewis, Civil Rights icon and US congressman, said:

"When you see something that is not right, not fair, not just, you have to speak up. You have to say something; you have to do something."[4]

These words resonate with our willingness to tackle social injustice, racism and inequalities from our own faith-based perspectives, as well as to address causal factors relating to crime and violence.

In recent years, there has been a steady growth of researchers exploring the extent to which faith organisations and their members contribute to social capital, and how they relate to achieving better education attainments, improvement of health, and lowering crime levels.[5] My own focus has been to explore critically the impact of faith-based and ethical approaches in working with black young men, and communities impacted by violence, crime and socio-economic challenges. It is from this research that have emerged perspectives and approaches that have positively impacted the lives of the black young men who have undertaken our *Damascus Road Second Chance Prison and Community Development Programme* – Bringing Hope's twelve-week programme in two West Midlands prisons.

Engaging with black young men's "realities" through acts of kindness

From the outset, we have been mindful that the very thought of having to transform or change oneself can and does strike fear into the hearts and minds of many of the men we work with. Based on this, we reassure the men that, "personal transformation" is a process that takes time, nurturing, and support. Furthermore, each individual on the programme is supported to have a sense that they are in a "safe space". Here there are opportunities to share and dialogue, centring on issues of mutual concern, socio-cultural heritage, masculinity, moral and ethical choices, faith, spirituality, family, community, and fatherhood. Men are also encouraged to participate in personal reflection on behaviours and lifestyles associated with their prison sentence.

Through our varied and interdisciplinary approaches (which include one-to-one personal development support, counselling, group work, mentoring, role plays and peer-support), we have built trust and confidence, allowing us to challenge, influence, empower and support individuals and their families towards positive transformation and change. It is worth quoting at length from the report on the evaluation undertaken by Coventry University, as it highlights the impact of our approaches on the lives of black young men:

> "A reoccurring theme in the data is how engagement in the Damascus Second Chance programme was a positive experience for those involved. Participants spoke candidly about the significance of participating in a programme that was specifically designed, delivered and targeted at black

men. The Damascus Road Second Chance Programme was described as a programme that was unique and empowering, in that it spoke directly to black men, understood the lives of black men, addressed black men's needs and specific barriers they may encounter inside and outside prison. Participants identified the approach, content and delivery as challenging but also refreshing, creating 'space' for personal reflection and development that was unthreatening. They welcomed the opportunity to speak openly about their experiences and valued the practical and emotional support provided during group activities and individually during one to one session.

The aspects of the programme identified as challenging were mediated by the programme being delivered by 'trusted' practitioners who offered unconditional support in a non-judgemental way. Hence, overwhelmingly the data illuminates positive feelings towards the programme and much of this reflected positive feelings in relation to the practitioners delivering the programme who were described as men who were 'genuine' and who 'genuinely cared' about the lives of black men. For participants, the uniqueness of the programme was that it provided an opportunity for Black men to meet as a group or individually (with practitioners) and provided a forum in which they were encouraged to engage in critical reflection, self-healing, spiritual, emotional and physical well-being, self-awareness and to consider the valuable contributions they could make to others (family, friends, community). Participants share how the Damascus Road Second Chance Programme provided a welcomed intervention that supported their personal development and wellbeing and equipped them with tools they could employ to navigate and cope with the prison regime. The one-to-one support and through-the-gate support aspects of the programme were important as they were considered evidence of practitioners' long-term commitment."[6]

Whilst this offers some insights into our work with young black men, it is important to acknowledge that we are undertaking this work within a context within which black men are still being misrepresented and misunderstood by individuals and systems that bear responsibilities to support them. Although a different context and located in the United States of America, it would be remiss of me not to draw parallels, and mention the pain, grief and anger witnessed, as millions, via social media platforms, witnessed the "professional" and merciless killing of George Floyd, in Minneapolis, on Monday 25th May 2020. Here, we see another black man, being the victim of racism, mistreatment and oppression, at the hands of officers paid to "serve and protect" individuals and communities. Even now, there are still tears as I remember Mr Floyd, grasping for his life, calling for his mother. I can still hear him pleading, "I cannot breathe"; "Please let me stand". I suggest, if those involved with George Floyd had decided to respond with a "kindness consciousness", as represented above, he would still be with us today.

Concluding thoughts

At the heart of our faith-based actions and activities are the principles highlighted earlier, namely: justice, love, compassion, kindness, integrity, humility, forgiveness and accountability. These principles are discussed and reviewed by our staff team on a regular basis. According to Martin Glynn, black young men are more likely to engage with individuals, organisations, institutions and systems that seek to support them within "safe spaces", where they can talk freely and share their "realities."[7] Bringing Hope has continued to be advocates of practices that are non-judgemental, antiracist and culturally competent. Consequently, we challenge systems, institutions and individuals that perpetuate injustices or oppressive practices. We act as critical friends to public service agencies whose policies have an impact on the families we work with.

Experience has taught us that effective and positive transformational work with black young men is rooted in developing genuine relationships of trust and respect, which usually emerges from implementing the principles above.

Our conviction of the vital role of love and kindness is shaped by our faith, but our methods and approaches are also multidimensional, working in partnership with statutory, community, faith and voluntary colleagues to provide responses to the cases referred to us that will be effective. If we are to influence criminal justice policies and research, it is our firm conclusion that faith-based interventions and approaches should be considered alongside other social scientific and criminal justice models and framework, seeking to contribute to crime and violence reduction in Birmingham and other UK cities.[8] Our ultimate aim is to preserve and enhance life and commit to "saving our sons".[9]

LOVE ACTUALLY: WHY WE NEED LOVE AND EMPATHY IN SERVICES AND SYSTEMS

Sarah Wilkinson & Anne-Marie Douglas

excited voice 'It's us. It's literally us!'

This is how the conversation went when we saw the title of this year's Monument Fellowship volume. If you cut Peer Power in half, you'd find kindness, hope and compassion in our DNA, along with two of our values: love and empathy. In our co-produced organisation, these values are explicit and lived; they drive our staff and Young Partners – as individuals, collectively and as an organisation to do what we do and work towards our vision:

A world where empathy-led services and systems support all children, teenagers and young adults to achieve their dreams and lead their best lives.

When thinking about the role of kindness, hope and compassion in the criminal justice system, we automatically think about the individual people within it – the transformational nature of trusted and caring relationships, and what young people repeatedly tell us: *'you just need that one person who will really care'*. We're sure that no-one reading this will need persuading of the central importance of relationships and connection! However, equally as important – but much less talked about – is the crucial role that kindness and compassion play at a systems level; where do we see these values demonstrated in public policy making, funding decisions, governance and commissioning?

Here, we'll explore the role that kindness, hope and compassion plays in criminal justice, both at an individual level and systems level; exploring some of the barriers that exist. We offer examples of how these can be overcome and the transformational impact that such approaches can have. Throughout, we've used quotes from our Young Partners[1], who we'd like to thank for the amazing contribution they make to influencing services and systems to be more compassionate and empathic. The thoughts and perspectives presented also draw heavily on the journey of exploration that Anne-Marie (Founder and CEO of Peer Power) experienced as part of her Winston Churchill Memorial Trust Fellowship on Empathy in youth support services (Peer Power, 2020 (forthcoming))[2].

Towards a system that heals

What might empathic organisations look like across health, education, justice and social care systems? If services were more empathy led, would this help systems to heal, rather than harm? And could that lead to more efficient services, leading to better outcomes and savings to the public purse?

Through her Fellowship journey, Anne-Marie wanted to explore these questions. She wanted to find out what the impact might be of increased empathy in the systems and agencies that support some of our most under-supported and socially excluded children, teenagers and young adults. Her journey of exploration took her to the USA and Canada, where she learned from individuals and organisations who were explicitly teaching and practicing empathic approaches in the fields of youth justice, social care, education, and health.

She found that people in the USA and Canada were more comfortable and open when talking about the need for empathy and love in services. It was accepted that these were 'must haves' for children who had experienced adversity. From her professional and personal experience in England, we appeared not to be as comfortable or explicit about it, despite the fact that this was what children, teenagers and young adults always said was '*the most important thing*' in engaging with services.

The intention with her research – and the reason she founded Peer Power as a charity in 2016 – was to help organisations and systems prioritise relational approaches above bureaucracy, to see opportunity rather than risk and be curious rather than closed. Above all else, Anne-Marie holds a belief that empathy, love, kindness and relationships can be transformational at a systems level and should be intentionally maintained as core values across *all* support organisations for children, teenagers and young adults.

"*Through exploring in the USA and Canada, I have found that the teaching of empathy, 'explicitly and deliberately' was being applied in schools, in prisons, in police forces, in justice agencies, and in health and social care agencies. I found that whole states in the USA are starting again with their multi-support agencies, understanding that it is whole system change that is required, and sometimes this can mean a long-term culture change strategy. Other times it means redesigning trauma and experience informed services, as is the case in California, and across school systems in New York and Washington DC.*"

I came to conclude... empathy is intentional, it is a 'doing' word, and that in fact empathy is the driver to love, kindness and compassionate action. It leads to 'empathic interactions' that increase connection and engagement between service providers and those who use the services.

The antidote to (or healing of) trauma, and the mitigation of the effects of childhood adversity and trauma comes from empathy, through human relationships, empathic interactions and connection, therefore: **the relationship IS the intervention**"

The relationship IS the intervention

Countless research projects, scientific and academic evidence, conversations with young people – they all show the same thing: trusted relationships are key. This is particularly true when working with young people in the criminal justice system, who have often been let down and traumatised by people, by society and even by the systems designed to help them. This means that time spent developing relationships and connection are even more important. It is empathy, trust and relationships, not programmes or interventions, that make the difference.

Some of the children, teenagers and young adults we partner with at Peer Power have described themselves as being 'abandoned by society'. They have experienced injustice and inequality through a range of social and economic factors, including race, class, poverty and disabilities, in addition to childhood adversity and trauma (individual, societal and systemic). Our Young Partners are passionate about using their experiences in positive and powerful ways to improve social care, justice and health services by voicing issues for and with other young people.

In a recent project some of our Young Partners reflected on their experiences of custody to make recommendations for what the future of youth custody should look like. One of the discussions that came up was whether there should be a role for love and care in youth custody. One of our Young Partners said: '*Yes, why would there not be!*', another said '*these are children and they need to be cared for*'.

They felt strongly that consistency, kindness, compassion and empathy were important practices for staff working with young people in the justice system. For them, recruitment of caring support staff was paramount. Many of them talked about staff members who they felt didn't care and were only there for their paycheck. However, all of them remembered at least one positive relationship that they had built. When asked what it was about those people that enabled a bond to form, the role of empathy, understanding and kindness came out strongly. Some of the key themes included staff who:

- were empathic and showed they could relate to them
- were believing and 'seeing the good' in them
- *'listened and understood how frustrating things could be'*
- go the 'extra mile', bringing in puzzles, snacks, sharing information and doing things they 'didn't have to do' in their role that demonstrated individual care.

Recommendations that Young Partners shared concluded similarly:

"They need to have someone who has consistency to give that love and care throughout their stay and even support after they have left. You should have a consistent worker for one young person for the duration of their stay."

"Just being kinder in the way you handle things. If you show some interest in young people then it goes a long way."

Barriers in the system

There are a number of barriers that exist and can limit the spread of such compassionate approaches, particularly in the criminal justice system. The inherent focus on management of risk, systemic power dynamics at play, and moral questions over the 'worthiness' of children and young people (who get into trouble with the law) receiving kindness and love – these all play a part. The media, the politicisation of criminal justice policy, and the need for political parties, institutions and organisations not to be seen as 'soft' on crime also has an impact and can instantly silence conversations and debates about the role of love and empathy in systems. There is a focus on 'hard' outcomes, key performance indicators and targets. The soft, relational values and outcomes around building relationships and trust are much harder to measure. Within the context of austerity – a system under pressure, targets, and ever-changing priorities – there can understandably be a tendency to focus on carrying out work that is a 'quicker win' and measurable at short-term intervals, to meet short term funding priorities.

Can commissioning be kind?

Surely, one of the hardest places to embed kindness and compassion is in the complicated and process heavy world of commissioning? In fact, we've seen how commissioning and procurement – in a health and justice context – can enable kindness and relationships to develop. For example, some of our Young Partners were invited to be part of the commissioning of a new health provider in a justice setting. The approach is steeped and modelled in respect, kindness and compassion and supports a trauma-responsive approach to involvement in commissioning. This means Young Partners are able to use their experiences positively and safely to help improve the system for others and influence the systems they have been a part of.

Working alongside Young Partners to help them prepare to participate fully and meaningfully in the process takes time, care and love. It is 'people over process', a 'people first, project second' and a trauma-responsive approach. We also work alongside professionals in the same way to build trust and respect for the value of co-production and champion both lived and learnt experience. Everyone needs to come to the party 'ready' for meaningful co-production and the sharing of power!

We can tell you that the time spent building relationships in order to influence systems is time well spent and it's always worth it! You will never have truly empathic systems until you have a mix of lived and learned experience at the top. This means developing young leaders from different backgrounds, with cultural competency; supporting them to progress in their careers, so that eventually a sustainable mix of lived and learned experience exists in leadership, commissioning, service design and delivery.

"Peer Power is about caring for people so they can care for themselves and for others"

This quote from a Young Partner epitomises our approach. We've seen encouraging examples of what happens when organisations and systems are open to learning about empathic approaches that value the role of lived experience. We recently worked in collaboration with NHS England and NHS Improvement to record a peer-led message about COVID-19 for children and young people who are currently in the secure estate.[3] Some of our Young Partners, known as the 'Peer Power Experts' fed into the script. They recorded an audio message which gave young people information about COVID and crucially, let them know that their peers in the community were thinking about them and care about them. The video starts with compassionate messages from the group:

"I've been to the secure estate so I understand what it's like not really knowing what's going on around you. I hope this information helps you guys a lot."

"We are a group of young people who've also been where you are and understand how you're feeling. We hope this five-minute message will give you some facts and provide you with a bit of clarity and comfort during this time."

Our Peer Power Experts were proud to have been involved in the recording because they really empathised with how children in custody might be feeling at this uncertain time and wanted to use their experiences to connect with them and go some way to reassuring them. Empathy is what drives our model and it has powerful results.

The time is ripe for change

We want to end by expressing our enormous gratitude to all those key workers, social workers, youth justice practitioners and managers, and others who've gone above and beyond to look after young people during the COVID-19 pandemic, that has been the context as we write this. This isn't about encouraging frontline workers to be more kind and compassionate – we know you are some of the kindest and compassionate people on the planet!

This is about making the case for radical systems change; for responding to the voices of young people and embedding empathy, love, kindness and compassion into systems, services and organisations. We agree with Julia Unwin CBE[4]: 'great public policy challenges of our time demand an approach that is more centred on relationships'.

As we write – during the COVID-19 pandemic and the global response to the murder of George Floyd and the Black Lives Matter movement – there has been powerful social activism and strong rhetoric around solidarity, kindness, empathy and compassion. These are the values that when translated into action can help us stand up and rally against structural inequalities and injustice, to make tangible changes in structures and systems. This is the time to press forward with sustainably embedding these values into the criminal justice system, into politics and into society more generally.

A Window of Turbulence, HM Prison Holme House

Image courtesy of Koestler Arts

CIRCLES OF SUPPORT AND ACCOUNTABILITY: REDUCING SHAME, BRINGING HOPE AND PREVENTING FURTHER VICTIMS OF SEXUAL ABUSE

Riana Taylor, CEO of Circles UK

Introduction

Circles of Support and Accountability ('Circles') work with individuals who have sexually abused others to reduce their risk of doing so again to prevent further victims. It is an approach which uses local volunteers to hold accountable and support perpetrators in the community, often following release after a lengthy prison sentence. Each Circle comprises four or five professionally trained and supervised volunteers and the 'Core Member' (the term we use for those that we work with who have been assessed as likely to sexually reoffend or have convictions for sexual offences).

Perpetrators of sexual abuse are often stigmatized and socially excluded from the communities they come from. Public opinion often favours a 'lock them up and throw away the key' response to them. Yet every day Circles operate with over 600 volunteers in England and Wales who meet with Core Members to help them manage their on-going risk and support them to live more positive lives. Core Members have told us that it is the fact that the volunteers receive no remuneration for their work and give tirelessly of their time and themselves that has been instrumental in their desistance from sexual reoffending; the fact that 'ordinary' members of the community extend a hand, build a relationship, are kind, show compassion and give hope in what may be an otherwise bleak life. This contribution will explain why Circles are effective in helping abusers to desist from further sexual abuse and how they are underpinned by a philosophy of hope versus shame, accountability versus denial and redemption versus lifelong exclusion.

Why Circles bring hope

The Circles methodology is designed to achieve the following:

2.1 Striking a balance between accountability and support

In most societies those with convictions for sexual offences are released from prison under stringent monitoring measures to prevent further victims. Stacey Dooley recently made a BBC documentary titled, *'Second Chance Sex Offenders'*, which asked whether *"sex offenders deserve a second chance."* The documentary focused on Bradford County in Florida, USA where people with sexual offences face restrictions for life after their release from prison. It is common to find a noticeboard at the person's home containing his/her name and informing the public that the person has a conviction for a sexual offence. As a result, vigilante attacks and public shaming are common, which has resulted in groups of people with convictions for sexual offences congregating together in separate 'communities' where they feel more safe. Stacey Dooley visited one such community called 'Miracle Village' which is a remote settlement where more than 100 people on the Sex Offender Register live together under extremely strict conditions.

In the UK, people with convictions for serious sexual offences are released on license to the Probation Service, are often subject to multi-agency public protection arrangements (MAPPA) and must be registered with the police. However, their identities are not automatically disclosed to the public and people can apply after a period of having been offence free to be removed from the Register. The Child Sex Offender Disclosure Scheme was implemented in 2013, allowing concerned members of the public to apply to the police for information about individuals that they suspect of being a risk to children. This followed a campaign for a 'Megan's Law' type of system after the tragic murder of Sarah Payne.

There is growing evidence that the effects of extreme monitoring and restrictions of people with convictions for sexual offences have detrimental effects by often preventing them from successfully reintegrating back into society after a prison sentence. It raises the issue of whether public protection measures have created unintended consequences that may encourage further offending instead of preventing it. The Core Members we work with experience significant challenges in accessing accommodation, education and employment due to their status as registered sex offenders. These obstacles, together with the high social stigma that is attached to their crimes, have also adversely affected their ability to re-establish and build support systems such as family and friends and to access community services. Although all people with criminal convictions experience these obstacles, it is well documented that people with convictions for sexual offences tend to experience higher levels of societal stigma which often result in a greater variety of forms of social exclusion. Ironically, when people experience such high levels of social exclusion and stigma, the potential for them to reoffend increases, which goes against the intended purposes of the legislation.[1]

There is always a tension between giving people a second chance and managing the risk of a relapse and potentially creating another victim. Core to the Circles methodology is the recognition of the devastating impact that sexual abuse has on victims and survivors. However, we also recognise that risk can never be completely eliminated and some people will relapse. All the evidence shows that a proportionate response between public protection, preventing further victims and giving perpetrators the opportunity to reform is the best solution to preventing further sexual abuse.

A Circle epitomises this proportionate approach as it rests on two key principles: accountability and support. The accountability aspects rests in the fact that Circles operate in close partnership with the statutory agencies. Any concerns, for example an escalation in risk to another person that is identified in a Circle by the volunteers, are reported to these agencies which when necessary, will take appropriate measures to prevent the person from reoffending. This is done transparently and with the knowledge of the Core Member as discussions of risk take place within the Circle. This is to support the person to adopt self-regulatory strategies and take responsibility for their behaviour. In fact, we have seen instances where Core Members shared with volunteers that their risk was rising and were fully cooperative in the enforcement action that resulted. At times it has meant that the Circle was stopped and resumed at a later stage when the risk has reduced. The accountability aspect of a Circle helps to prevent further victims but without intensifying the shame that the person may experience.

The other key principle of a Circle is to provide support through the volunteers' relationship with the Core Member which addresses the specific needs of the person. This can involve practical help with accommodation, employment and financial advice, but also includes a focus on helping to develop appropriate relationships, access community support networks and reduce social isolation.

Research has shown that the combination of 'accountability and support' helps the person take ownership of their behaviour, feel positive and motivated to change. As stated by Carich et al, 'It is only through a relationship that defines itself within the context of humanity and care that the Core Member is likely to accept the relationship of being held accountable by the Circle as anything other than positive.'

2.2 Counteracting the lifelong label of 'sex offender'

The Core Members we work with often say that they would like to be seen as more than the sexual offences they have committed. Instead society and some parts of the media often use stigmatising and shaming labels and narratives to describe people with convictions for sexual offences. Labels such as 'pervert', 'paedo monster' and others have been used to describe individuals having perpetrated acts as diverse as having had unlawful sexual intercourse, viewing illegal images of children, public indecency, date rape, sexual assault of a stranger, incest and sexual homicide to name just a few. By aggregating these criminal behaviours under a single label, we lose sight of the variety of behaviours that are involved; the similarities and differences between the types of perpetrators; the range of seriousness differentiating those and the various legal, social, and developmental contexts in which those behaviours occur.[3] Dehumanising language makes it acceptable to hurt, to shame, to exclude and to deny a second chance. Dehumanisation does not allow for any social justice.

Somehow, we find it harder to forgive perpetrators of sexual abuse for their crimes in comparison to other types of perpetrators like murderers and robbers. Even a self-confessed, non-offending paedophile who has not harmed a child but is coming forward to ask for help is ostracised and we, at present, in the UK offer only very limited support services for such individuals.

The overarching sentiment also seems to be, that once labelled a 'sex offender', one will forever be seen as such, although research evidence has shown that not only is the reoffending rates of people with convictions for sexual offences lower than for other types of offenders but they also do not continue to commit sexual crimes throughout their lifetimes.[4]

Circles take a strengths based and desistance approach and try and instil in Core Members the idea that they are more than the label that has been bestowed upon them from society. Circles bring into focus other identities that Core Members hold such as parents, grandparents, citizens and fellow human beings. However, often the public has not acknowledged their other "identities."[5] The desire of human beings for punishment and retribution when they have been harmed through another's actions is universal and often understandable. It is therefore no surprise that the philosophy of punishment and retribution is such an integral part of most criminal justice systems. But how far should punishment and retribution go, especially once a person has served a prison sentence and all available evidence suggests the person to be law abiding and compliant? How long before the punishment is done and we allow forgiveness and redemption?

2.3 Bringing hope versus shame

Most of the perpetrators we work with in Circles tell us that they experience high levels of shame about the abuse they have committed. When this is revealed, it may be an extremely vulnerable moment in the Circle and takes great courage from the Core Member. By showing empathy and compassion during this process, the volunteers create a safe space where the Core Member can share.

Kaufman describes shame '...*an entrance to the self. It is the affect of indignity, of transgression, of defeat, of inferiority and alienation... Shame is felt as an inner torment, as a sickness of the soul. It is the most poignant experience of the self by the self, whether felt in the humiliation of cowardice, or in the sense of failure to cope successfully with a challenge. Shame is a wound felt from the inside, dividing us both from ourselves and from one another.*'[6]

Cavicchia writes, 'The experience of shame contributes to a contraction of the space for inquiry, dialogue, and thinking together. Experimenting with new behaviours, or imagining new possibilities, become extremely difficult to the extent that individuals are often acutely self-conscious, primarily preoccupied with being acceptable, and unwilling to risk anything that might make them look bad or simply different.'[7]

Shame is the opposite of hope. Hope is essential for positive living, for having a sense of purpose. You cannot have hope if you think you can never be seen as a person apart from the crimes you have committed. I am reminded of an interview of Brene Brown with Marie Forleo on 'Belonging, Courage and Constructive Conversations' (2017) in which Brene says that connection is our ability to form meaningful relationships and is key to the human existence. This is key to experiencing and exercising empathy. On the other extreme is shame which prevents us from having or forming human connections. Shame in a therapeutic or restorative setting only results in fear and withdrawal. As soon as shame comes into the room it kills the conversation.

On the opposite extreme, an accepting and 'safe' environment such as within a Circle, can reduce this sense of shame and encourage a different way of relating. Cavicchia comments on the positive impact of such environments: 'Far from being a way of avoiding accountability, reducing the fear of exposure can make it easier for individuals to take fuller accountability for the part they have played in any situation, reflect, learn, and make them less likely to pass accusation and blame elsewhere.'[8]

2.4 Allowing restoration through re-entry into the community

It is well documented that people with convictions for sexual offences often tend to be socially isolated and this isolation is enhanced through the labelling, stigmatisation and social exclusion they experience as described in 2.2. Core Members tell us that the Circle is often the first group that they are a member of where they feel safe, accepted and not judged. The Circle is the place where difficult conversations can happen, where support can be obtained for a range of issues and can take the place of a family or circle of friends when these structures are absent in the person's life. Probably most crucially, through the volunteers, the Circle represents a crucial community structure. This creation of community is an integral aspect of Circles as they facilitate the positive reintegration of the Core Member back into the community. Once the person is familiar with the Circle as community, the volunteers facilitate other appropriate community groups that the Core Member can access and join. This is an important part of the restoration process after punishment and why Circles are often described as a restorative solution. As Katherine Fox writes: '*Active civic engagement between offenders and citizens teaches community values explicitly via interactions designed to guide and support offenders as they transition. In addition, community values are transmitted implicitly by expressing the values of inclusion, citizenship, fundamental human rights and forgiveness.*'[9] When these values are applied to practice, there is a significant change in the way that justice is being delivered and it becomes transformative.[10]

Conclusion

The Criminal Justice System can be experienced as cold and harsh by those who have been found guilty of crimes and serve sentences. Key rehabilitative and desistance concepts like kindness, compassion and hope are often not found within its structures. When Core Members first come into a Circle, they often express a sense of hopelessness, of being full of shame and fear that they will carry the label of 'sex offender' for the rest of their lives. Circles counteract this sense of hopelessness as they teach Core Members that people can and will give them a second chance and that they are worth something as people. This increase in self-worth and self-belief, in itself, can be enough to move them away from reoffending.

I'll conclude with a powerful statement by Grant Duwe, '*At a more profound, individual level, Circles also speaks to the power of compassion, friendship, and love. Many of the Core Members who participate are aware of how sex offenders are perceived by society. For these individuals who have offended sexually, the Circle not only provides them with much-needed sources of pro-social support but also offers hope and a path to redemption.*'[11]

COACHING: TOUGH QUESTIONS, BRAVE ANSWERS

Ben Amponsah, Clare McGregor & Jules Roberts

Coaching Inside and Out helps people improve their own lives and the lives of others. CIAO's coaches offer kindness, have hope that everyone can change and act with (com)passion. It takes courage to answer coaching's hard questions, but there's laughter, as well as tears.

Everyone deserves to benefit from great coaching, regardless of their ability to pay or position in life. That's why we coach adults in prison and on probation in the community; as well as children who've been locked up or are on the edges of the criminal justice system. It's never too early and never too late. CIAO also coaches staff working with our clients. We started in 2010, when a Google search implied no organisations were coaching in prisons anywhere in the world. Now it's increasingly widespread.

Being asked to reflect on kindness, hope and compassion in our work with men and boys builds perfectly on the book about our beginnings in HMP Styal: '*Coaching Behind Bars: Facing Challenges and Creating Hope in a Women's Prison.*'

These attributes existing in criminal justice may surprise some, and possibly even more so with male clients. It's a tough world to share them in. People can be mocked and despised for it. It can be a challenging place for these qualities to be accepted too. Coaches have the luxury of being outside 'the system' and are very aware of the additional challenges faced by those in different roles; often in environments beset with drugs, fear and violence. However, you'll find examples here of kindness, hope and compassion by coaches towards our clients and, far more importantly, by our clients towards themselves and their peers, families, coaches and staff.

What's in your toolbox?

Mentors can advise and show how to fix things or even do a job for you, whereas coaches bring a toolbox full of transformational questions to help clients work things out for themselves.

We all need more tools, if, as Maslow said: *"It is tempting, if the only tool you have is a hammer, to treat everything as if it were a nail."* Coaching helps you discover tools you've forgotten, tools you never knew you had or tools you aren't quite sure how to use yet.

How might we change the world if we believed everyone has their own answers, if asked the right questions? What if people could focus their energy by choosing what they want to change and what tools work best for them?

No tool required?

You can be human in a coaching session, not 'male'; no longer playing a role but being yourself, often for the first time. If you've spent a lifetime being told not to cry or show weakness, this belief is cemented. Sometimes you don't need to be asked a question. You just need space to work things out.

One man wept his way through half a box of tissues and said: *"Oh my god... I've filled the bin! You'll have to tell them you've been really busy and had ten clients today and they've all cried!"*

He'd paced back and forth with his head down. At times he lost his breath from crying so hard. It was a totally new experience. He'd never been seen crying and hadn't ever cried like this. Tears of shame, hurt, sadness, loss... He only managed to sit down for the last 10 minutes.

A calmness came over him and he said: "*What's just happened to me?*" On leaving he immediately began to address his addiction.

Allowing so much time for silence may be surprising, not least when we limit our work to six hours with each client to concentrate thought and action, but that space can be as powerful as any question.

Suspicion of Kindness – Why are you doing this?

Great coaching means being open, genuine and straight-talking, as well as showing vulnerability. Being human and patient fosters trust and a safe environment for exploring thoughts, feelings and future actions. Knowing the immense part luck plays in our lives means we also work without judgement.

The power is with the client, which makes coaching a very different experience to most criminal justice interventions. Suspicion about kindness can lead clients to test us, whether by sharing their history or through current behaviour (anger, swearing, not turning up etc.). Instead of being pushed away we work through challenges and show up repeatedly regardless. Curiosity about issues like 'Anger Icebergs' means looking at what's below the surface, addressing the emotions that generate behaviour and reframing them.

This isn't soft or easy. CIAO coaches are tough but flexible and expect clients to work hard. We hold them accountable. If anyone plays games we'll work with that with curiosity: What's the game and is playing it really working for you?

We try to model bravery and don't avoid the powerful questions, but we don't encourage bravery above all else. We go deeper or just work at surface level, depending on where people are at that moment. While coaching can be challenging, uncomfortable, difficult and scary; you can go far further with someone alongside you being kind and encouraging you to be kind to yourself.

How's that working for you?

A young teenager was extremely kind to others and put all his energy into thinking and feeling about them but not about himself. "*I like to be kind to others; it hurts me when people aren't and I get into trouble as I do things to help them like starting a fight. I don't want people to feel sad when they're told bad things like: 'You're gay, black and stupid.'... Most people don't think I'm kind, they think I'm bad. What can I do about that?*"

> Coach: If being kind is your superpower how is fighting being kind?
> Client: Oh!
> Client: What else could I do?!
> Coach: Let's work that out...

He recognised he was feeling empathy and talked to his friends about how they actually felt and how his fighting then made them and him feel. His mum called the next day: "*I wanted to thank you as I had no idea that this was the motivation to fight – to be kind... I feel ashamed I didn't know this and that my son's also been bullied. I can offer him support from now on.*"

In his last session he gave his coach a piece of paper: "*Please never forget to BE KIND I won't!*"

Beyond Hope – What would you make if you could make anything?

Some clients had hope taken away from them on imprisonment and many have never had a hope, which is part of why they're in 'the system'. Working with children can feel more hopeful as they're just starting their lives, but forgotten adults also need support. Hope means there's a future worth living for in places where many feel they're at a dead end and some take that literally by contemplating or attempting suicide. Hope brings light into this darkness and despair.

CIAO coaches often have no faith, in a religious sense, but bring love and an abundance of hope grounded in the hard reality of life that clients share. Many clients don't start with the determination and motivation to change things, whereas we know we all have the capacity to think differently. Coaches may come with greater hope, but it doesn't just transfer to clients, hope grows once they work out what's stopping them think and take control of their lives.

What materials have you got?

CIAO's first male community client said he only had five minutes but stayed for thirty. He'd never had any 'meaningful use of time' in all his 29 years and was first arrested aged 12: "*I had to look after myself all my life. I've never had a penny.*" He'd no hope and couldn't see how he could change anything, so he went in at the deep end uncovering his strengths and values (that included kindness and hope). The raw materials of energy and self-esteem were all he needed. "*People do things because of the hand they were dealt, who they're around, who they mix with and how they were brought up. Now I'm putting my cards back in the pack and giving them a good shuffle.*"

Coaching had to stop after just two weeks because he got a job. As importantly, he was also now "*minding the kids a lot more and taking responsibility. I told my ex 'I can't have the kids with me' and that killed me. But I could. I just needed to sort me head out.*"

What assumptions are stopping you start?

Another client shared that he'd lost his get up and go. "*I really want to make the changes but I just don't know where to start.*" When asked what he was doing or thinking that was stopping him move forward, he covered a wall in sticky notes with negative assumptions of people's views of him, but he couldn't say why he believed that.

He recognised he held the power to make the changes he wanted to happen. *"How crazy is it that I was the one who was stopping myself from moving forward? I decided from session 3 that I was going to stop this. Once I'd worked that out I started immediately to change and move forward in my life. Things that I hadn't ever seen were all around me. It was as if I'd stepped into a new world. I learnt that I was supported, I had my place and people recognised that I was good at what I did. I have a new way of dealing with things now, which is brilliant for me."*

This officer's story shows how we're all human before we are anything else. It's common to read accounts and need to check if the client is a prisoner or a member of staff. Clients of all sorts share doubts and fears, as well as bravery.

No Forgiveness, No Compassion – What dead wood do you need to let go of?
"Scum", "worthless" and "FEAR".

Judgement and prejudice hold us all back. These words are what some men in prison wrote on a flip chart to describe themselves. Self-judgement is something coaches challenge to enable clients to move to a better state. We want people to demonstrate compassion towards themselves. Otherwise we shore up anger, pain and hurt inside us; with no solid foundation to build on. We want our clients to feel self-compassion, not self-hatred and shame.

Passion is more vital to what coaches do than compassion. Although coaches might feel sorrow or want to relieve suffering, it's essential that we don't coach in anger or pain, whether ours or transferred from clients. We need to be able step in and out of clients' emotions and we use clinical supervision and other help to support that. None of us is super-human. Treating ourselves, as well as others, with compassion is fundamental.

What are you assuming that's holding you back?

Coaches challenge invisible assumptions to break negative patterns of thinking or self-sabotaging. This positive questioning can be the first time many have done this form of reflection.

A client nearing release developed new strategies for old situations, which prompted this exchange:

> Client: If people look at me funny in the street, when I'm out, then obviously I'll...
>
> Coach: May I challenge you on the word obviously?
>
> Client: Yes.
>
> Coach: What's obvious about that? What if someone's just having a bad day?
>
> Client: That never occurred to me! That's going to stay with me that is.

We also explore 'Blind Spots' in perception and others' possible intentions: What don't you know about yourself that others do? How can you use this to change what you want?

An older boy really struggled with anger issues. He turned up angry once and when he realised the coach wasn't condemning or annoyed, but instead was going to be compassionate and work through his anger with him, something clicked. His coach modelled how things could be if he used his attractive personality for good. He realised he could forgive his family and treat himself with compassion too. He applied this and could see the change in his family's reactions. Once he'd cottoned on to this he took off and was elated. He had options, power and control. He opened up with his family, explained how he was feeling, and they supported him. The vicious cycle became a virtuous one.

CIAO coaches always write certificates and this client chose to adapt his in return. This is one of the points:

Coach: You haven't been afraid to be challenged even when you were feeling down and irritable - that takes real guts.

Client: You haven't been afraid to challenge me even when I was irritable, hilarious and the rest... that takes real guts!!

This response shows how kindness and compassion, and both giving and accepting challenge, leave us all with greater hope for the future.

Who can you share your tools with?

One man always talked of having three plans and whenever he mentioned Plan 3 he'd give a cheeky smile:

Plan 1: Get a Job

Plan 2: Go to College

Plan 3: Go back to my old life but try not to get caught and locked up again.

In his last session he shared: "*Okay, I want to help other young lads like I was, to learn from my mistakes. I now know what it is that I need to do... I've made a mistake but that's not my life ended... I'm still only 24 years old... but I'm going to be kind to myself, not judge myself and hate myself. That way didn't work so good for me. There is no Plan 3: I'm never coming back!*"

Coaching is a two-way relationship and, whilst we clearly learn and benefit immensely from our clients, they often want to give something more back to their coaches and can struggle with being unable to. However, they can pay it forward in different ways instead, and they do, including recommending coaching to others. Showing greater care for staff is another kindness that results: one officer was shocked when asked: "*How are you?*" – "*That was a first!*"

What are you taking away from this?

Reflection makes us all better able to improve our lives and the lives of others. It takes years of experience to hone deep coaching skills, but everyone can benefit if we all ask more questions and listen more deeply. The questions in these headings can be used by everyone, inside and outside the criminal justice system, to change what we want.

Kindness, hope and compassion allow the belief that change might be conceivable and that an aspiration just might be achievable. Brave answers to coaching's tough questions can then provide all we need to make the most of our potential and what life has given us, whatever our situation may be. We cannot afford to waste resources, wherever they are. Thankfully though, some resources are renewable and the most powerful of these is hope.

THE COMPLEXITY
OF COMPASSION

Alice Dawnay

Compassion needs to be at the heart of the justice system because human beings need to be at the heart of the justice system. In meting out justice, as a society, we give ourselves the authority to ask others to be better humans. And as humans, we need to do this through recognising the humanity both in the victims and the perpetrators.

A kind, compassionate, hopeful justice system can only exist through the lens of a shared humanity. Here are the stories of three real people[1] I have worked with that speak to this truth.

Wayne

A funny, charming, irreverent 23-year-old, Wayne had been in and out of prison for some years by the time I met him. Highly likeable and very outspoken, he was skilled in entertaining people and getting them on side. He told me all about how much he wanted a future that was different to his past. To have a stable home and real job prospects. To be admired for having achieved things. He could picture it.

Devastatingly, however, Wayne suffered from what I term as 'Good Boy Really Syndrome' which is a condition that left his life in stasis. What I mean by this rather glib phrase is that Wayne was stuck in a situation where he felt he had to present as only good in a society that saw him as only bad. His mother believed very avidly that her son was a victim, that he wouldn't hurt a fly, but that the police were always on his case. The fact she felt he was so misunderstood and that she had to take his corner, entrenched her beliefs that much more.

He was an angel in her eyes. In the meantime, the police saw him as trouble. Getting high, burglaries, stealing, dealing… an irredeemable opportunist. They saw him as 'bad'.

The truth of course, is that Wayne could be both. He was many things, as we all are. But the myths on both sides – and sadly, especially on his mum's side – kept him where he was, unable to progress. It's not possible to authentically connect with someone with 'Good Boy Really Syndrome'. It doesn't work. It makes them impermeable.

There is an important chain of cause and effect which involves admission of causing harm, taking responsibility, facing the consequences, making reparation, forgiving and being forgiven. It applies to us all. If the part about admission of doing harm and taking responsibility is missed out, the rest doesn't follow. You can't just skip it. And for someone whose mother believes he's a Good Boy Really, there is a terrible fear that this is the only reason she loves you. That you are loveable because you are untarnished. So it is too frightening to admit guilt. You can't do it. You know very well that you've caused harm and made mistakes but you will deny it until the ends of the earth, in the belief that that will leave you unloved. You have no reason to believe you could still be loveable if you were what you are: both kind and funny and affectionate AND an opportunistic drug-user who makes casual use of violence and intimidation.

That same mother – that loving mother - who would have been ringing the school to complain about mistreatment by teaching staff when you were sent home for bullying as a kid; by making you a Good Boy Really, has created such a level of shame and fear around allowing you to be honest with yourself and her about who you are that you cannot move forward from past behaviours.

This bottomless sympathy and victimising of the perpetrator takes away from the real victim. It hurts everyone more.

The justice system needs to stand alongside the humans at the heart of it – both victim and perpetrator – in recognition that they can be both, and that they need the space to be fully human and to grow. To be a compassionate agent of change in that system involves being able to stand with someone being all versions of themselves. It's complex.

Jack

Of course, there are other people caught up in the justice system who consider themselves to be so entirely bad that they have lost all self-compassion. There are people who have gone into prison and actually found some form of kindness and hope inside those walls, because there is so little of it for them out in the world. In some cases, getting 'sent down' somewhere where you are fed and watered, can have a break from misery and chaos on the streets, and shown care – even if that's just being given a meal and a bed – is your best chance at getting the scraps of compassion needed to sustain you.

I have worked with people in the last twenty years for whom things have got so bad in life that - having come to the conclusion there is no place for them in their family or in society - have found themselves in chronic despair. One of those young men who comes to mind – considering his life to have been a failure, and feeling his death would be unmourned – felt that his final moments might be his only opportunity for acknowledgement, for recognition. That he might get in the papers. He attempted something I have seen a couple of times: suicide by cop. Being seen to be committing acts of serious violence, in broad daylight, he felt sure he'd be shot if the police thought he was going to shoot someone else (he wasn't – his was a replica firearm). Thankfully he wasn't shot but arrested and given a hefty sentence. A long enough sentence, with sufficient evidence of psychological unravelling, through his increasingly disturbed behaviour, that he was deemed eligible for HMP Grendon. Grendon is a prison that is also a therapeutic community. It is a beautiful example of how compassion in the justice system is absolutely not a soft option. Quite the reverse.

Facing your demons, looking deep into the 'why' of your offending behaviour, is a tall order. It is perhaps as 'tough' as real justice gets. Revisiting harrowing childhood experiences and piecing together a puzzle of both what was done to you and what you've done… there is perhaps nowhere where the lines between perpetrator and victim are more blurred than in the human stories of Grendon prison. And the men there have caused enormous harm and damage.

But, critically, in that prison you are made to feel 'more than just a number and a surname' and Jack's journey through much darkness now has light days too. In understanding himself better and having the courage to look at the pain he's suffered, he can become overwhelmed by the weight of the pain he now understands that he's caused others. This is a man who once asked me how anyone could care about the person they were robbing when they didn't care about themselves. And told me about plummeting to a level of self-contempt where empathy for anyone was entirely theoretical.

But the human-centred process at Grendon made him kinder to himself and therefore kinder to others. A complex, sensitive and fiercely intelligent man, he is profusely empathic and a true friend to many. He has qualifications now that mean he can build a career in healthcare, which means when he is released he is in a position to spread healing not harm.

Reuben

Reuben came bursting into the office to see me one day after his front-of-house shift in a training café. He'd only been released from prison a few weeks before. "When I smile at people, they smile at me!" he exclaimed. He was 21.

This was a young man who clearly found social interaction very difficult. Quiet and gentle, he struggled to express himself. He didn't have the words. This breakthrough moment of understanding how to positively interact with other people was happening at age 21, because it hadn't happened through a reciprocal relationship with a caregiver in babyhood. Reuben had been subject to neglect as a baby and hadn't been cooed over in a cot or given attention that would have helped develop his emotional and interpersonal behaviour.

Growing up, the attention, feedback, 'nurturing' he longed for was found through the bigger boys on his estate. Everyone simply graduated to selling drugs to put money on the table. And that's what he did. He didn't see it as a choice. His identity wasn't bound up with gangsterism. The local boys were his family and source of income; it was a sort of 'cupboard love'. And he accepted the reality of being something of a disposable resource to this family.

When I met him on the wing in Rochester prison and asked him how he wanted his life to look when he got out, he didn't understand the question. He had no evidence that it was possible for life to look different to how it always had - the idea that he was someone who could develop skills, get a job, be a present father and a stable partner, pay the rent was beyond him. But he could, and he did. Step by small step. Learning to smile, to say good morning, to converse. To see himself as someone of value and to be seen that way by others. An extraordinary transformation. And without the intervention of the justice system and the compassion he was shown by a skilled voluntary sector practitioner, at a time when prison had pressed pause on the chaos of his life, he wouldn't have known any different. The justice system can play an important role in scooping up and rescuing those young people who have been failed by others... unparented, slipping through the cracks of overstretched social worker provision and school pastoral care. Those who haven't been shown kindness in the past can thrive and grow in the sunlight of compassion.

Many of the inhabitants of our prisons are there because of this lack of critical 'sunlight', and if we are interested in a system that rehabilitates, we must recognise that this needs to be built in so that they can forge a different path.

Compassion as characteristic of a shared humanity

So for people like these – this critical ingredient has either been misinterpreted, or unavailable to them in childhood. People like Wayne – who never experienced the 'tough-love' of compassion but only the misguided one-sided abundance of acclaim that he couldn't live up to. Those like Jack who've been so stifled by the effects of multiple traumas and shame that they can't find a way forward. And indeed for the Reubens of this world, who've had to wait for 21 years, to come out the other side of a custodial sentence, to be shown compassion through a resettlement programme. These are only three examples, but I have worked with hundreds of young men over the years and have seen the damage that this void of compassion and self-compassion has done to their life chances. The damage that this void has imparted on their victims. The urgent importance of true, complex, human, nourishing compassion *from and therefore towards* society, family, and consequently self.

Real compassion is not soft. It often involves difficult conversations. Hard truths. The courage to keep believing things can be different. Having high expectations against the odds. It is not indulging in narratives of victimhood, or excusing away past harms, but neither is it ignoring the profound effect of social context. It's not about telling people things are going to be ok when they're not. False hope and loose boundaries in the name of kindness can be the cruellest blockers to growth and fulfilment.

A real system of justice must insist on individual responsibility and accountability whilst demonstrating the compassion that people need to nourish themselves with. It serves no one to release people from prison who don't care about themselves or the world.

By accepting and working with the complexity of true compassion, we can guide people out of the justice system into a society where they belong. We all need this. Compassion needs to apply to any of us who have ever done anything we're ashamed of. And if it does, it can engender forgiveness and new possibilities. Wracked with shame, we cannot become the people we are capable of becoming.

If we believe behaviour change is at the heart of the justice system, and humans are at the heart of behaviour change, we cannot perpetuate a 'them and us' universe that fails to recognise that we all have the potential for doing both good and harm. Only with a general recognition of the innate humanity of people in the justice system will we have communities that forgive; open-armed communities that see release from prison as an opportunity to welcome people back to a better future. An opportunity not just for the prison-leaver to have a 'second chance', when it's likely he never had a fighting chance to begin with, but for society to have a second chance to do right by its members.

'THE TRANSFORMATIVE POWER OF RECOGNISING SUFFERING'

Jo Hobson and Keziah Poultney

Introduction

'Every human being is worth more than the worst thing they've done.'
SISTER HELEN PREJEAN

Crime, understandably, stirs up strong emotions. On an individual and societal level, we can feel moral outrage, fear and anger about the harm and hurt caused by crime. We can feel hardened towards those who have committed crime, as though their actions disqualify them from receiving positive qualities including compassion, hope and kindness. This is especially true of those who have committed violent crime and sexual offences. Yet, having worked with women aged 18-25 in prisons over the last eight years, through a faith-based mentoring and education project, we have seen firsthand the desperate need for those who have committed crime to experience compassion, hope and kindness when in prison and after their release. The majority of the young women we've supported have committed acts of violence at some point. However, this does not make them unworthy of these three qualities. Every individual we've worked with has a story that proves that to see the world in terms of 'victims' or 'offenders' is a false dichotomy; they are both.

As a population, women in prison have experienced hugely disproportionate levels of rejection and suffering compared with the general population. We have seen how compassion, kindness and hope are vital in helping them begin to heal and move on from the pain that arguably led them to the point of causing pain for others. In this chapter, we consider the qualities of compassion, kindness and hope, examining what they are and imagining what part they could play in the criminal justice system. Although this chapter centres on women in prison, our firm belief is that these qualities are of the utmost importance for all stakeholders in the criminal justice system. Until compassion, hope and kindness have a more prominent role, the justice we administer will be limited.

Compassion

> '*Compassion is not religious business, it is human business, it is not a luxury, it is essential for human survival.*'
> THE DALAI LAMA[1]

The power of compassion has long been recognised in religion and philosophy as a fundamental quality for humanity. Deriving from the late Latin *com*, meaning 'with', and *pati*, meaning 'to suffer', compassion is about recognising another person's suffering and doing what you can to relieve it – even if that involves nothing more than acknowledging their pain.

What makes compassion pertinent to a criminal justice context is that it does not ask if the person suffering is *deserving* of help, it simply considers *if* they are suffering. It is a quality which, like the classical symbol of justice, wears a blindfold; it does not consider the character of the person, it considers the situation of suffering. As philosopher Elizabeth Anderson summarises, 'compassion seeks to relieve suffering wherever it exists, without passing moral judgment on those who suffer.'[2] To practice compassion, then, means to seek to reduce the suffering of everyone, not just those we might deem morally worthy.

This means understanding that everyone in the criminal justice system suffers; those who have committed a crime, their families, their communities, those who have had a crime committed against them, their families, the witnesses. The reach of compassion in such a context should extend as far as the suffering to which it bears witness, including to those in the system as 'offenders'. Since compassion is not based on a 'moral judgement on those who suffer', those whose actions have contravened the law are still deserving of compassion if they are suffering. Committing a crime does not, and must not, exclude them.

You need not look far into the backgrounds of those in prison to see the depth of their suffering. Independent of their current imprisonment, those in prison have suffered disproportionately compared with the general population. This is especially true of the female prison population. According to the charity, Women in Prison:

- 'Seven in 10 women in prison reported that they had been a victim of domestic violence.
- 53% of women in prison report having experienced emotional, physical or sexual abuse during childhood.
- 31% of women in prison have spent time in local authority care as a child.
- Women in custody are five times more likely to have a mental health concern than women in the general population
- 46% of women in prison report having attempted suicide at some point in their lifetime. This is twice the rate of men (21%) and more than seven times higher than the general population.'[3]

Every woman we have worked with has been living proof of these statistics. As we have developed trust with our course participants, we have learned about the different kinds of suffering each one has endured, often a combination of:

- exposure to violence from a young age;
- traumatic bereavements;
- sexual assault;
- violence in relationships;

- school exclusion;
- rejection, physical abuse or neglect from people they should have been able to rely on, and the list goes on.

Whilst every story is different, the consistent thread for each woman is deep and traumatic suffering.

The pain caused by these experiences is not isolated to each woman's past. It is carried with them into prison and is often exacerbated there. Without access to usual methods of escapism, past experiences can haunt a person in prison and the constant feelings of powerlessness and exclusion that come from imprisonment means it is a (re) traumatizing environment for many.

This needs to change. Far from being the point at which compassion runs dry, entering prison is a crucial moment at which to compassionately intervene. Recognising suffering and meeting it with compassion can begin the process of healing and transformation so necessary for all affected by crime to move forward into positive futures.

Kindness

'Kindness is a language that the deaf can hear and the blind can see.'
Helen Keller

Kindness is 'the quality of being generous, helpful, and caring about other people, or an act showing this quality.'[4] Like compassion, kindness is not concerned with who deserves it, rather whether an individual chooses to extend it. The character or behaviour of the other person in question is immaterial, they are still 'worthy' of kindness if the individual views them as such.

We teach about kindness in our education sessions in prison, encouraging our participants to explore the importance of being kind to others through thoughts, words and actions, as well as being kind to ourselves. Many of our participants feel kindness is irrelevant to them or their context, making it a difficult quality to nurture in prison. Without much experience of being treated with kindness themselves, the women we work with can have a warped view of what it means to be kind. For example, we often hear the women we work with associating kindness with vulnerability - "I used to be kind," a woman might say, "but here people take my kindness for weakness." Prison seems to be an environment that teaches people that the value of kindness holds little to no currency. For as long as prison is not seen as a safe place to be kind, and indeed is not an environment where many would say they receive kindness, those in prison will continue struggling to see it as a quality worth developing.

Although encouraging kindness alone will not solve society's problems, to not encourage kindness in the system of criminal justice feels like a sorely missed opportunity. If kindness is about showing care and consideration for other people, its power must not be underestimated in the process of holistic intervention and change. In the words of Albert Schweitzer, 'Constant kindness can accomplish much. As the sun makes ice melt, kindness causes misunderstanding, mistrust and hostility to evaporate.'[5]

Hope

'Hope is being able to see that there is light despite all of the darkness.'
DESMOND TUTU

The European Court of Human Rights (ECHR) and the British Government have come head-to-head in the past on matters relating to criminal justice and those in prison. One such instance was in the case of Vinter and Others, when the ECHR ruled that it was against a person's human rights to be given a prison sentence without any prospect of release.[6] This caused some issues for the Conservative Party's pre-election manifesto at the time, in which they were wanting to propose a new 'US-Style' 100-year-sentence to ensure that those who committed the most serious crimes would have no hope of freedom.

An article written in response to the Conservative party's proposals that 'life should mean life'[7] cited the case of Vinter and Others, quoting Judge Power-Forde:

> Hope is an important and constitutive aspect of the human person. Those who commit the most abhorrent and egregious of acts and who inflict untold suffering upon others, nevertheless retain their fundamental humanity and carry within themselves the capacity to change. Long and deserved though their prison sentences may be, they retain the right to hope that, someday, they may have atoned for the wrongs which they have committed ... To deny them the experience of hope would be to deny a fundamental aspect of their humanity and, to do that, would be degrading.[8]

The author powerfully ends the piece, stating '[the government] should make clear that even the worst offender has the right to hope, for with hope, a person can change.'[9] In a system that seeks to change the likelihood of reoffending, the need for hope is vital.

In The Book of Joy, Archbishop Tutu describes hope as the 'antidote to despair.'[10] In the context of standing up against the Apartheid regime, '[w]hat made people want to go on going on', Tutu explains, 'was not optimism but hope – dogged inextinguishable hope'[11]. Change is difficult at the best of times, but without hope it is practically impossible. And without hope in the criminal justice system, what's left? To remove hope is to invite despair, and to accept that things will never change and the cycle of crime will always continue.

For many people in prison, their tendency to hope is likely to have been gradually eroded over their lifetime. Hope erodes every time someone is not believed in, or are told they are not good enough. Hope erodes each time a person is excluded, or labelled from a young age - 'gang member', 'violent', 'aggressive', 'criminal', 'antisocial'. Hope erodes every time someone is abused or mistreated. Hope erodes when someone feels they are consistently not seen, heard or loved. If we are not working to counteract these barriers to hope and developing new narratives of hope for change, then how will change ever come?

We have seen through our work on the ground that hope is often the harder quality for us to encourage within the criminal justice context. There is so much working against people in prison in their attempts to change; both externally, through the stigma they face post-release, and internally, through the wearing thin of confidence, aspirations and self-esteem. However, we continue to strive to grow hope in our participants. For someone to be able to change, it is vital for them to genuinely hope things can improve, for without hope it is often too hard to find the courage to try.

The 'Other'

A problem for people caught up as 'offenders' in the criminal justice system when it comes to applying principles of compassion, kindness and hope, is that society labels them as 'other'. When those separate from the prison population harden themselves towards offenders by viewing them as fundamentally 'different', this sense of 'otherness' is perpetuated. Society consequently compromises its capacity to do the compassionate work of recognising the suffering of people in prison and their human need to experience positive qualities. Extending positive qualities to those who have committed crime can often be seen as undermining 'justice'; as making excuses for people in prison and absolving them of responsibility for their actions. There can also be an underlying belief that compassion, kindness and hope can go either to the 'offender' or the 'victim.' Not both.

Disrupting cycles of crime, though, requires society to move away from this view. We must work to replace it with the understanding that extending compassion, kindness and hope to a person who has caused harm is not to deprive these qualities from the person who has been harmed, nor is it to ignore the harm itself. Extending them to one person does not take them away from another. In fact, the more you work to foster these qualities, the more you see that they are boundless; kindness breeds kindness; compassion breeds compassion; hope breeds hope. These qualities do not require the giver to ignore a person's harmful actions; one can treat someone with compassion, kindness and hope whilst still asking that they take responsibility and make amends for their actions. They allow for the suffering a person has caused, and the pain a person has experienced, to be recognised equally and held alongside one another.

Need for change

If we allowed compassion, kindness and hope to influence criminal justice, the system could become more effective for everyone. The quality of compassion would allow the 'whole person' to be engaged within the context of their wider narrative, their suffering could be better recognised, leading to healing and positive transformation where needed. Kindness could be modelled as a relevant and worthwhile quality that is beneficial to those on both sides of crime. Hope could grow the motivation, strength and endurance needed for a person to do the hard work to move away from crime.

We have found that we are effective at engaging young women in prison precisely because we strive to demonstrate these three qualities (amongst others) in our work. When we ask our course participants what they like about working with us, the same themes come up; they don't feel judged, they feel understood, they are treated with kindness. We still challenge them, helping them to take responsibility for the harm they have caused, but we do this from a place of care and concern. Instead of just seeing them as 'offenders' we recognise it is never this straightforward; we allow space for the realities of their own pain and suffering as well.

We regularly see these qualities have a positive impact on a micro level. What might happen if they were taken seriously on a macro level? If we seek change in the justice we administer, and recognise the fundamental humanity we all share, we must treat all stakeholders in the criminal justice system with qualities like compassion, kindness and hope. Extending these qualities to all who are suffering as a result of living in a broken society, and dissolving the misleading distinction we draw between 'offenders' and 'victims', will open new opportunities for transformation in criminal justice. It won't be easy to do, but there are already some good examples of models of justice that allow more space for these qualities, for example, restorative justice.

Compassion, kindness and hope are three of the most powerful things we can offer to one another. These qualities have the power to transform people and situations - why wouldn't we try to make them a part of our criminal justice system?

Window of Opportunity, HMP YOI Parc

Image courtesy of Koestler Arts

SUPPORTING PEOPLE TO BE OUT, OUT

Tracy Hammond

A while ago, the comedian Micky Flanagan had a set about going 'out, out'. In it, he took the audience through the stages of popping out for some groceries, bumping into a few friends, going to the pub with them, meeting others and then having a 'proper night out'. Whilst his audiences rolled in the aisles at the thought of someone who had gone much further from home than they originally envisaged, I considered the changes in the person's mind-set, and the influence and acceptance of others that had to take place for someone to go 'out, out'.

I pondered that when a person is released, they need to be as far from prison as possible in terms of their thinking and affiliation with custody; they too need to be 'out, out'! This entails a progressive distancing from the identity that comes with a prison number, changing their internal dialogue and finding a place of value in their neighbourhood.

This idea was reinforced as I spoke to a man who was coming to the end of a long prison sentence. During the conversation, we spoke about his hopes for release. He had some money and was in a position to buy a house. He knew what he wanted from a property; the number of bedrooms he needed, the garden he had planned and the type of dog he would share his life with.

The conversation changed and he started to talk about life in prison. He lit up as he spoke with humour about his fellow prisoners and the good-tempered prison officer who had helped him settle on transfer. There was a stark contrast between the two conversations; the first was about bricks and mortar, the second was about community. This man had given thought to what he'd have on release; but not who he'd be. I pondered that in his thinking he wasn't yet 'out, out'; he hadn't thought about how he would develop the friendships and connections that would be instrumental to his new life and help him to identify as part of his new community.

As an organisation that supports vulnerable people, including ex-offenders, to live in the community, KeyRing knows how seemingly small acts can generate a lasting change both in how people are seen by others, and how they see themselves. Although difficult to measure, we know that acts of compassion and kindness create a virtuous circle; which supports long term desistance and generates an often indefatigable hope for the future.

The Virtuous Circle – Small acts that change lives

I'd like to introduce you to two people: The first person is Danny (not his real name), a softly spoken gentleman, always smartly dressed and now in his 60s, he has served a total of 22 years in prison. He had a chaotic childhood, which included time in care and culminated in borstal. Danny speaks of his early life without emotion and certainly without humour. Whatever his early days were like, it is clear that the adults around him modelled anger and frustration more often than kindness or compassion, and that the conditions in which a child learns hopefulness were in short supply.

Danny's Story

Danny also had a secret; he struggled with things that others could do easily. He had a learning disability, he didn't know what it was called back then, but he couldn't read or write, found arithmetic difficult and the world perplexing. His first prison sentence was for non-payment of a fine for being drunk and disorderly but he lacked the skills to make the payment and so entered the prison system. Here, he found that the things he struggled with didn't matter so much; he had no home to run or bills to pay. He learnt the rules the hard way as he couldn't read them, but once he knew the ropes, prison seemed a welcome break from the complexities of life outside. This precipitated a life of revolving door crime, which saw Danny serve 22 years in prison over approximately 30 years of his life. At times he was desperate to return to the 'safer feeling' prison environment. For example, even after hiding under a kitchen cabinet during riots at Crumlin Road prison, he was sufficiently driven to return to prison such that - upon release - he put a brick through his own solicitor's window and called the police himself.

When he entered prison in the 70s, although staffing levels were comparatively good, Danny says there was a strong focus on discipline, and marching, rather than relationships and rehabilitation. However, as time went by, Danny saw a change of focus and had the opportunity to develop catering skills that would eventually be recognised by others and stand him in good stead for the future. However, he didn't have much of a vision for that future…

The last time he left prison was unremarkable. There was no moment of epiphany or great determination to go straight. It was a chance encounter, with someone who saw Danny for who he was, that changed his trajectory.

Shortly after his release, Danny's hostel was visited by someone who ran a soup kitchen. He began volunteering there, bringing with him the valuable chef skills that he learnt in prison. Although he didn't know it then, this volunteering and the sense of self-worth it brought, started him on his journey to being 'out, out'. Danny says the realisation that he was never going back to prison didn't hit him for another four years, when he was much further down the road.

Danny's volunteering soon extended beyond the soup kitchen and he began offering his services to the British Hearth Foundation, where he worked in a local shop sorting the clothes. With formal volunteering under his belt, and with his confidence and standing in the community increasing, Danny started to go shopping for his neighbours.

As people got to know him, they noticed that Danny sometimes found things difficult and so as he approached his fiftieth year, Danny was tested for learning disabilities, and finally received a diagnosis that would open the door to the support he needed. After diagnosis, Danny was supported by KeyRing who helped him find settled accommodation and to organise his daily life. Although sorting out the 'bricks and mortar' is undoubtedly important, KeyRing has a strong emphasis on community connections and mutual support. This enabled Danny and those around him to develop a very different narrative. When asked now what others see in him, Danny says that people appreciate his dry wit and humour; he describes himself as a bit of a comedian. His reply would have been much less confident and self-aware when he first left prison.

When asked about kindness, Danny describes the prison officers who brought him some fruit and tobacco at Christmas. He says that no one ever believed in him until he met staff at KeyRing. He says that only after meeting the staff from KeyRing was he seen, for the first time, as a person – rather than just a risk.

Kim's Story

The second person is a woman called Kim (not her real name). She has done much less time in prison than Danny. Kim is younger and informal, outspoken and frank but with a ready laugh and a keen sense of fairness. Kim likes to travel and will often save up and take herself off on a UK seaside break for a few days.

In her younger days, like many others, Kim was unhappy and often depressed. Her life course took a turn for the worse when she made a number of suicide attempts, which often required her rescuers to place themselves at risk.

Her story was splashed across the national press as she received a court judgement for these suicide attempts, when campaigners believed she should have been offered support. The publicity around her case did little to help her situation and her behaviour was labelled as attention seeking – whilst the autism that contributed to her actions went unrecognised for another decade.

The punishment doled out by the first court was clearly ineffective as Kim breached her conditions. She later found herself back in court and with a custodial sentence for an unrelated offence. This sentence did nothing to improve Kim's trust of authority figures and had little impact on her behaviour. It was the approach of a police officer - who Kim describes as being kind - that caused her self-destructive behaviour to stop. This police officer took time to explain the impact that her actions would have on the children in her extended family if her behaviour continued as they reached school age. At that point, she understood that her choices influenced the lives of those she cared about.

Kim is lucky enough to have a good network around her. She has a supportive family and has been a member of a local church all her life. She has also been a Brownie leader since the age of 18, only stepping away for a while when circumstances dictated that it was right for her to do so. Kim is now 2nd in charge in the Brownie pack. This work is important to her as it gives her a sense of self-worth and a chance to positively influence the children she meets. Kim has friends whom she has known for a long time and also speaks of her involvement with a project called Genesis which runs a variety of activities and events.

'Professional curiosity reveals the power of (kindness and) humanity'

Both Kim and Danny have turned their lives around and they now have strong and positive connections to their communities. The common thread linking them is a seemingly random encounter with a professional who took time to see beyond their behaviour, recognise their potential and show them some compassion and kindness. The messages they received about themselves were ones of value that painted a more hopeful picture for the future and allowed them to develop a life connected to those around them.

Others report the same pattern. Someone believed in them, saw their potential and made it their business to walk beside them for a while. Sadly, few professionals get to know the depth of the impact they have had:

- the probation officer who refused to give up on the angry young man who numbed his senses with alcohol. He never got to know that the diagnosis of autism that he helped that man get was transformational. This person hasn't been in trouble since. He understands that others see the world differently to him and is comfortable in his own skin. He now runs a group for people with hobbies similar to his own;

- the community worker who redirected the car thief's hyperactive energy into sport probably doesn't know that his support enabled this man to end his revolving door involvement with the criminal justice system. He went on to become a leader in his community, enabling things to happen, rather than causing danger and frustration through constant joy-riding;

- The manager who waited tirelessly for the chaotic young man, who was imprisoned for not paying his debts. He also doesn't know that - although he failed to turn up for scheduled meetings many times - her patience was part of this young man's journey. He has now faced his fears of the unknown and is a highly effective volunteer.

Almost anyone who has been around for a while will have similar stories up their sleeves. We will also be starkly aware of the times when people have slipped through the net. How can we get it right more often than we get it wrong? How can we free staff to do the right thing in an environment where risk and safeguarding are never far from our minds? We know that it is difficult to legislate for such things and that many formal programmes do little to effect the sort of internal dialogue that create genuine and lasting change. All the professionals cited above worked within the rules of their respective organisations but showed the humanity to reach out and make a huge difference to the people they walked beside. They were prepared to take a different type of risk; one that involved investment in someone who may not show gratitude, immediate change or even receptivity to, or recognition of, their efforts.

In order to have the emotional resilience to do this, people have to be well led, feel supported and be working in a culture where professional curiosity is encouraged. The term 'professional curiosity' is often but not exclusively used in a safeguarding context; but this simple term describes the capacity and communication skills to explore and understand what is happening for a person, rather than making assumptions or accepting things at face value. This is what led to Danny getting his learning disability recognised which in turn led to him getting the relevant support. It's what led to Kim having a transformational conversation when someone was sufficiently curious to 'find a way to reach her' on an emotional level.

Once professionals feel empowered to be curious, they need the resources and knowledge to do the right thing at the right time. They can do this by knowing their patch and their people. This means understanding the people they work with, updating knowledge on disability and mental health as needed, and getting beyond a list of statutory provisions, to understand what makes the heart of the community beat. Thus equipped, they can support authentic connections that are led by a deep understanding, not just of the geography of the community, but also of its nature and personality. Much of this is about bringing the 'whole self' to work; maximising every contact and conversation and making links that would otherwise be lost.

There are a number of tools to help people do this. Professor John McKnight of North Western University Illinois, is famed for his asset based community development work and this has been expanded in Ireland and the UK by Cormac Russell of Nurture Development. Community Organisers in England also offer a range of information and training to empower local people to bring about change in their neighbourhoods. Whilst tools such as community mapping will be of direct relevance to the work of supporting people to become embedded in the community, these organisations' wider focus is important because without welcoming and diverse communities, it will be more difficult for people to truly be 'out, out'.

COMPASSION IN THE CRIMINAL JUSTICE SYSTEM

John Bayley

> *"We are in great need of people being able to stand in somebody else's shoes and see the world through their eyes."*
> BARACK OBAMA

I've been involved within the Criminal Justice system for just over thirty years, in two separate capacities. Firstly, as a Buddhist Chaplain at three prisons in Dorset, I work under the auspices of Angulimala, the Buddhist Prison Chaplaincy Service, (angulimala.org.uk) which makes available facilities for the teaching and practice of Buddhism in Her Majesty's Prisons and other places of lawful detention or custody.

In addition, I worked for eleven years, on a mentoring project at a prison in Dorset for young offenders (18–21 year-olds). Initially I was one of three full-time mentors, who worked with young men prior to their release from prison and then for a period of 6–12 months, following their release into the community. As the project evolved, I recruited a team of volunteers from London, Hampshire and Dorset, who were trained and matched with young men. They too worked with their mentees prior to release and then for a period of up to a year following release.

> "Compassion can be defined in many ways, but its essence is a basic kindness, with a deep awareness of the suffering of oneself and of other living things, coupled with the wish and effort to relieve it."
> PAUL GILBERT, THE COMPASSIONATE MIND

I remember sitting in a hugely palatial office at a multi-national bank in Canary Wharf, where I had an appointment to meet the bank's Corporate Social Responsibility Director. I was asking him to consider having some of his staff, released from work once a week in order to become mentors for the project and for the bank to part-fund the project. I showed him a short film I'd had made about the project. He was very complimentary about the work we were doing, especially as one of the areas in London that we were concentrating on, was a stone's throw from the bank's building. But he then proceeded to say, "John, I really admire what you are doing but the bottom line is that it's not sexy. We need pictures of starving children in war-torn countries or villages in Africa with no water. That's what makes people feel like giving and that's what my bank wants to be linked with. Nobody wants to be aligned with a 19-year-old drug dealer from South London. And the bank can't be associated with that social group."

He was implying that it was easy to show compassion to starving children in Africa but not for young men in prison in the UK. Compassion is, therefore, in his world view, and many others, conditional. We can pick and choose those to whom we can be compassionate. I wasn't surprised by his statement. After all, it's easy to be nice to nice people. I'd faced hostility, somewhat surprisingly, from some friends and family members who had the view, "Lock them up and throw away the key." "They don't deserve help after what they did." "You should be supporting the victims not the perpetrators."

The heart of Buddhist teaching and practice emphasises the importance of compassion. Compassion towards oneself and to every sentient being. It's not conditional. And that is a real challenge. It's relatively easy to empathise and be compassionate towards an elderly lady who has fallen over in the street and dropped her bags of shopping. Most of us intuitively would rush to help. But what about a young man who has just mugged an old woman? The longer I worked with young men in prison the more I got to realise, firstly, that we cannot generalise about "young offenders" and stereotype them and silo them into a convenient social group. What was common to all of them and all of us, is that we all have a story, a history, which often defines us. I remember sitting in my office taking down the details of a young man from Southampton, who we'd taken on to the project. "What's your address in Southampton?" I asked. He gave me the name of a block of flats I knew well. "And what's the flat number?" "Oh, it's not a flat, it's the stair well on the third floor." He was 19 and had been kicked out of his mother's flat because her new boyfriend didn't like him. The story was not untypical. He was a street criminal, thefts, muggings and dealing drugs. Compassion?

World over, the single most desirable trait in your partner, friend, parent, teacher, neighbour, colleague, or child is kindness. Kindness is the daily practice of compassion.
Amit Sood, Professor of Medicine at Mayo Clinic College of Medicine, Rochester, Minnesota, and serving as Chair of Mayo Mind Body Initiative.

A 19-year-old from Peckham who has been sentenced to a 4-year custodial sentence might not have experienced much in the way of compassion shown towards him. But how do we, should we, interact with him? After all he was dealing crack. Does a compassionate approach work? That same 19-year-old talked with me in the car when I drove him back to London on his day of release. I'd got to know him fairly well in the 6 months since we'd taken him on to the project, matched him with a mentor, who had travelled down to the prison twice to see him and prepare a plan for his period on his Probation licence. He opened up to me about just how frightened he was in prison especially at night when he was alone in his cell. "You know what was nice - when you used to come and get me from my cell and take me down to your office. You always offered me a cup of tea or coffee and it wasn't prison tea bags or naff coffee. And your biscuit tin only had chocolate biscuits, proper KitKats and Jacobs Orange bars not fake ones. It was like you treated me normally. You and the other people on the project didn't judge me. And when you said my mentor was coming down from London, a 3-hour train journey, to see me and it was voluntary! I had only ever had people care for me who were paid. I couldn't get my head round that. And now you're driving me to London. Why?"

> "I believe that at every level of society - familial, tribal, national and international - the key to a happier and more successful world is the growth of compassion. We do not need to become religious, nor do we need to believe in an ideology. All that is necessary is for each of us to develop our good human qualities. The need for love lies at the very foundation of human existence. It results from the profound interdependence we all share with one another.
>
> I try to treat whoever I meet as an old friend. This gives me a genuine feeling of happiness. It is the practice of compassion."

This quote from His Holiness the Dalai Lama, sums up to me, the essence of compassion. It is not the exclusive property of any religion or ideology, nor should it be. It is simply what we have, within ourselves, to offer each other and very importantly – ourselves, should we choose to subscribe to this way of living, with compassion as a guiding feature.

We also have it within ourselves to be the opposite – **merciless**. Or even somewhere in the middle – **dispassionate**. I would suggest that initially we should not be concerning ourselves with "**society**" or the "**criminal justice system.**" Whatever we decide to do, however we feel we should act to ourselves and others, it is not a separation from the criminal justice system. That system is merely a reflection of the society in which we live, individually and collectively. Dostoevsky famously said that "*A society should be judged not by how it treats its outstanding citizens but by how it treats its criminals.*" By constantly reflecting on our own personal thoughts and actions regarding others, that will inevitably influence the way we deal with those men and women who enter our criminal justice system.

Observe how it feels to be compassionate. How does it feel? What does it do for you?

SEEING THE PERSON

Tanjit Dosanjh

I choose to work with people in prison because my father served a long prison sentence. By visiting him in prison, I gained an insight into this world from a young age. I now train prisoners on how to make prescription spectacles, the anatomy of the eye and how spectacle lenses correct vision problems such as Myopia, Hyperopia and Astigmatism.

I thought the most important thing that I would give them is practical knowledge about the optics industry. Most of the prisoners, called learners on our programmes, enjoyed learning about optics and worked hard to pass qualification exams set by the Worshipful Company of Spectacle Makers. Then, when some of them started getting jobs in optical practices whilst on day release they were extremely happy. They were given an opportunity, worked hard to achieve something and they succeeded – something that may not happen too frequently if you're a prisoner.

Alongside the training, we spend time talking to them about their worries and struggles. Listening to them shows our learners they can trust us and have someone willing to be a friendly ear. In schools this is called pastoral care but if you offer the same to a prisoner it's considered too soft. Most prisoners have not gone to great schools so they've never had great pastoral care.

Prison is a tough place to be in. Usually the people in prison come from the most opportunity deprived sections of our society. Prison just makes them harder because soft people are bullied.

We believe kindness and compassion are key to getting through to even the hardest prisoners. If you show a normal person kindness then they will engage with you and prisoners more so than most given the deficit of kindness and compassion found in prisons. Prisoners may be opportunity deprived but they struggle to engage with new people because they are distrustful of authority. Imagine for a moment if you were imprisoned and there were 500 people there telling you how bad the judge, the barrister, the police and the prison officers were – eventually you too would become distrustful of authority.

I did not think that this is how I would be making a difference. I am not a counsellor but I know that listening to learners and giving them my time made a big impact on both them and me. The truth is, family members of prisoners also struggle with similar issues so with my dad being in prison, it was easy for me to empathise with the trainees.

A prisoner once said to me, "How can prison officers rehabilitate me if they are the ones punishing me?" I believe the majority of prison officers today still have that mindset – it is shifting slowly to more about rehabilitation but the shift is slow.

I've had my own struggles with getting the balance right. You need to be kind but you also need to challenge learners when necessary. If the person trusts you then you can challenge them while still remaining kind. If you don't challenge them then they, just like normal people, will not know where the boundaries are and all people try to push the boundary lines in their favour – prisoners are no exception.

Prisoners are normal people therefore should be treated like normal people. The only issue is in prison kindness is equated to weakness. So prisons are devoid of kindness, and then you have practitioners and volunteers like me who try to help but 'do-gooders,' as we are called, are viewed with suspicion because the prisoners don't know if they can be trusted or not. It takes time to build that trust. Kindness and compassion are not only key elements of this trust-building process, they are life-changing.

I'm glad that I've been able to help a small number of people and hopefully we will continue along this path helping more in the future. Kindness will always be central to our training as without it nothing can move forwards.

I am sure that you can only change people for the better with kindness and compassion. I am speaking as an optometrist, trainer, and father of two young boys.

Free, Guernsey Prison
Image courtesy of Koestler Arts

ON KINDNESS AS "BEING SOLID": VISIBLE PRESENCE AND ICONS IN INSTITUTIONAL CARING

Father Richard Rene

At the heart of the word, "kindness" is a sense of solidarity. To be *kind* in its original sense was to affirm one's shared *kinship* with another. In the pastoral context in which I work – chaplaincy in Canada's federal correctional institutions – many incarcerated persons express this sense of kindness using the prison-slang phrase, "Being solid," which means simply behaving in such a way that demonstrates one's sense of solidarity with those of one's group or *kind*, specifically, other inmates.

Correctional staff typically view "being solid" pejoratively, as part of a culture where inmates discourage other inmates from "ratting" to prison authorities about their criminal activities, while ostracizing and punishing those who do not comply. Kindness in this sense is seen negatively, as reinforcing a culture of criminality, and hindering the reintegration of offenders into law-abiding society.

There is, however, another dimension to the notion of "being solid." Using the theology of icons in my Eastern Orthodox tradition, I contend that being kind in the sense of "being solid," when practiced as "visible presence" by carers in the correctional system, can enable personal transformation for those we serve.

In the "Statement of Work" that forms the mandate for Chaplains in its institutions, Correctional Services Canada (CSC) defines "visible presence" as the manifestation of the "spiritual dimension of life" to inmates. During my tenure as the Site-Based Chaplain at Kent Maximum Security Institution in British Columbia, I faced challenges in fulfilling this mandate. While inmates at lower security institutions can simply walk over to the chapel, inmates at Kent are locked in their cells up to 20 hours a day. Thus, while Chaplains at other institutions could be "visibly present" just by sitting in their offices, I had to take a different approach. In the institutional schedule, known as Standing Order 566-3, I found the solution in a single line: "*1105-1205: Chaplain and Elders may make rounds in the units to speak with or hand out information to inmates as their cell doors.*"

My first efforts at "visible presence" in the living units had mixed results. Many inmates were taken aback to see me. Initially, I knocked on each door to make myself known, but soon abandoned this practice when one fellow politely informed me that this felt like an invasion of privacy, like a salesperson soliciting at one's front door. Others were less polite. Eventually, however, I developed a routine, and simply walked down each dimly-lit hallway, calling out a couple of times, "Chaplain here!"

On a given day, I had a number of conversations with inmates, some of them "spiritual", but many of them not. As inmates requested, I distributed Bibles, Qur'ans, address books, greeting cards. I took note of other requests to be fulfilled later. However, I learned that the real value of those walks had less to do with what I actively accomplished, when one of the inmates later told me, "When you come around, I don't always get up to speak to you, but I hear your voice and I know you're there. That's important."

Speaking as a Christian, visible presence in this sense is not just important, but vital. The name given to Jesus, "Emmanuel", means "God with us,"[1] so that the Gospel is the proclamation of God's visible presence with humanity. Christians themselves declare, "It is no longer I who lives, but Christ lives in me" (Galatians 2:20), thus committing themselves to practicing the visible presence of God in their own lives.

Eastern Orthodox icons (such as the one depicted above) offer further insight into the practice of visible presence. The media of icons—pigment, cloth, wood, stone, tile, or metal—represent an affirmation of the fundamental goodness of the material world. As John of Damascus puts it in his definitive treatise on the subject:

> "*I do not worship matter; I worship the God of matter, who became matter for my sake, and deigned to inhabit matter, who worked out my salvation through matter. I will not cease from honouring that matter which works my salvation.*"[2]

Inseparable from the "good matter" of icons are the images themselves, rendered according to clearly defined, formal conventions, which are not merely aesthetic, but symbolic rendering God's transcendent divinity. Together, the media and image of icons are theology in visual form, demonstrating God's visible presence in Jesus Christ expressed as the *solidarity* of the divine with the material of human life. So, icons embody God's kindness, understood as kinship with all human beings. To put it in prison lingo terms: icons show us that God is "solid" with humanity.

There is, to be sure, a certain passivity to icons. By the simple fact of their existence, they express God's kindness. But the icon's passivity is not inactivity; it is transformative, silently inviting the viewer to see their material existence as inscribed with the presence of a transcendent divinity. In the Orthodox view, the visible presence of icons shows that God's kinship with human nature simultaneously offers the possibility of kinship with God's divine nature,[3] and through that kinship, our self-transcendence. In this way, icons can speak powerfully to inmates, both of the passivity of their experience of incarceration, as well as to their aspiration to transcend their current condition, finding kinship with a greater awareness of who and what they can more truly be as human beings.

For the ultimate icon is no less than the human being itself. This has an important implication for carers in the justice system, which is that "being solid" need not be pejorative. When re-purposed to a life-giving end, "being solid" with those we serve can assist them in personal transformation, by offering a vision of mutual solidarity and care as well as a foundation for self-transcendence. At this basic human level, no intentional religious or educational or correctional program is needed; no particular faith commitment is required. One person's presence with another is sufficient to show them that they are not alone, and that something beyond themselves is attainable. In caring for one another, a practice of visible presence is itself a demonstration of solidarity; solidarity, a demonstration of kindness; and kindness, the basis for self-transcending personal freedom.

SEARCHING FOR HOPE, KINDNESS AND COMPASSION IN THE CRIMINAL JUSTICE SYSTEM? FIND YOUR LOCAL WOMEN'S CENTRE

Angela Collins

My PhD involved a six-month ethnographic and narrative data collection phase in a women's centre in the North of England. I ran a crochet club whilst at the centre and through that I met many amazing women. Women who had experience of the Criminal Justice System (CJS) and who told me incredible stories about their lives both within and outside of our Justice System. At crochet club we talked about anything and everything including politics, Brexit and voting in the run up to the 2019 General Election.

The time I spent in the women's centre and the stories women told me about their lives profoundly affected me. My data collection period coincided with Brexit and the winter General Election 2019 (GE19). Pre-election, there was potential for change and a reason to be hopeful, but the whole time it felt like believing in change was foolish. Hopefulness would mean more pain later down the line. There were parallels in the political climate and the lives of women I was spending time with and getting to know. These parallels can be personified in one woman I interviewed. The first woman I interviewed. Gemma.

Gemma was a prolific shoplifter but had had run-ins with the law for other crimes, including taking without consent, since her teens. Gemma had two children, similar in age to my own children, and throughout our conversations I discovered that her children were similar in character and behaviour to mine too. It has to be said her children had more material 'things' than my own: personal iPads, mobile phones, the latest PlayStation consoles and games. Nevertheless, our kids sounded similar, behaved in a similar way. Anything and everything that Gemma's children wanted, she would have provided, in the belief that this made her a good mum. We could easily have been friends. I knocked around with a few 'Gemma's' in my late teens and early twenties.

Why women's centres are important

Women's centres received major investment following the publication of *A Review of Women with Particular Vulnerabilities in the Criminal Justice System* written by Baroness Corston in 2007. The Corston report called for:

"A distinct, radically different, visibly-led, strategic, proportionate, holistic, woman-centred, integrated approach."[1]

It did not deliver 'new' information to those already working in the CJS and was not the first report to highlight women's particular needs within the CJS, but it did come at a time when the government was listening and they indicated their welcoming of the report with acceptance of the majority of the recommendations it provided. In 2009/10 the MoJ provided £15.6 million for a two-year period for a 'new opportunities fund' for female offenders.[2]

The conception and implementation of women's centres was hopeful. For the first time an attempt was being made to understand the needs of women in the CJS in a gender responsive way. Although some said the investment didn't go far enough (see Fawcett Society, 2009), the fact that women were being listened to and the Ministry of Justice (MoJ) was investing in gender responsive services, was positive. The aim to provide women with the support services they needed to live fulfilling lives was hopeful, kind and compassionate. Originally designed to help all women, those in the CJS and those on the margins of it, this changed as funding decreased. At the time of the Corston Review (2007) the country was facing a financial crisis which resulted in a period of recession in the UK. The coalition government set about reducing public expenditure and a period of austerity began. In the 2010 coalition agreement, the Government said it would introduce a 'rehabilitation revolution.'[3] (MoJ, 2010; 1) To implement the proposed revolution to justice in England and Wales the Ministry of Justice (MoJ) published Transforming Rehabilitation: A Strategy for Reform in 2013.[4]

Some of the proposals suggested within the Corston Report were progressing, for example by 2010 there were approximately 40 women's centres operating across England and Wales.[5] However, the Transforming Rehabilitation (TR) agenda resulted in the commissioning of services on a value-for-money and payment by results basis. Making commissioning decisions based on value-for-money is not compatible with small scale, intensive support for low-level offenders, as proposed by Baroness Corston. Therefore, TR created an environment whereby commissioning for small numbers of women, who are low risk but with complex needs was simply not viable; given this, it was difficult for TR to work for women. This approach to commissioning is largely driven by budgetary pressures and perpetuates a large, punitive and intrusive criminal justice system which, as Roberts states, might be 'inherently pointless or problematic.'[6]

Originally providing access to a range of services including housing support, the benefits system, addiction services, domestic violence support and so on, women's centres needed to refocus their work and as a result had to prioritise working within the contractual boundaries of the MoJ by focusing on the requirements placed upon them by probation.

One of these contractual agreements for the women's centre I was based in was the delivery of court mandated RAR (Rehabilitation Activity Requirements) days and supervising unpaid work by giving opportunities for cleaning and generally helping out at the centre. On the surface this may seem like a simple contractual agreement between the women's centre and the CRC (Community Rehabilitation Company) operating out of the centre. In reality, this is an example of the women's centre, and wider CJS, showing kindness to women who have been given court mandated unpaid work hours. Completing their unpaid work in a supportive and non-threatening, all female environment means that women are more likely to attend and continue to meet the requirements of their license. The motives behind the decision to enable women to complete unpaid work hours at the women's centre may not be intentionally or purposively compassionate, but the resulting experience of women is experienced with kindness and compassion.

During some unpaid work/ crochet lesson time Gemma and I got talking about politics. The women often gave me space and time to talk about politics and showed a vague level of interest. Gemma asked questions along the lines of "I don't even know what Brexit is. What even is it?" To some, the sheer notion that a person living in the UK in 2019 would not know what Brexit was is unfathomable, evidence of a disengaged underclass. In reality, Gemma just had too many other things going on to allow a complicated political endeavour to occupy any of the space left in her head. I wanted the women to trust me enough to sit down and tell me their life stories and so I always gave them space to talk. I was already fighting against the tide as an 'other'; I didn't want to give the women any reasons to alienate me and as such I was always neutral. The only time I waived from this was around issues of women's rights and feminism, I made it clear in all interactions with women that I was pro-women, a feminist who believed that women in the CJS sometimes got a bit of a shitty deal. I was able to back that up with facts and figures, so it didn't seem controversial, although some women disagreed and believed that women were treated less harshly because they had children, for example. This may or may not have been the case for individual women at the centre. I didn't argue with that.

Creating space for hope through every day interactions

During a discussion about the GE19 I spoke passionately about my belief of the importance of voting. Gemma asked, "How do I vote?" I helped Gemma register to vote there and then. She made plans to go and vote with a friend. It was an invigorating moment and one of the highlights of my time at the centre. I fully engaged with any activities I could, enjoyed crafts at the Arts Club, collected clothing from friends to be distributed to women in need, baked biscuits for fundraisers, talked with staff like I was an employee about the television I'd watched and talked with women about their children, and partners and estranged parents. I was intentionally interested in what people had to say and made a lot of effort to be someone that people felt comfortable around. Naturally, this approach meant that I was as kind as I could be with all the women and staff and volunteers and partners I encountered. I was not fully in either camp (woman receiving support or staff member) and because of this was able to openly chat with anyone about anything. I believe that because I showed women respect and I was kind to them they repaid me in being open and frank in their conversations with me. I benefited personally in a range of ways from my time at the centre including building meaningful relationships with women, and occasionally through snacks from Anne, a dedicated volunteer, without whom the centre would offer a much-depleted timetable. I helped Anne, she helped me. We were kind to each other. Although this started as a way to build bridges and make sure I was not causing any resources to be spent on me, it ended with my genuine care for the people, what they needed and how I could provide that. The kindness displayed by volunteers such as Anne paid dividends when it came to how women engaged at the centre. Not only did Anne run a breakfast club to feed the women, she was also a trained and skilled domestic violence worker helping women whenever they needed. I witnessed compassion in action everyday whilst I was at the women's centre, between peers and key workers and volunteers and towards me as an interested outsider.

I knew Gemma was going to vote. It did not matter which way. She was excited to vote for the first time and I felt proud for playing a small part in igniting something in her.

A week or so after the GE19 I realised that I had not seen Gemma since election day. I had been looking forward to talking to her about her experience of voting. On a Thursday, I ran my crochet club. Also working that day was the hairdresser, Kerry, who was serving her sentence in open prison and was let out on day release to volunteer at the centre cutting hair, doing nails and plucking eyebrows. The women really valued this service and I realised quickly that if I ran crochet club in the same room as her, I would be more likely to see people, introduce myself and if they fancied show them crochet, or just sit and talk and drink tea with them. This was a deliberate move to expose myself to as many people as possible at the centre in the hope that they would then happily take part in an interview with me. It worked well. Women saw me as part of the fixtures and fittings of the centre but knew that I was independent of it. I engaged lots of people to interviews following my interaction with them during Thursday morning sessions of crochet and hair cutting. I also got to know Kerry the hairdresser well, as sometimes no one would come for haircuts and no one would come to crochet. It would just be me, Kerry and whoever was doing their unpaid work at the centre that day, often Gemma. I asked Kerry if she had seen Gemma recently. She replied, "Haven't you heard?". Gemma was not a drug or alcohol user, she was not (at that time) in an abusive relationship so I was not so concerned about her coming to some kind of untimely death. I knew it was the run up to Christmas though, and that she was keen to get everything her children wanted for Christmas and so my heart sank. Gemma was still under the requirements of her licence following a shoplifting conviction, hence the unpaid work at the women's centre. This meant that any breach of her license, including an arrest for shoplifting, could and probably would mean she was recalled to prison. Kerry explained:

"She got caught shoplifting. Last time I saw her she was waiting to find out what was going to happen"

I haven't seen Gemma since. I am yet to find out the details of what happened to Gemma as staff are, understandably, reluctant to talk about individuals and none of the women accessing services at the women's centre knew Gemma outside of the context of the centre.

How the system can be an impediment to hope, kindness and compassion

After finding out that Gemma was more than likely recalled to prison, I experienced my lowest point of the whole data collection process and my time in the field. Gemma, who I really liked, was going to be spending Christmas in prison. Away from her children who she so clearly wanted the best for. Her desire to provide them with everything she thought they needed and the capitalist society in which she felt the best thing to do would be to steal gifts for them, had meant her children would be waking up on Christmas morning without her. Searching for compassion, I could not find it.

The news of Gemma's (most likely) recall to prison came during the fall out of the GE19 which saw the red heart lands of the North East, my home, turn blue. Gemma had registered to vote, had the motivation to organise a trip with a friend to go and vote and had been recalled to prison before she had the opportunity to do so. It felt impossible to be hopeful. The whole thing hurt.

The CJS is a system based on rules. It is full of people complying with those rules and of people breaking those rules. There is little space for nuance, thus leaving little space for compassion and kindness. Certainly, a probation worker could be sympathetic when they recall a woman to prison for stealing toys for their children but nothing about the decision is kind, or compassionate. This is not the fault of the probation worker, the system dictates what they must do. Gemma's story tells us that if the system had the flexibility to show empathy towards the circumstances of Gemma – stealing Christmas presents or her children – perhaps it could be kinder and deliver actual justice. The systemic punitive approach of the CJS does not allow space for this to happen. The non-statutory workers, therefore, such as key workers operating out of women's centres, are essential in supporting women in the CJS with kindness and compassion. Women's centres take a one-stop-shop approach and as such offer hope. They are hives of activity where people eat, and laugh, and talk and learn together. The atmosphere in the women's centre I spent time in was very hopeful. Keyworkers would do anything they could to get that domestic abuse sufferer on the programme that would offer her support, or feed breakfast to the women who had not eaten so that her children could.

If you're looking for kindness, compassion and hope in the CJS, find your local women's centre (before a funding crisis closes it).

The Offender Rehabilitation Act 2014 introduced a one-year mandatory post-custody supervision period for all people sentenced to less than 12 months in prison. As women are more likely to receive shorter prison sentences, they have been disproportionately affected by this change.

Numbers of women recalled to custody in 2015 = 1,155, in 2016 = 1,378, in 2017 = 1,651, in 2018 = 1,924, in 2019 = 1,609 (up to September 2019 – number likely to breech 2,000 for the whole year) (MoJ, Offender management statistics quarterly)

A PEACEFUL OASIS IN AN UNFORGIVING DESERT

Deborah Murphy

Six years ago, I began setting up an Occupational therapy service for men with mental health problems in a pre-existing day centre, in a Cat B local prison. The independent monitoring board (IMB) deemed the environment incompatible with maintaining humanity and dignity, highlighting cells without lighting, hot water or functioning toilets; cockroaches resistant to insecticide; and mouldy showers. They suggested this neglected environment directly contributed to an increase in violence, drugs and self-harm.

My unit had filthy, graffitied walls, and broken or 'specialist' furniture bolted to the floor, communicating the anticipation of violence. Whilst understanding the need for such precautions, I questioned whether it was preferable to create an environment where we motivated people not to throw furniture. The social environment presented its own challenges. With no prison officers allocated to our wing, the health staff had taken on a harsh discipline approach. Basic choices such as choice of drink were denied. In an environment where people were already stripped of so much autonomy, restoration of dignity felt vital.

It is well documented that environment influences behaviour, motivation and mood. In an environment so devoid of beauty, we wanted an environment that communicated to people their worth. If we were to support people to engage with the better aspects of themselves, the furniture, the décor, the walls themselves needed to reflect their humanity to them.

Giving the wing a heart

Occupational therapy theory is based on the premise that we need to harness skills in self-care, to engage with leisure activities that bring meaning to our lives; and we need a role in which we can offer contribution, and experience belonging. It is important that people retain an identity beyond being reduced to a 'prisoner'. We need to provide opportunities in which people experience themselves as having agency, have opportunity to master skills, and experience success. To do this we provide a series of groups including creative sessions; sessions that help people self soothe and ground; or assist them to develop skills for life.

Participation in shared activity allows exploration of how we cooperate with others; of our likes and preferences; and gives structure and purpose to our time. They provide us with a medium through which we can converse and connect, and experience what it is to be human. It's hard to keep up meaningful human exchanges when nothing ever punctuates our day, and it is difficult to hold a sense of identity and a narrative of who we are in the world, if our world is reduced to a 12ft by 8 ft cell. We deigned an environment to open people's worlds back up. Service users frequently express that it is helpful to get out of prison for the day; despite the barred windows enclosing them. We discovered that being in prison, and the feeling of being in prison, could be disentangled.

In recognition that the kitchen is frequently the heart of a functional home, we decided our wing needed a heart. We secured £25,000 innovation funds in a local completion, to create a kitchen, art and music studio. We decided to approach cooking beyond an activity for practical skill learning, recognising that the preparation and sharing of food has an important function for forming social bonds, as well as nourishing ourselves. We approached food as a sensory pleasure; an act of compassion to self; and kindness to others. We look beyond the end-point of the meal, to the journey we create together. We consider how we can support those less skilled than ourselves to learn. Participants need to be willing to take a lead, and to be led. Such shared tasks stretch our ability to see beyond our own individual needs, to let go of a preoccupation that our way of doing things is the right way, and to develop our ability to compromise.

Two different cohorts of men attend the centre daily, each week alternating between morning and afternoon attendance. Each week the morning cohort create a large vat of soup to feed those present, and the afternoon cohort. This encourages kindness and generosity to those whom we don't know. In the interests of reciprocity, the other cohort returns this favour the following week. Attempting to imbue such qualities as kindness is not problem free, but kindness is a practice, something we all need to work on, and to notice our resistances too. We are at least clear about our anticipated direction of travel.

A man once told me of how assuaging his hunger through eating dry white bread in his cell signified to him how far he had fallen, solidifying his lack of self-worth. The offering of good food arguably communicates that we matter. We are literally choosing to nourish another person. Foods we eat can denote our place in the social hierarchy. We chose to operate outside of such stereotypes eating 'high class' foods. More recently we started growing our own.

In our previously old dilapidated kitchen, the atmosphere was chaotic, with food approached as a perfunctory activity. We thought we would need to shape behaviour following the refurbishment; but change organically emerged. The cue of a nice tablecloth and a well-laid table indicated that meal times were to be cherished. We invite passing visitors

who drop in to dine with us. This has included officers, chaplaincy and IMB members. All appreciate this levelling experience. We now intend to formalise invitations, so that 'prisoners' can experience relationships with staff in a different way. Service users often comment on how sitting together makes them feel part of a family.

Bringing nature inside

As we cannot readily get our population out into nature, we decided to bring nature in to them. We created an 'outside inside' room which mimics a forest like environment with walls of plants. Research suggests that humans are hardwired to respond positively to that which we experience in nature. We secured funds to create a wildlife garden. The presence of plants, butterflies and bees gives a sense that we are not separated from the cycles of life, despite the prison walls. Witnessing life emerging signifies hope, which contrasts to the stagnant concrete surrounds. Learning to read a plant's needs provides a helpful analogy to the empathy we need to develop for other humans. Understanding how we care for the organism on which we depend feels like the most urgent of skills for us all to develop. We have therefore offered education on environmental issues, exploring ways of being a responsible citizen, who offer contribution to future generations, as well as to the earth itself. Opportunities for increasing empathy are put out there, though it is acknowledged that some people may not be in a place in their life at present to take these up.

Compassion requires understanding

We need to take a particular kind of responsibility for introducing beautiful things into an environment where beauty is largely absent, to a population who have so little. Temptation is ignited for people to want that which they don't have. Theft is largely prevented through all recognising that once items are taken, they may not be replaced, to the detriment of all in the community. It is seen as every individual's responsibility to contribute to maintaining that which they cherish within the department. We emphasise that we could readily default into being the same as the environment that they are so keen to get away from, if we fail to sustain our efforts to nourish what is different in it. A culture has formed where stealing from the department is akin to stealing from oneself.

On the rare occasion that thefts occur, they are met with derision, and disbelief from the community's members. Of the rare occasions that people don't play by the rules, the offering of an amnesty generally makes missing items materialise. Preventing 'vigilante' action against those who transgress is important. Staff need support not to take thefts personally. Our egos can protest when we sense that people whom we offer so much to are taking from us. But compassion demands that we move beyond our personal ego needs. It demands that we depersonalise such incidents.

It is doubtful that people who take things from the department conceptualise this as stealing from an 'us', they are simply taking something of beauty to line their bare cell with, or acquiring items to trade to free themselves from debt. It is not for us to judge and condemn, but it is for us to provide clarity regarding what we are prepared to tolerate within our community. We must acknowledge those times we have taken an item of work stationary home, the times we used the office printer for personal purposes, and how we've all taken something that wasn't strictly on offer. We need to observe how quick are we to label behaviours in others, which we aren't prepared to look at in ourselves. If we are to exercise compassion, we need to be honest about who we all are, and how we would all likely behave given a particular set of circumstances.

But compassion cannot be woolly, a sentimental notion that lacks clarity. It is unkind to allow people to walk over you, if you wish to support them to learn to have relationships based on mutuality. There are valuable lessons to be learnt in not getting what we want as a consequence of our behaviour. If you steal from someone's home, it should not be a surprise if they don't invite you back. We operate on similar principles. Time out can be effective for a period of reflection on the behaviour that led to exclusion. Returns are negotiated through re-committing to the community's rules. This in itself can be a useful process for those who do not have patterns of healing relationships once ties are severed.

Kindness and compassion can be bold and fierce

Initially we noticed that offering kindness could be confusing to those for whom kindness was a novel experience. Kindness could be misinterpreted as stupidity, naiveite, something that could be exploited. But kindness isn't an insipid passive behaviour which involves capitulating to those who shout the loudest. Kindness can be bold, solid, grounded and unwavering; and compassion can be fierce. It is an act of kindness to communicate where boundaries lie. It would be unkind to avoid confronting behaviours that society finds unacceptable. If we are to be truly compassionate, we need to not shy away from difficult conversations. People need to know which of their behaviours may be contributing to their being ostracised and isolated, and to be supported to work on these. Some need help to understand where people's bottom lines are likely to be situated.

It is also important for us to model an act of kindness to self, though communicating clearly when enough really is enough. We need to balance how generous we are to others struggles and challenges, with what's helpful to the community as a whole, and to what is realistic for us to tolerate on a day to day basis. Of course, if a person's behaviour means we can no longer support them within our service, holding compassion regarding their not being in a place to engage positively with others at present, is a given.

Creating a culture of kindness and reciprocity acts as one of the main protections for managing risk and for reducing staff burn out. As the community establish their own culture of the expectations of positive behaviour, the staff team can step back a little. I recall an occasion when faced with a particularly distressed and hostile man invading my personal space, his peer stepped in, gently placed his hands on his shoulders and informed him "you don't need to do that here, we talk to sort out our problems here". Such interventions are a norm, people notice when we are short staffed and offer a little more assistance, people pick up on the arrival of newcomers and help them settle in. Openly discussing with us what is disrupting the community is no longer viewed as 'grassing' as we reduce the sense of a 'them and us.' We have instilled that if we are to have a successful community, there is only an 'us'.

Offering more carrot and less stick

Such cooperation, leads others to suspect we may have cherry picked 'model prisoners'; this is far from the case. We frequently take regular visitors to the segregation unit, and many frequently miss sessions due to adjudications. We take some of the most vulnerable men in the prison, who have some of the most volatile behaviour, but we witness how their behaviour improves in an environment that offers more carrot and less stick. If we hope for positive change in people, we cannot leave them with nothing to lose.

We can appear to have a blessed existence, sitting around doing artwork and cooking. In truth, there are wonderful days like this, but for much of the time, beneath the smooth surface appearance, our legs are paddling frantically to keep things afloat. One of the reasons humans fall into dominating others through brut force and control, is that it can be a lazy shortcut to getting what we want with relative ease. Developing cooperation and containment, explaining decisions, nourishing positivity and compassion demands significant energy. If we lose our momentum, or have an off day, the environment quickly reflects chaos back at us.

Our office is the wing where we remain for eight hours, bar lunchtime. There is no escape when we are having a bad day. Parts of ourselves that we might prefer to hide get triggered and reveal themselves. But this too can be used to advantage. It feels unhelpful to present oneself as a perfectly contained superbeing. Real life isn't like this, and human beings are not like this. We demonstrate that we mess up, we get it wrong, we need to apologise and to model humility. We demonstrate that we too are working with the messiness of being human, because attempting to create social automatons is certainly not a kindness, and neither is modelling an unrealistic version of the 'perfect person'. If we are expecting people to behave with humanity, then we need to model what humanity looks like. We need to provide something we can belong to, something we can take ownership of. On entering our wing, the physical environment itself communicates that this is a different space and something different is expected and likely to occur here.

The potential for such environments in prisons is getting recognition. In their 2019 report the IMB described our work as outstanding and awe-inspiring, the royal college of GPs acknowledged us with an award for the best clinical team in secure services, and commissioners and managers from other

prions have visited to learn from our experience. At least three other prisons having now replicated the service. Most importantly for us however, the service users themselves frequently thank us for helping them to feel human, for accepting them for who they are, and for seeing them beyond the crimes that they have committed.

Ward B11, HMP Low Moss

COURTESY OF KOESTLER ARTS

Arterial is red
venous is blue
I've met lots of nurses
but few as nice as you

From the hundreds I've known
many liked to lecture, put down and shun
but I met no nurses like that
on ward B double one

I came in wearing handcuffs
I had three guards at my side
carried out from the prison
another failed suicide

Staff nurse Bradgate was my favourite
because she spoke to me the most
told me all about her hobby
visiting castles and the coast

Not one of you seemed judgmental
all tried real hard to call me "she"
no hunger, you filled my belly
you eased my pain with D.H.C

Often months at a time
denied TV or radio in my cell
I feel I'm forced to harm myself
for a short escape from this hell

I spent a lot of years locked up
most of it in segregation
sometimes many weeks can go by
without a real conversation

And you make a simple gesture
letting me know that someone cares
like coming in for five minutes
pulling up a couple of chairs

I don't think that you nursing staff
will ever understand or know
how much it really means to me,
when I feel so alone and low

So please keep up all the good work
for the many of us like that
who just need to be acknowledged
with a simple smile and a chat.

Just a few minutes of chit-chat
can ease the hurt inside my head
and I suddenly start doubting
all of my wishes to be dead

LESSONS ON KINDNESS, HOPE AND COMPASSION FROM A PHILIPPINE PRISON

Trevor Urch

Davao Prison and Penal Farm

The Tagum Development Company (banana plantation) is a joint venture between a private Philippine company and the Bureau of Corrections. This generates income for the Bureau while giving prisoners the opportunity to bolster their dietary intake by engaging in paid work. The detainees are paid 370 PHP (£6 approximately per fortnight). This enables them to club together to buy meat, fish or rice. Due to the fertile environment, an abundance of varied food is grown including veg and fruit to further supplement the diet.

I visited the site in August 2019. As I entered the prison, I found myself taken in by the sheer scale of the facility. Local people sold their wares in stalls alongside prisoners. For the tour, I was assigned a correctional officer who would escort me to the minimum, medium and visiting areas of the maximum-security compounds. Little did I know that my escort party would include up to eight trustee residents equipped with a range of nightsticks, to keep order. Known as watchmen, these peers are monitored by an elaborate system of accountability. Each area has a lead detainee (Bosyo/Mayor) who runs their Barangay (area) within a resident local government process.

I found myself a source of curiosity as I entered all three secure locations. Each separate facility appeared to view my arrival with a sense either of indifference or as someone that may be important, (sorry for the deception)! Each detainee wore a different coloured t-shirt depending on their location or status. Brown t-shirts for minimum secure areas, blue for medium and orange for maximum. I observed little difference between each compound. Everything appeared open within the confined areas; dormitories had an open entrance (no doors or gates, helping to dissipate the intense heat). Detainees carried out the roll count (people are arriving back from work from the plantation). Each dorm held three tiers of floor to ceiling bunk beds from one end of the living space to the other, with a walkway in between. Each dorm held 250 people and the only source of privacy was a curtain hanging over the beds.

Comparing the English and Philippine prison experience

There is an overall misconception that incarceration in a UK prison is a world apart from the Philippines. Yet at HMP Birmingham, where I work, overcrowding and poor conditions recently led to the closure of three wings. Gang culture can be rife in such conditions, as well as addictive behaviour, overcrowding and debt.

However, the main concern seems to be that we have a similar congestion due to the war on drugs. In the past year, HMP Birmingham has seen the number of residents incarcerated for drug offences nearly double in number to just over 20%. If you add this to the largest offending category, which is 'acquisitional', then over half the population seems driven to crime for financial gain. The challenge in both countries is how people maintain desistance after the process of rehabilitation returns them to a state of normality, given social deprivation looms in the background.

Contributing factors for the current stability now at HMP Birmingham includes HMPPS taking over responsibility for the prison just over two years ago and adopting a systemic approach to safety that included the move to shut down the three aforementioned (old Victorian) uninhabitable wings. This facilitated extra officer numbers as well as a reduction in the prisoner population. Such options are perhaps not feasible for Davao prison, but I understand that there is a long term plan to renovate the prisoner living quarters.

The Corrections Senior Superintendent Atty. Melencio S. Faustino informed me that their current population is close to 7,000 residents. The national war on drugs implemented by President Duterte has intensified the high level of prison congestion.

This coupled with the low number of prison guards and other non-custodial personal are some of the constraints faced by this penitentiary in particular. There are around 400 staff in total. It is anticipated that the number of internees to the regions facilities will continue to grow. As the war on those that use and sell drugs intensifies, people are handing themselves into the police rather than face reprisals that often result in fatalities. A conservative estimate suggests that up to 70,000 people have voluntarily presented themselves to the police. This has increased overcrowding while putting pressure on access to appropriate quantities of food, adequate sanitation and to minimise exposure to diseases.

Some would read this and find it hard to believe that prisoners should choose incarceration over freedom. However, in the UK, we now have the ridiculous scenario of men manufacturing their own capture so they can return, full of concealed drugs, in order to extinguish drug debts.

How hope is engendered in this setting

I was pleasantly surprised to see the extensive range of group work and employment opportunities on offer in Davao prison. Most people chose to work while in the prison which is hardly surprising; it enabled them to buy extra items (food for example) that are sorely needed. These opportunities running alongside moral & spiritual programs appeared to engender hope in residents. They allowed them to gain new skills that supported their long-term aim of resettling back into their community while gaining skills that enhanced their employment opportunities upon release, opportunities that would be central to their desistance.

The therapeutic community within the prison also evidenced some outstanding work including detailed carvings being created in the visiting area of the maximum security facility, with residents in the process of sculpting large dragons, gargoyles and eagles for example from wood. I was lucky enough to be given a small carved wooden eagle by a detainee and correctional officer in the medium secure area.

Kapwa – Kindness and compassion in practice

The one thing that will stay with me from this visit is the humility, humanity and respect shown by the correctional officers. They all possessed the core Filipino value known as Kapwa.

The nearest English equivalent of the word Kapwa is "others", however a more accurate translation is "both" or "fellow being" (Kapwa-Tao). Enrrquez, 1994, refers to the unity or oneness of a person with other people. Hindi ako iba sa aking Kapwa (I am no different to others).

Individuals who are guided by Kapwa can be recognised by their genuine people-centred orientation, their service to those around them and their commitment to their communities. It is common practice for Filipinos to come to the aid of, assist, or help others without the expectation of getting anything in return. In English, this is best translated as "altruism."

I was lucky enough during my visit to witness Kapwa across a range of engagements that embodied a high level of compassion and empathy. This virtuous and moral stance had obvious benefits to those residents they were there to serve. All of the staff spoke perfectly good English and had an ease of connection with people, which shone through their interactions especially with residents. The small tangible things make a difference. Making sure you are available for example, listening to understand and warmth of approach. This is a quality in my opinion that we can learn from and develop across UK prisons as such qualities play an important part in making a criminal justice setting work for all parties.

There is no quick fix when it comes to rehabilitation and the potential to reduce reoffending.

However, prisoners who are treated with dignity and respect are provided with a foundation for growth. For many this can be an alien concept, as they may have only ever known disrespect and abuse. Acts of kindness engender hope and inspire people to take control of their lives as opportunities arise. This may be by a way of being able to access meaningful training. That enables people to be upskilled in terms of work specific activities in the prison; leading to actual employment opportunities within the community, be that in the Philippines or back home in the UK.

Kapwa in the Philippines makes a difference as it shows there is another way and helps people survive; with a view towards truly understanding where a person has come from. Just as importantly where or what they may be going back to. It can help people regain their cultural and spiritual identity.

Conclusion

To break out of the cycle of poverty, crime and prison, you need a will to do so and somebody to help you. Whatever strategic approach the government takes to reduce re-offending, whether it be the temperate encouragement of self-efficacy in the Philippines, or work to address the recommended pathways in the UK, anybody who has an understanding of the population in their care knows that the gaps in the current provision have to be filled by human compassion. This is where the Filipino value of Kapwa is inspirational.

Whilst our plights may be similar, the warmth of approach of the Filipino correctional workers is admirable. The guards have an understanding of the life circumstances of those they are trying to help. By bestowing their strengths and talents into the redemption of the men in their care, they commit their time and energy into what they regard as a truly authentic profession. They have the social conscience to recognise that their work will have lasting value if they can stimulate hope and self-belief, and by implying the men are worthy of their support they empower the prisoners to consider their own social and moral deficits before they re-integrate into society. Used in this way, Kapwa is an advisable example of human kindness that stirs others to desist.

The challenge in both countries is how we get people to maintain desistance, after the process of rehabilitation returns them to a state of normality, given social deprivation looms in the background.

The correlation between desistance and stable employment is undeniable, especially when it allows men to build strong relationships, both personal and societal. Being given support, acceptance and compassion in the workplace, irrespective of their past, is vital if ex-offenders are to cultivate a new and positive identity.

However in England, when we discuss the paid employment opportunities that could interrupt our own crisis of inequality, a new term "incentivised altruism" has arisen. Rather than considering their social duty, corporations here worry about a perceived negative impact on their organisational reputation, and only when given national insurance contribution holidays as a reward for recruiting ex-offenders, so they are forced into the implementation of social value measures in public sector tendering, do they consider their ethical responsibilities. A more natural altruism, without reward, is needed. Our society needs to facilitate the possibility of social mobility because it is simply the right thing to do adopting if you like the Kapwa mentality that we are no different to others.

HOPE: THE ROLE OF THE LAW IN MOTIVATING CHANGE

Juan Periago Morant

Introduction

One of the main challenges that every advanced society faces is the question of how to ensure the best conditions for future generations. Ensuring good and sustainable future outcomes requires not only good governance but also social consciousness that permeates all levels of society: from individual level through buy-in from average citizens, to the institutional level where government policies are translated into action. It goes without saying that this undoubtedly requires a determined commitment from a variety of actors.

It is part of the human condition to yearn for a better and happier world for our children, grandchildren, and grandchildren's children. One area where changed attitudes have translated into changed actions (albeit at a relatively slow pace) is in our response to climate change. The focus on environmental sustainability means that – as a society – we care about preserving biodiversity – even if at some levels a resistance to change remains, rooted in preserving economic and social progress.

However, with all our care for *environmental* sustainability, there is an argument to be made that our drive to create a positive future for children does not extend to the areas of our society that need it most. For example, ask yourself – How 'sustainable' is the way we treat children in the criminal justice system? They are part of our future generations and are especially vulnerable. They have more risk factors than most other children do. Yet we distance ourselves from them and often treat them with limited kindness and compassion.

My specialty is not sociology or public policy. Professionally, I have dedicated myself to the legal field: firstly as a jurist in a juvenile detention centre and currently as a university professor of Criminal Law. Yet, as a mere spectator, with careful examination of juvenile justice legislation, I can assess the ideology of criminal policy supporting juvenile delinquency in Spain.

In Spain, young people in the criminal justice system continue to face a turbulent reality; with the most vulnerable groups experiencing the greatest difficulties in finding necessary support to meet their needs, pushing them still further towards social exclusion.

Citizens and the system

The life journey of these children is notoriously influenced, not only by the greater or lesser success of public policies, but also by the behaviour of other citizens. I want to focus on the latter: the behaviour and attitudes of the public.

We know public opinion can sometimes be very belligerent to those seen as being different or in conflict with the law. It is often easier for the public to distance themselves from interacting with the root causes of why young people commit these acts - especially when they are constantly bombarded with news of crimes committed by children, the consumption of which can create the right environment for punitive populism. We see repeatedly how this in turn motivates the legislator to create regulations emphasising punishment over the purposes of reintegration.

While some actively take a belligerent position against those in conflict with the law, others choose inaction and silence, refusing to engage. Resignation is a comfortable position. The direct consequence of this, however, is sympathising with those who install themselves in postulates of vindictive justice and resist offering opportunities for change to our young offenders. At the very least, we make their arguments stronger.

What have we left? We still have a body of citizens who, with determination and daily action, almost inadvertently, could still do a lot for our children in conflict with the law.

I want here to make my small contribution, avoiding the academic rigidity and investigation that accompanies a research article. I will share my own personal testimony instead.

I started working in a Spanish juvenile detention centre in 2001. In that year, my new professional career in the field of care for juvenile offenders coincided with the first year of operation of Organic Law 5/2000, the law that currently regulates criminal responsibility of minors in Spain.

Much has changed in the years between those early days in a juvenile detention centre and my first days in a university law school classroom.

The role of the law

Organic Law 5/2000 (regulating criminal responsibility of minors), was a paradigm shift in how the Spanish justice system administers justice to minors in conflict with the law. It not only incorporated technical improvements to how the law was apply but also inspired principles that rightfully protect minors.

Organic Law 5/2000 ensured cases of all children (aged 14–18 years) were treated as a matter of child protection, rather than a justice issue. According to this law, all sentences would include a punitive education measure aimed at re-socialising young people to reintegrate into society and encouraging desistance from further engagement with the criminal justice system – especially the adult justice system.

The previous guardianship system made the interests of children a secondary consideration considering them to be passive subjects, justice administered to them. As a comparison, this is analogous to a hospital patient who receives care from medical services (in this case from the administration of justice in a broad sense) but whose role is simply to follow the instructions provided. In other words, the law was applied by rote with no room for case-by-case nuance.

Organic Law 5/2000 changed this to make the child the central character, focusing on the child's interests whether they were a victim and/or offender. The aim of the law is to ensure the child believes there is hope for change in their life path – that there is another way.

While this may be the intention, can a law - a regulation - achieve this? A law in principle is nothing more than a few drops of ink on paper, which trace a series of words. Indeed, certain regulations demand a certain conduct, punishing non-compliance.

Complying with law requires belief that it works

Continuing controversial debates exist, as to why citizens comply with law. Some believe intimidation – fear of experiencing punishment – is what refrains us from failing to comply. Others (myself included) consider that regulations have a pedagogical and motivating function that cannot be ignored. We believe the main function of regulations is to teach us what we should do, what behaviour is most appropriate to live in a better and fairer society; inviting and motivating us to act in a way that helps us progress as individuals and as a group. This function of regulations ultimately reaffirms positive law and the justice system in general.

As I said previously, the law by itself is inert; people are its driving force. We are the ones who put it into operation. We give it meaning by behaving in compliance with it, with a decided conviction about its functionality.

How do we reach that belief? How can we transfer that conviction to those in conflict with the law? That belief contains the engine of change, the hope of aspiring to a society that is more just and caring towards its citizens. We can all contribute.

Organic Law 5/2000, which organises the system that determines criminal responsibility of children, has undergone reforms since enactment in 2001. Each reform has brought important changes. Some of these changes, in my opinion, go against the initial educational philosophy of law, and encourage an approach to more punitive postulates.

Despite this, the system continues to place the minor as the central character. These legal instruments can provide minors with tools to convince them that of the goodness of the system. The aim is to engender hope in them that their future is in their hands, they can live a life free of crime, there is hope for a better life. Engendering this belief, and subsequent desistance from crime, is however dependent on the law being implemented in a way that shows them the system works to protect them and their interests.

One way we do this is by implementing the principles to act in the best interests of the child and give flexibility; which allows young people - on the condition of improved educational attainment - to move from restrictive measures in their sentence to others with fewer restrictions to their affected rights.

Another way is through restorative justice, which allows young people to make reconciliation or reparation to the victim, in a way that serves both young offender and victim.

Minors in conflict with the law in Spain are subject to a system of criminal responsibility that is both sanctioning and educational. The system aims to make minors feel responsible for the greatest offense they can commit toward those around them: a crime. But the answer we must offer them as an advanced society does not have punishment as its main function. Truthfully, the measures at our disposal have a punitive component, since they deprive minors of the effective enjoyment of certain rights. However, punishment is not the primary objective - what is important is to educate young people, to help them grow as people. The fact they are children or adolescents makes this easier, as there is a greater margin of hope for them to realise this and redirect their life.

This is equally true for victims, whether or not they are minors. The way the system treats them must show they are cared for and understood by the system. This is key to ensuring they feel comforted and convinced about the effectiveness of the treatment provided by justice, in the hope of a more just society. In other words, for the system to work, we have to extend principles of kindness, hope and compassion to victims as well as offenders.

I return to the idea that the law needs people to be its driving force, people persuaded by its functionality. When a society decides law does not work, it diminishes its applicability and we seek alternatives within the system, rather than recognising that implementation of law is the issue, not its underlying ideological foundations.

Hope is not ethereal, it is shown with evidence

One must take responsibility for one's mistakes. I make them just as everyone else does, we can always do something more, better. In 2006, when the Spanish juvenile justice system was reformed by modifying the law, one of its ideological foundations was attacked. The potential for flexibility became hindered. This reform allowed for the possibility of limited access to the legal instrument that – as previously stated, allowed modifying sanctions imposed on minors – assuming their positive development complied with their educational and sanctioning measure. This reform even established that minors convicted as juveniles could be transferred to serve their sentence in adult prison upon reaching a certain age (18 years or 21 years), under certain conditions.

This reform appeared after an increase in juvenile offending, which created social panic, after a series of serious crimes committed by children. The voice of those demanding tougher sentences prevailed, thanks to punitive populism driven by the media.

Some, like me, could have done more to prevent this from happening. I suspect we did not understand sufficiently how to defend the benefits of the legislation in place. Despite having enough data to refute the argument in favour of a more punitive justice system, the legislature was carried away by the sensationalist and excessive media hype over certain crimes perpetrated by minors. This included evidence based arguments with statistics highlighting that the actual increase in crime was miniscule and there was, in fact, no escalation in serious crimes committed by young people.

Those of us against the changes made to the law lacked the skill to make people aware of how well the system already worked: that our minors were reintegrating into society – the recovery of each minor was a success to be shared and widely understood.

My failure back then has driven me to ensure I no longer miss the opportunity, as a juvenile justice specialist, to show how the commitment and good work of those involved in juvenile justice bears fruit in the reintegration of many young people.

As a legal advisor in a juvenile detention centre, I have worked with almost a thousand young people. Of these children, few reoffended and returned – the majority rearranged their lives successfully. On various occasions, while walking in my city, I meet many of those children and we exchange knowing smiles. When they confirm they are doing well, I have no doubt, seeing their sincere gaze. I met them as delinquents. Now they are students, workers or even parents who honestly support their families.

Some recall their journey through the centre, we exchange anecdotes about experiences shared. Almost all tell me that having people alongside during that difficult period of their detention helped them, like their educators and the example that they set for them; and how these professionals showed them there were opportunities, but that ultimately the choice of what to do with their life depended on them. The testimony of those young people who have rearranged their lives and the joy with which they talk about it is something we must not forget. These types of conversations do not just happen to me – my colleagues have similar experiences.

In each academic course I teach, the first thing I do is ask my students what they know about juvenile delinquency. I am never surprised by the distorted image they share in their responses. That is where my work to dismantle this erroneous perception begins, using technical arguments, objective data and testimonies from minors and professionals. I simply ask that they question their perception of juvenile crime using healthy criticism, and generate a new perspective on the citizens with whom they interact.

I approach each article or public speaking event in this way. I no longer remain silent. I tell people: The system is not perfect – there are things to improve - but I have the conviction that a system with the interests of children at its heart, is the real engine for engendering hope in young people in conflict with the law. Treating them with kindness and compassion and implementing the law in a way that places their best interests at the heart is essential to helping them to discover a life outside of crime, as those young people I know have done.

Conclusion

The role of a law is to create a system providing sufficient tools for convinced and committed professionals, so they can equip children with the necessary skills to be capable of choosing the most suitable destination for their lives and those of their loved ones. But the success of a law – making real change – is dependent on how it's implemented. Kindness and compassion are key to showing young people the system works to protect them and their interests. That is what creates the hope that drives desistance.

As for how we influence public opinion, a lesson I learned over the years is that those of us in the system, must use evidence-based arguments to make the case for what works in the system. We must not be silenced by attitudes driven by sensationalist media influences. After all, the lives of our children are dependent on it.

A PERSONAL JOURNEY OF KINDNESS, HOPE & COMPASSION

Gary Stephenson

I write this piece from the perspective of having worked in the criminal justice system for the last 45 years in a variety of roles – including general policing, counter terrorism, major crime, developing and delivering restorative justice, and as the volunteer chair of a charity which engages and supports vulnerable young people who are at risk of offending.

This is a personal account of my journey over the years.

A 'rooky' officer

I have to start the journey with an abiding memory of my first week as a young police officer. Following months of training and preparation, I began my career at the raw age of nineteen. I was primed and trained to fight crime.

Like everything in life, you learn the most by actually doing the task in hand so I was directed to the 'warrant drawer.' This had all the outstanding warrants. All you had to do was find someone and arrest them – a nice easy non-contentious way to make my first arrest. I did not particularly sift through them but just chose one at random. I looked at the address and the name on the warrant and off I went. The warrant was for non-payment of fines and the subject of the warrant was to be taken straight to jail without a further court hearing. Easy, or so I thought. I knocked on the door with the authority bestowed to me and the door was answered by Lilly (not her real name), the subject of the warrant. She had seen the police car outside and had put her hat and coat on in readiness, saying "*I have been waiting. What kept you?*"

Lilly was eighty years of age, rather frail, bespectacled and very much similar in appearance to my old Gran. I was challenged to say the least, but took a deep breath, boldly cautioned her and told her she was being arrested. She replied by saying "*Bobbies are getting younger these days.*" I blushed.

The warrant had no details of the crime, so on the way to the station I asked what she had been fined for – thinking it must be something serious for the warrant to have been issued by a magistrate. Lilly told me she had not paid her TV Licence, was subsequently fined and had been unable to pay the fine. I began to think, "*Is this what I joined the police to do?*" But duty called and we continued to the police station, where she would be detained before being taken to prison for thirty days.

With my first 'collar' under my belt (a term used in reference to when you make an arrest), I had mixed emotions, but deep within me was a massive discomfort. I had neither the skill, knowledge nor experience at that stage to fathom this out. Refreshment time came around, where we would play cards and discuss our 'captures' of the day (a pejorative term used back in my early career when the landscape and environment was very different. These would typically include burglars, shoplifters, robbers and so on. It then came to me to tell them about my 'collar' of the day.

There was a collective silence around the room as the rest of the team all glanced at each other with disbelief. Frank, the sage Station Duty Officer, put his head in his hands. I immediately realised something was wrong, but I had followed the letter of the law and treated Lilly with dignity and respect. Jack broke the silence, saying they had all been purposefully avoiding that one. The warrant was about to expire and the plan was that once expired, it would probably not be renewed, due to the (then) failings of the system. To say I felt bad is an understatement. Here I was with my first arrest, which should be a very proud moment, and I felt deeply ashamed of what I had just done. However, what happened next was to stay with me for the rest of my life.

Lilly could not simply be un-arrested and released, that would be subverting the course of justice – I had lawfully executed the warrant. To my surprise, my colleagues – who were all seasoned cops – had a whip round, raided the tea fund and raised enough money that morning to pay Lilly's fine. She was duly released and I took her home and made her a cup of tea. We chatted for a while and began to form a friendship that would last until Lilly's death.

A human approach: the most effective form of policing

The collective kindness and compassion of my more experienced colleagues taught me more about discretion and humanity than my last six months in the boot camp style training centre. This incident would stay with me throughout my 32 years of policing. It informed and shaped my thinking throughout. It is a fact that when policing, you encounter people often at their worst. The ability to treat someone with kindness and compassion and to engage with them thereafter to give them hope that they can change (often just moments after they have tried to knock your head off), is one of the many great attributes of British policing to this day.

Giving hope and treating people with kindness and compassion are some of the highlighted success factors of the public health approach in Scotland. This has led to a significant reduction in violent crime over a period of 10 years. Many other police forces with Police and Crime Commissioners are taking a similar approach in their government funded Violence Reduction Units. This reminds me of one of the early restorative justice conferences I facilitated. The offender was known as an extremely violent man and had a fearsome reputation. I introduced myself and he launched a verbal tirade at me shouting and bawling at me, he was screaming, 'What do you want with me?' Once he had run out of breath, I simply said to him, "I am here to help you." To my surprise, he threw his head on the table and began to cry out loud. He eventually told me that he had been committing a crime more or less every day since he was eight years of age and no one had ever offered to help him. Unfortunately, the conference never took place due to other reasons beyond our control.

I spent the next 32 years fighting crime, witnessing and having to deal with some of the worst crimes of humanity and often arresting the same people time after time. Often I'd see generations of families over and over again.

So the question is – How did this crime fighter end up as an advocate, practitioner, author and campaigner for the use of restorative justice – which at its' very heart exudes kindness, hope and compassion?

Challenging the status quo – A restorative perspective

Like most things in life, chance and opportunity combine to determine your future. I had risen through the ranks and found myself in the position of Divisional Commander in the Northern Division of the Lancashire Constabulary. I ended up at a national conference held by the Restorative Justice Council (RJC) and listened to a presentation by Sir Charles Pollard – the former Chief Constable of Thames Valley Police and a truly inspirational restorative justice pioneer. I had a light bulb moment and was sold. I got it.

This approach actually solves problems, changes offender behaviour and reduces harm by providing kindness, hope and compassion. Restorative justice is by no means a soft option. Any offender – or harmer as we prefer to call them – will tell you it is the hardest thing they have ever done. They are not supported by lots of people in wigs; they are confronted directly by the person they have harmed – the person who shares the pain and agony they have gone through as a consequence of their behaviour. An outcome is agreed between the harmed and the harmer. Often the outcome agreement contains actions for the harmer to address their behaviour. Hope is given to both the harmed and harmer. The process is emotional and compassionate. All parties have an opportunity to have their say and often the parties involved display kindness to each other at the conclusion of the conference. Currently Restorative Justice is available to every victim of crime in England and Wales. That is good news and great progress. Unfortunately, however, many victims are not made aware of this and often have a misunderstanding around what restorative justice entails. Once the approach is explained to them properly, we get a good take up from victims and offenders. At the moment, whether you get the offer of a restorative conference is a bit of a postcode lottery. A more consistent integrated and universal approach with the offer of restorative justice will ensure that kindness, hope and compassion will become embedded in our justice system.

Kindness, hope and compassion have a great role to play in our criminal justice system, as my first experience as a rooky police officer demonstrates. Perhaps today this is even more necessary, given the current flaws in the system.

Lighting up my sky

COURTESY OF KOESTLER ARTS

I really appreciate your kindness
More than words can say.
Lighting up my way;
If I feel lost in my madness
Your caring smile makes me remember
Self-kindness

You are so humble
So sweet, like apple crumble
Those eyes warm like a loving mum.

I might be no one special
Or maybe I am,
And you make me believe it
And I know you mean it.

You put sunshine in my world
You make me feel hope
Where there's hope no more.
I can't ever see you as an enemy
In fact you are my hero

Life is a journey,
Every day we are learning something new.
There's always sunshine after rain.
Thanks again to you that are my main.
Just keep passing by
Lighting up my sky.

HOW CAN KINDNESS AND COMPASSION SHAPE PROBATION?

Rhian Metcalfe

This is an interesting question. For those of us working within the criminal justice system, kindness and compassion are integral to working effectively with service users while supporting their rehabilitation.

What this chapter intends to highlight is the importance of kindness and compassion being extended to criminal justice practitioners. As a probation officer myself, I believe this is key to the effective provision of the services required to help our clients make meaningful change. The traditional ethos of the probation service was often referred to as '*advise, assist and befriend.*' Whilst in modern times this message is no longer considered an accurate representation of the service we provide, it is arguable that the central message attached to this remains significantly relevant. Developing meaningful, supportive and purposeful relationships continues, for many practitioners, to be an essential requirement to supporting desistance. Moreover, we understand the importance of being supportive figures who assist service users to make necessary personal advancements; such relationships enhance the likelihood of a reduction in the risk that our clients pose within the community.

I believe a greater focus on manageable caseloads and the avoidance of a practitioner experiencing compassion fatigue could assist officers in having the creative freedom to explore and promote overall service user advancement whilst developing meaningful relationships.

To understand why extending kindness and compassion to probation professionals is vital it is important to understand our operating environment:

- 65% of NPS staff and 67% of CRC staff believe there is low morale at their workplace.
- 47% of Probation Officers and 32% of Probation Service Officers found that they were regularly unable to cope with their workload.
- While 43% of POs and 32% of PSOs said that they regularly suffer from work-related stress.[1]

Manageable workloads

As the above research suggests, probation staff are under significant strain due to unmanageable workloads. A more compassionate approach, one which prioritises the wellbeing of staff, would not only help mitigate the effects of this strain, it would have positive effects on the outcomes our clients achieve.

We know for example that the HMIP has previously criticised probation staff for not carrying out OASyS reviews within appropriate time-frames, highlighting that when completed, such assessments were often characterised by a lack of involvement from the offender despite policy and practice instructions.[2] There is an argument to be made that this is invariably due to the high caseloads the average probation officer deals with on a given day. Often, practitioners are 'fighting fires': addressing critical need or meeting hard targets.

Probation officers are held accountable for ineffectively managing risk – after all, it is our job to manage the risk posed by our clients. Unmanageable caseloads however, make doing this very difficult. Research shows that probation officers who challenge this are often perceived as not 'doing themselves favours' in terms of career progression or performance reviews) leaving many in a difficult situation.[3] This is true across all levels – senior management staff within the probation service face the same intense workloads and emotional stressors, with many citing service budgetary constraints, a lack of fundamental resources and staffing issues as factors contributing to the situation which we find ourselves in.

Staff well-being

The result of these pressures, in many cases, is compassion fatigue. People with some of the most complex needs in our society pass through the criminal justice system every day. They have often sustained adverse childhood experiences and significant trauma in their lives. Working with people who have such complex needs can, and does, have a significant effect on practitioners. Not having the time to properly reflect on these issues because of a never-ending conveyor belt of cases can, and does, lead to staff burnout. This in turn can have a detrimental impact of clients as the time and energy required to positively influence and provide relevant intervention work with service users is drastically reduced.[4]

When considering kindness and compassion to staff, Westaby et al. examined practitioners' desensitisation to crime and the impact that this had on their wellbeing and home lives. The research suggested a 'spill over effect' in cases where practitioners did not have a solid work-life balance. They found that such practitioners developed a skewed, pessimistic and negative perception of the world around them because they worked in a field with a high concentration of disturbing subject matter and did not have the time to reflect on and separate their work life from their home life. The research found that a significant number of these professionals spoke of 'worrying at night' because of work-related stress, increasing caseloads and target pressures. This is suggested to have contributed to many incidents of staff 'burn-out' and staff sickness, alongside other issues such as privatisation which led to many skilled and experienced practitioners vacating the profession.[5]

In recent years, there has been a significant shift in organisational practice which has focused on enhancing staff well-being. An example of this involves national support, such as making counselling sessions readily available for staff. These are fully funded and entirely confidential. Another example of good practice in this area includes regional well-being activities, such as charitable team walks and well-being days. Since a focus has been placed on practically enhancing staff well-being, I have noted a significant increase in staff discussing feelings of appreciation for direct management and business structures. I would argue that whilst this has not assisted in decreasing workloads, management teams showing care and considerations for the emotional and general well-being of staff has served to increase their current sense of loyalty, and a feeling of being 'in it together'.

Knight and Modi argue that, in order to deliver effective supervision and engagement, a practitioner needs to be able to emotionally regulate their own feelings.[6] This ability allows a practitioner to be more receptive to assessing the emotions of others. Improved staff wellbeing, combined with a reduction of emotional stressors, is shown to enable staff to develop increased emotional resilience – something that empowers staff to develop relationships that are more meaningful with clients, a key ingredient to achieving better outcomes.[7]

The distribution of time

In contrast to theoretical notions expressing the importance of meaningful work, Phillips notes a leaked and restricted MOJ report confirming results of a 2008 survey, where probation staff spent less than 24% of their time conducting work with offenders.[8] The report found a large proportion of offender managers' time was consumed by administrative tasks and computer-based work. It may be argued that whilst recording information and completing assessments are integral to a probation officer's role. It is equally true however, that delivering purposeful supervision sessions and truly building up relationships with clients to support desistance is the prime focus of our role. Desistance and reducing risk is unlikely to derive from a lack of face-to-face engagement with our clients. In fact, Burke and Collett suggest that probation targets, which are primarily computer based, are arbitrary in the sense that they lack a person-centred focus.[9] As with many things, the truth is more likely to be found in the middle. National standards are integral to our work and form a level of client protection. But we must have a conversation about how our time can be best spent to achieve meaningful outcomes for our clients.

Resilience and schooling

An offender manager's role is multi-dimensional. We play a caring role in the lives of offenders whilst also working with them to help them control their behaviours. It is a role that encompasses psychoanalytical casework to improve behaviours while also providing common-sense advice as an advocate for the court. Mawby and Worrall argue the procedure of enforcement and punishment is in fact an 'act of strength'. They argue that the credibility of an Offender Manager is dependent upon their ability to enforce and draw boundaries where necessary when conducting 'dirty work' – something they describe as work that carries significant emotional stressors and is figurative of solely negative aspects of society.[10]

A certain prestige is involved in criminal justice work, in the sense that it has high value and purpose as those who work in this system often aim to reduce harm. I have experienced in the service, that as practitioners we are 'in it together', working for the greater good of our communities, which in itself encompasses high morality and ethics. Within this, despite difficult days, there is always a draw to go back and try again. Mawby and Worrall highlight this sense of loyalty, stating that criminal justice employees have an attachment to their profession.[11] Individuals within our organisation can become skilled in reflection and emotional resilience. Experienced practitioners often school other perhaps less experienced workers through delivering constructive criticism and care. Our occupation has a propensity to lead to emotional exhaustion. Academics reference the resilience required to maintain control in situations resembling complete chaos - situations that would be regarded socially as uncontrollable. Academics also infer a practitioner's work entering a realm that is clearly a threat to an ordered existence, in terms of mental and physical well-being. There is almost reassurance in these recognitions, that in fact feelings of overwhelm, exasperation and emotional fatigue are biohazards of such a profession.[12]

What works

When considering 'what works', as a practitioner I would acknowledge the benefits of true relationship building. Certainly, within my career thus far, I have noticed meaningful change and personal reflection derive directly from spending positive and pro-social time with an individual. I have been part of pioneering projects within Approved Premises. I have also witnessed other areas of our service (often jointly funded with the NHS and/or Police) offer increased services to clients offering a multitude of varied psychological, practical and educational support, alongside allowing practitioners freedom and time to engage on a one-to-one or group basis with clients.

If I were to provide a recommendation towards improving results within the criminal justice system, (however seemingly unrealistic, given current working pressures and budget restrictions), I would suggest a need to reduce caseloads by half, allowing practitioners to effectively perform the job they are trained to do. As I have heard many practitioners suggest over the years, we would significantly benefit from increased funding and better community integration of resources. This could be achieved by better funding of services and an increase in staff numbers.

One way of extending kindness and compassion to practitioners, which arguably has a strong relevance to the outcomes of service users, would be the provision of training aimed at helping professionals develop their emotional resilience and positive coping skills as well as the provision frequent clinical supervision and reflective sessions. Reflective work is a key aspect of a practitioner's role and is embedded with desistence theory. Staff would also benefit from this. Whilst there is certainly a greater focus on staff well-being in modern times, this is not supported by a reduction in workload. A reduction in workload would support staff to engage with psychological services that are arguably necessary to support effective practice. Research suggests that staff currently feel unable to appropriately engage with imperative professional support because it often comes at the expense of appropriately concentrating on their own caseloads.[13]

Conclusion

To conclude, I would reflect that a greater focus on kindness, hope and compassion towards staff, in the form of manageable workloads, is key to enhancing staff wellbeing and subsequently the achievement of positive outcomes for the service users that we work with. Staff should be encouraged to maintain a strong work-life balance. I would suggest that practitioners developing emotional regulation and resilience skills is an essential factor for effective probation work. It is perhaps arbitrary to suggest this, when it is likely that staff already possess such skills, but to successfully utilise these skills, they need to be working within a manageable environment. I believe it is critical to perform meaningful and individualised one-to-one work with our client group rather than solely addressing critical need. Arguably, a primary way to support this is to increase staffing levels and to reduce administrative and computer-based tasks for criminal justice practitioners. Additional effective one-to-one work is what is needed to rehabilitate effectively. This is not an unfounded assertion, but an argument grounded in desistance research. Whilst the sector has advanced internally in recent years, austerity and the current political climate is having a damning effect on the ability for a criminal justice practitioner to create meaningful change.

In addition to this, whilst national service efforts have been made to support staff well-being, there is a need to take this further. Clinical supervision and a reduction in workload to engage with psychological support work is arguably a desirable ambition for the service to reduce the likelihood of professional compassion fatigue and 'burn out'.

If possible, I would like to dedicate this extract to all of the criminal justice staff that I work with, across all grades. In honesty, I feel utterly privileged to have met and worked with such kind, professional, supportive and intelligent individuals, who have a genuine passion to help people and to create safer communities. You all inspire me every single day. I am so grateful for you. Thank you.

A THERAPEUTIC LENS ON COMPASSIONATE CARE: ENCOUNTERING THE INNER CHILD IN A FORENSIC MENTAL HEALTH SETTING

Belinda Sherlock

'Compassion,' writes Christina Feldman, *'speaks of the willingness to engage with tragedy, loss, and pain.'*[1] Tragedy, loss and pain are hardly strangers to those of us who live or work in the criminal justice system. As a dramatherapist working in a forensic mental health service, it's my job to turn towards these dark and difficult feelings and offer creative ways for clients to navigate through them, without neglecting the self-compassion I need to do this. For me, the inner child is one of the most effective gateways to cultivate compassion in settings where trauma is the norm. Here, I share some of the approaches I've found most helpful for bringing compassion into the work, and exploring how a compassionate space enables the healing, creative side of the inner child to manifest.

The Traumatised Inner Child

We know trauma – whether a single event or ongoing neglect or violence – can significantly alter one's physiological, cognitive, and emotional processing. Unless offered appropriate support, those of us who have experienced trauma may become "trapped" in it in some way, perhaps experiencing flashbacks, poor mental or physical health, or difficulty in building relationships.

For most of my clients, trauma began in childhood and their experiences have caused them to feel somehow 'stuck'. Many live in a constant state of hyper- (overactive) or hypo- (underactive) arousal, and have difficulty regulating – or even recognising – their emotional states. Many have missed out on the developmental stages that enable a healthy sense of self and independent, meaningful engagement with the world. Many professionals, too, working in this environment have experienced trauma; some of us have taken caring roles because of this, desiring to heal others alongside ourselves. 'In each of us,' writes Thich Nhat Hanh, *'there is a young, suffering child.'*[2]

How we do (or not) tend to our wounded inner child depends on the resources, community and support available. Some are lucky to have enough safety, security and care to develop a more-or-less healthy relationship with ourselves and the world, to feel enough trust and curiosity to tend to our pain and make meaning from it. Others suffer within cycles of hopelessness and self-destruction, as bell hooks writes:

> *We could not choose healing because we were not sure we could ever mend [...] We comforted ourselves by acting out [...] More often than not we became addicted to living dangerously.*[3] (2001: p.212)

As well as speaking directly to my own experience, this provides a helpful framework for understanding the traumatised teenagers and adults I work with, all of whom have histories of acting out through violence or "living dangerously". Whether through disconnection from a terrifying or chaotic reality (dissociation, addiction, psychosis) or seeking to gain a sense of control (eating disorders, OCD, violence) the wounded child is always *'trying to get our attention. The child says, "I'm here. I'm here. You can't avoid me."'*

'Child ego state', writes transactional analyst Thomas Harris, comes to the fore:

in situations where we are faced with impossible alternatives, where we find ourselves in a corner, either actually, or in the way we see it. These 'hook the Child', [...] cause a replay of the original feelings of frustration, rejection, or abandonment.[4]

This is immediately recognisable in my place of work, where clients frequently perceive themselves to be pushed into a corner, as do we as professionals (probably more often than we care to admit). Our clients are involuntarily detained, with little control over their living environment and community. Most have histories of being abandoned, abused, and minimal (if any) control or protection. Most have also faced challenges of economic deprivation, social disadvantage, and/or racial discrimination their whole lives.

As psychiatrist Gilligan writes:

' *the most vulnerable, those who lacked any non-violent means of restoring their personal dignity, such as educational achievements, success, and social status, might well see violence as the only way of expressing [their] feelings.*'[5]

Violence, we could say, is the wounded inner child's way of communicating, 'I'm here'.

Harnessing Compassion

I'm taking compassion here to mean '*awareness of the suffering of oneself and of other living things, coupled with the wish and effort to relieve it.*'[6] Unlike empathy, compassion '*implies a warm, sincere feeling of concern, but does not require that one feel the other's suffering.*'[7] Ricard points out that, whereas empathy can lead to '*emotional exhaustion and distress*', compassion '*reinforces our strength of mind, our inner balance, and our courageous, loving determination to help those who suffer.*'[8]

This can sound pretty far-fetched in our work – it is immensely challenging to maintain strength of mind and inner balance when clients' unmet needs are expressed as violence, bullying, chaos or outright rejection of care. In these moments, our own inner children can surface, replaying responses and coping mechanisms that – maladaptive as they might be – have been carried into adulthood. I notice this particularly when I feel disrespected, attacked, harried, or ignored. However, I've begun to find that by cultivating self-compassion, I can tend to my inner child and her needs, restoring the courage and 'loving determination' I need to tend to the needs of others. Here is the practice I currently use:

Stage one: recognising my own need for compassion - I regularly check in with my own trauma exposure responses so I can start to address them. *In Trauma Stewardship* Van Dernoot Lipsky and Burk outline sixteen 'warning signs', including feeling helpless and hopeless, diminished creativity, inability to embrace complexity, minimising, chronic exhaustion, inability to listen, numbing, anger and cynicism, sense of persecution, and guilt.[9] Looking at this list, it's easy to recognise these traits in my clients too.

Stage two: finding my own compassionate presence - I create a comfortable, safe, quiet place to sit, focusing first on my breath to calm the nervous system. I then remember an experience of receiving compassion, whether this be from a person, animal or simply the feeling of the sun warming my skin. Often this can bring up complicated feelings, and I try for now to focus on the essence of feeling cared for.

I then bring to mind a compassionate being that embodies this quality of care, one that resonates with my own background, culture, and belief-system. Gilbert offers a helpful guideline: '*If you could design the ideal 'compassionate other' for a child,*' he asks, '*what qualities would they have?*'[10], suggesting wisdom, strength, warmth, and non-judgement as a start. Resting in the presence of this compassionate being for a moment, I bring to mind the person for whom I want to develop compassion and invite them to rest in that presence too. I usually complete this practice by bidding them goodbye and taking a little more time by myself in that space.

Stage three: transforming my suffering into relief - Going a stage further, I stay in that compassionate presence and identify some physical or emotional pain I'm holding. As I breathe in, I imagine I am breathing that pain into the compassionate space I have created. As I breathe out, I breathe out a sense of warmth, acceptance, and relief. This is based on the buddhist practice of Tonglen. After a while breathing in this way, I start to notice subtle changes in how I perceive the pain: it becomes less of a problem, more of a curiosity.

I can then extend this practice to someone else, noticing the suffering that comes up when I think of them and breathing that in, then breathing out warmth, relief and acceptance towards them. I'm always amazed how energising and effective this practice is, and I love that *anyone* can do it at *anytime*. '*Start where you are*', says Pema Chödrön, '*You might think that there are no others on the planet who hate themselves as much as you do. All of that is a good place to start.*'[11]

Stage four: creating a compassionate microculture - We can also build a more compassionate external community. Van Dernoot Lipsky cites this as vital in addressing our trauma exposure responses. She invites us to consider who in our lives supports us by '*showering us with encouragement and holding us accountable.*'[12] What can we change in our living and working environment that contributes to our wellbeing? How can we support our clients, limited as their options might be, to create their own compassionate microculture?

The Creative Inner Child

My hope is that the dramatherapy space becomes part of my clients' compassionate microcultures. Two elements are paramount here:

1. **Safety:** the dramatherapy space is (ideally) physically and emotionally safe. By creating a contained space – unlikely to be invaded, offering exercises to build a sense of safety and co-creating a therapeutic contract with clear boundaries established – clients develop the sense of the space as a 'secure base' from which to explore.[13] The therapist creates, holds, and protects the space for their clients, mirroring the role of a care-giver.

2. **Play:** dramatherapy is about enabling rediscovery of our playfulness. Because play is how we explore and make sense of the world around us, it is essential for cultivating the imagination, creativity and curiosity need to develop new meaning for our existing reality. Play taps into the aspect of our inner child that has natural propensity to learn, connect, and heal.

Encountering the inner child, then, is integral to the dramatherapy process, and by providing a compassionate space that acknowledges suffering and aims to relieve it, both the wounded and creative inner child can be welcomed, expressed, witnessed, and explored. Bessel Van der Kolk extols the use of drama and play in healing trauma, noting how reframing one's experiences imaginatively can create *'an alternative memory in which your basic human needs are met and your longings for love and protection are fulfilled.'*[14]

Bill's story

Bill (not his real name) has generously consented for me to talk about his journey. Spending the first few years of his life in an orphanage, and then – once reunited with his unwell mother - abused violently by his step-father, Bill grew up lacking trust that others would care for and protect him. He joined the army, but at 16 was sexually abused and started to develop an aggressive and psychotic presentation. Finding solace in spending time with animals, who were easier to love than humans, Bill eventually bought his own pet. Bill also began to find solace in drugs and alcohol. One day, a neighbour teased Bill about his pet. They got into a fight and Bill ended up killing the neighbour. Sentenced for wilful murder – Bill maintains it was accidental – he served twenty years in prison, where he attempted to take his own life, and expressed more obvious signs of psychosis. Having served his time, Bill – now in his fifties – was transferred to a low secure forensic and specialist mental health service. Six months later, I began working with Bill.

In his dramatherapy assessment, Bill articulated his difficulty in trusting others: "I've built up a very strong wall around myself as protection. People are bad, people want to hurt me. I also have great power and knowledge – I can't tell you what that is – which I need to protect. If the bad guys get their hands on this, the world is done for. The only things I can put my trust in are animals, science, and logic." Bill was courageous enough to tell me he'd started building the wall due to the childhood abuse. He expressed anger that no-one protected him. I acknowledge Bill's anger, and noted, "It's a very compassionate thing you've been doing, trying to keep yourself and the world safe from harm". "People aren't compassionate," he responded. "A least, I've never seen that." "But you are," I offered, "we've just seen you have a compassionate side. I wonder if it's possible for others to have compassion too, then. And to have it towards you?" Bill was sceptical. Nonetheless, he agreed to join a dramatherapy group. I hoped aloud that this might support him to experience trust and compassion.

Bill proved a force to be reckoned with in the group. He tended to monopolise, to centre on his needs, frustrations and difficulties and to shut down or sabotage group exercises. I started to dread sessions, wondering each week how to manage Bill's needs whilst ensuring others had a meaningful experience. It often felt draining and fragmenting. With Bill in the group, the group's capacity to think and be creative – and indeed my own – felt under attack. *The space can become,' writes dramatherapist Seebolm, 'both terrorised and terrorising, sometimes leaving the therapist holding the shattered pieces of debris, as in the aftermath of war. This may echo the patient's own life experience, which has left them struggling to hold together the debris of their own history."* [15]

After sessions I would reflect with the Arts Therapies Assistant (part of my compassionate microculture). "Poor Bill", she would say, "he has an overwhelming need for people to see how much he's suffering, and yet such a need to protect and control so that we don't see his suffering". We held hope that the safer and more seen Bill felt, the more we might encounter his creative, curious inner child, and support him to contain and harness his destructive tendencies through play.

Over the next 23 group sessions (7 months), Bill gradually became increasingly open to and confident in using the dramatic techniques offered to explore anger, difficulties with trust and his need for protection and nurture. Four sessions stand out in particular:

Week 11 – Bill shared something about his beliefs - a big step for him in terms of trusting the group. Later in a group improvisation he chose to play a child crossing the road with his mother, who protected him from an oncoming car. Reflecting afterwards, he noted the importance of the mother protecting the child, something he wished he'd had.

Week 20 – In an exercise celebrating ourselves and important people in our lives, Bill felt unable to identify anything to celebrate. He appeared moved when, during my turn, I chose to celebrate him, noting how much effort and courage he had taken to build trust in the group.

Week 22 – Bill arrived angry, and found an image to represent this, plus an image to ease this anger ('creative flow'). Each group member was guided through embodying their chosen feelings/qualities. Bill managed the exercise well, being witnessed and mirrored by others. At the end, he picked two images to reflect. The first said "ready to face the unknown"; the second, "tenderness and kindness". "I felt moments of tenderness and kindness with you all today," he said.

Week 24 – Bill shared something traumatic from childhood, and needed support in thinking how to re-imagine this. The group helped Bill by role-playing what he needed to support him in that moment as a child. Bill appeared to find this useful, reflecting the trauma had been big deal for him – this was accepted and held by the group.

Final Reflections

Holding Bill's traumatised inner child in mind enabled me to understand the needs he was communicating – to be seen and protected. Through regular compassion practice, I felt able to continue holding Bill's destructiveness in the group and, together with the group, we

showered him with warmth and acceptance. Gradually, this brought
out his more playful, creative side, and he could share his vulnerability.
Being received with compassion, Bill felt increasingly safe in the group,
to trust us, and experience 'tenderness' and 'kindness', something he
had dismissed as impossible.

Twisted trolls or special souls?

HMP Low Moss, Poem courtesy of Koestler Arts

Two women had turned up to see me,
"They're psychologists," the staff informed
Oh well! Here we go again I thought,
My opinion was already formed.

One was Irish, the other ginger
(No this ain't the first line of a joke!)
They'll be trying to get me off-guard,
Then my future ruined with one pen stroke
They made being suspicious hard to be,
Their smiles caught me off-guard somewhat
I looked for reasons to dislike them,
But so far they'd given diddly squat
They didn't at all seem threatening,
Both were harmless looking pretty souls
Ignore those smiles, I told myself,
Behind those faces hide two Twisted Trolls.

One week later, one of them came back,
Couldn't even remember her name
Though I doubt it mattered anyway,
She'll turn up twice then never again
And honestly, that was the second,
I'm surprised she'd even came to that
I was bored and lonely anyhow,
It got me out my cell and a chat
She'd still not tried to screw me over,
Mess about with or deceive my mind
Clearly still pretending to be nice
But I know she ain't caring or kind.

Two weeks passed and she's back as promised,
This time I don't dread her stopping by
I seemed to have a niggling feeling,
Though unsure of what it meant or why
I then noticed something else as well,
Her name was Lisa, I recall
It didn't feel like she's tricking me,
She spoke to me, always with respect
Asked me how I was, not what I'd done,
I kept trying to find the trap
No matter how long I spent thinking
I found no attempts to cause me crap.

So yet another fortnight went by,
And she turned up right on time once more
As soon as the screws said, "Lisa's here,"
I worked out these niggling thoughts before
They weren't cause she's out to get me
But because the contrary's what's true
Neither were duty bound to come back,
After that initial interview
But they chose to, Lisa most of all,
Spent her precious time with worthless me
Her kind and caring helpful manner
Cannot be taught, comes with no degree.

I'd demonised jail psychologists,
But I guess I'd found two exceptions
Now I felt like a bit of a twat
For suspecting lies and deceptions
They helped free me from my painful thoughts,
Gave me a break from my f-d up brain
Just having someone there to talk to,
Numbed hurt like a tooth by Novocaine
So from then on I looked forward to,

Rather than dread my future sessions
It's a relief to have a normal chat
}Random stuff, not just my transgressions.

So, jail psychologists? Take a punt,
You may well discover Twisted Trolls
But like me, you might just get lucky,
And meet two kind caring Special Souls

Be me to understand me
J STORELL

To me, compassion is not pity. It's the understanding that those of us in prison have done wrong and maybe even need to be punished but we should be punished fairly not continuously; not for being a second late to my cell door or having my television taken away with stern words for minor infractions.

Be in the system for a day to understand the life we live.

We Will Meet Again, HMP The Verne
Image courtesy of Koestler Arts

CONTRIBUTORS

Alan Jermey

Having completed a BSc in Criminology and Psychological studies and a Masters in Development Management, Alan has found a calling in the Sport for Development field as a way to help others. Alan is now pursuing the possibility of carrying out further research via PhD. As a son, father, brother, uncle and friend, it has also given him the opportunity to repay the years of love bestowed upon him through the good as well as the bad times.

Alice Dawnay

Alice Dawnay is Founder and CEO of Switchback: an award-winning charity enabling young Londoners to find a way out of the justice system and build a stable, rewarding life they can be proud of. For 12 years, Switchback's radical, relational approach has been getting results. Switchback Mentors do more than manage prison-leavers' crises and build employability: they work to totally refashion attitudes, behaviours and self-narrative. Now Switchback is using its evidence and experience in seeking to actively inspire more human, more effective policy and practice across the justice system.

Angela Collins

Angela Collins is a PhD candidate in Social Policy and Criminology at The Open University. Her research examines the stories women tell about their criminalisation and is grounded in ethnographic fieldwork from her time at a women's centre in the North of England. Angela has worked in research for over 20 years. In her previous role as a Research Director, at an independent research organisation, she completed a range of research projects for voluntary sector organisations working within the Criminal Justice System.

Anne Fox

Anne Fox is CEO of Clinks, the national infrastructure charity supporting voluntary organisations working in the criminal justice system in England and Wales, a member of the Monument Fellowship.

She has worked in the voluntary and community sector in the UK and Republic of Ireland in campaigning, policy, public affairs and communications roles since 1998, the same year Clinks was founded. Together with Dr Alison Frater, then chair of the National Criminal Justice Arts Alliance, Anne edited the 4th in the series of these books, "Crime & Consequence- what should happen to people who commit criminal offences?"

Anne-Marie Douglas

Anne-Marie has worked in the voluntary and statutory sector for twenty years, locally and nationally supporting the meaningful involvement of young people who are least heard. Anne-Marie's belief in empathy and personal experience of peer led services led her to found the charity Peer Power in 2015. Anne-Marie is passionate about positive changes to support excluded children and young people. Her work is underpinned by a belief in supporting individual choice, the importance of empathy, nurturing, and a person centred therapeutic approach.

Belinda Hopkins

Belinda has been pioneering restorative approaches in youth settings across the UK and beyond, for over 20 years. In the mid 90's she founded Transforming Conflict to offer training and consultancy to schools who wanted to develop a restorative approach. It now also works in the fields of social and community care. Belinda gained her doctorate in 2006 with research into the implementation of a whole school restorative approach. She is passionate about sharing how the ethos, principles and practices of Restorative Approaches can transform communities and institutions. She runs training courses, writes books and articles, develops training materials and resources, and speaks at conferences nationally and internationally.

Belinda Sherlock

Belinda is a dramatherapist working in forensic mental health within the NHS, soon to be moving from an inpatient focus to a forensic community team. She is starting to research the role of dramatherapy in forensic mental health recovery. Alongside this, Belinda runs Playful Wellbeing which offers therapy, clinical supervision and workshops to individuals and teams with a focus on growing connection, creativity and compassion (for more information, see www.playfulwellbeing.com). She enjoys performing and is a member of the London Playback Theatre Company, a trained therapeutic clown and a hobbyist musician. Other passions include meditation, tai chi and storytelling.

Ben Amponsah

Ben Amponsah, an ex-army officer, is both counsellor and coach. He qualified as a counsellor in 2004 and took his life coaching qualification in 2011. Ben has worked for several charities both as a practitioner and as a Trustee and then Chair – he very much values this work and has a keen eye on social justice. In his free time Ben considers himself an amateur creative writer, is a published contributor to a psychology book and is active on many fan fiction gaming forums as such and is a published writer.

Brenda Birungi

Brenda, who also goes by the name Lady Unchained, works to prove that there is life after prison. Through poetry she tells her own personal story and the stories of those with experience of the criminal justice system; stories that are often left untold because of shame, stigma and negative labels. With the support of her friends, she was inspired to set up Unchained Poetry, a platform for artists with experience of the criminal justice system. She regularly works with a number of charities & hosts Unchained Nights in partnership with Artsadmin at Toybee Stations, a night of inspirational storytelling, through poetry and music, performed by artists with lived experience of the justice system.

Callum Hutchison

Callum Hutchison is from Glasgow. He was an active Gang member for 15 years and has had contact with the criminal justice system since he was 16 years old. He has now turned his life around and works for the Scottish Violence Reduction Unit as a Development officer.

Reverend Dr Carver Anderson

Dr Carver Anderson is a practical theologian and social scientist. He is a qualified social worker, with over 35 years' experience, working with individuals, families and communities plagued by multiple and complex challenges. He is one of the Executive Directors and cofounder of the Bringing Hope Charity which works to support individuals and families impacted by crime and serious violence, which includes perpetrators and victims. Over the years, Carver has chaired and been part of numerous committees and conferences regarding family and community associated issues. He has lectured across the world about his approach to practical theology, youth crime, black young men, social ethics and faith-based interventions governed by a Christian ethos.

Clare McGregor

Clare McGregor is an experienced independent advisor, speaker and author who was 30 before she realised it's better to help people solve their own problems, rather than telling them what to do. As Founder and MD of Coaching Inside and Out (CIAO) she wrote 'Coaching Behind Bars', which is used internationally and recommended in The Times as a "remarkable book" with "dark humour". Clare's always worked at the hard end of social justice, focusing on those dealt the toughest hands in life, and is keen to connect with others who share her desire to make change happen.

Charlie Rigby

Charlie has been working with young people since 1996 in a variety of settings including: activity camps, youth centres, social services and youth justice. He is the Founder and CEO of the VIP Project and currently works with young people involved in serious youth violence, delivering practical and emotional outreach support to help young people move forward positively with their lives.

Dave Nicholson

Dave Nicholson is a former Probation Officer, currently Director of Ex-Cell Justice Solutions, a co-operative of people with lived experience of the Criminal Justice System, campaigning for a fairer justice system and developing innovative justice solutions for victims and people who commit criminal offences. Dave read Social and Political Sciences at Jesus College, Cambridge and has a Masters in Applied Criminology, Penology and Management from the University of Cambridge Institute of Criminology.

David McGuire

David joined Diagrama on leaving university and spent his first five years as a Social Educator in a secure establishment for the Diagrama Foundation in Spain, also achieving his Social Educator Degree during that time. In 2006 he led an after-care programme which helped over 400 children and young people who had been through the justice system. He established links with all the relevant community agencies and organisations which support the young people to reintegrate into society. In 2008 he moved from Spain to the UK with his family to establish the Foundation in the UK and was appointed Chief Executive in 2009.

Deborah Murphy

Deborah Murphy is an Occupational Therapist and who manages a therapeutic day service in a Cat B remand prison in London. She has 25 years experience of working within mental health services, with over a decade of this specialising in working with those with mental health issues who have committed offences. Alongside her undergraduate in Occupational Therapy ,Deborah has undertook postgraduate training in leadership and management; and Psychosocial Perspectives of Personality Disorder. She is currently studying for her masters in advanced practice in Occupational therapy with the aim of contributing to research regarding Occupational therapy in prisons. Deborah recently qualified as a Mindfulness teacher with Oxford university, and has worked in partnership with Oxford for four years to develop the practice of mindfulness within prisons.

Gary Stephenson

Following a thirty two year career with the Lancashire Constabulary, Gary has been working with Restorative Solutions a Community Interest Company, which is committed to developing and progressing innovative restorative approaches and services in the public sector and communities for the last twelve years. Gary has managed a number of national programmes aimed at implementing and developing restorative practice in a diverse range of sectors including Prisons, Health, Policing, Neighbourhood Management, Housing, Police & Crime Commissioners. Gary has provided evidence at the Select Committee hearing on the effectiveness of Rrestorative Justice. Gary has a B.A. (Hons) in Public Administration M.Sc. Investigative Psychology

Gerard Lemos

Gerard Lemos is the author of The Good Prison: Conscience, crime and punishment. He is also the lead non-executive director and chairs the board of HM Prisons and Probation Service. He is a partner at social researchers Lemos&Crane, a member of the Monument Fellowship.

Greg Berman

Greg Berman is the former director of the Center for Court Innovation in New York. He serves as the chair of the Centre for Justice Innovation UK and writes a column on nonprofit leadership for New York Nonprofit Media.

Jayne Richards

Before release from prison, in 2014, Jayne achieved a BA (Hons) in Humanities with the OU, The Barrow Cadbury Scholarship award with Koestler Arts, and began a voluntary position on ROTL with the creative charity Only Connect, based in London. In 2018 Jayne was awarded with by Princess Anne, Catch 22's patron, who presented Jayne with an award for "Outstanding service to Catch 22" at Hertfordshire police headquarters, after she had been nominated by the police and crime commissioner, followed by the Rehabilitation award for 2018 by HMPPS Wales. In 2020, Jayne was featured in the HMPPS online communications, titled 'Progress in partnership' for continued commitment to contribute to helping people lead law-abiding and positive lives. Since 2015 Jayne has worked in a variety of areas of Catch22, culminating in her current role as Operational Support Officer, supporting teams across the breadth of their services that build resilience and aspiration in people and communities.

Joanna Hobson

Joanna is one of the founders and Project Manager for Essence, a small faith-based project working with those aged 18-25 in women's prisons in London and the South East since 2012. Joanna has been involved in prison work for just under 12 years and has an academic background in Theology (BA Durham University) and Criminology (MA Kings College London).

Jules Roberts

Jules Roberts is a founder member of Coaching Inside and Out (CIAO) working as a coach supervisor and coach coordinator in men's and women's prisons. She also coaches children, young people and staff in the Youth Justice Service. She believes that everyone should have the opportunity to be coached to support them to live a more fulfilling life. Jules is also an independent qualified therapist, facilitator and coaches a diverse group of professionals both 1:1 and in teams. She supports her clients to create insights, develop strengths and take action to achieve their goals in times of change and uncertainty.

John Bayley

John's background was mainly in Education and after training as a teacher, worked in schools in Hampshire, Dorset and Surrey with children from 5 – 16, before moving to Finland as Deputy Principal of the International School of Helsinki. On returning to the UK, he became Headteacher of a school in Weymouth. His commitment to Buddhism was furthered when he joined Angulimala, the Buddhist Prison Chaplaincy Service, where he has served as Buddhist Chaplain at three prisons in Dorset. Currently he works at HMP The Verne, Portland. After retiring from teaching, he worked in prisons in Dorset and London managing an innovative mentoring project for prisoners aged 18-21 He is a trained psychotherapist and worked in a clinic in Weymouth using the Human Givens Approach.

John Samuels QC

His Honour John Samuels QC was a Crown Court judge for 27 years; a judicial member of the Parole Board for his maximum tenure of 10 years; and is a Vice President of the Association of Independent Monitoring Boards. He is also the President of Prisoners' Education Trust; Vice President of UNLOCK and Tempus Novo; and a Patron of Prisoners' Advice Service and of Revolving Doors Agency.

Juan Jose Periago Morant

Juan José Periago Morant is Assistant Professor of the Department of Public Law of the Faculty of Legal and Economic Sciences of the Universitat Jaume I. He currently instructs students studying degrees in Criminology and Law. His specialisation is in mediation and family intermediation.

Keziah Poultney

Keziah is an English Literature graduate from Warwick University and has been part of the Essence team since March 2019. In addition to her work with Essence, Keziah also has a background in coffee and training within different criminal justice settings.

Dr Peter Neyroud CBE QPM PhD.

Peter Neyroud is a Lecturer in Evidence-based Policing. He is is the Deputy Director of the M.St. Police Executive Programme. He has been at the Institute since 2010, following a 30-year career in the police service. He has been a Resident Scholar at the Jerry Lee Centre for Experimental Criminology managing a major research programme, Operation Turning Point; a randomised controlled trial testing offender desistance policing. He has taught senior police leaders and advised governments across the world and in the UK on criminal justice reform. His research interests centre on field experiments in policing, pre-court diversion, crime harm and the implementation and leadership of change in criminal justice agencies.

Malcom Carter

Having studied and completed a BSc in Criminology and Psychological Studies and a Masters in Development Management. Alan Jermey has found a calling in the Sport for Development field as way to help others. He is no pursuing the possibility of caregiving out further research via a PhD. As a son, father, brother, uncle and friend it has also given him the opportunity to repay the years of love bestowed on him through the good and bad times.

Marianne Moore

Marianne is an entrepreneur and strategy consultant specialised in criminal justice reform. In 2011 she founded the social justice consultancy Justice Studio, through which she has worked for clients such as the UK Government, UNICEF and the Council of Europe. With 18 years experience, Marianne has worked extensively in the UK, and in over 30 countries internationally. She is passionate about revolutionising the criminal justice system, and consistently strives to improve its child and gender sensitivity. She holds an MSc in International Non-Government Organisation Management from Cass Business School, an MA in Applied Criminology and Youth Justice from the University of Middlesex, and a BA in Modern History from Oxford University.

Mr Gee

Mr Gee has performed poetry for two decades. Perhaps best known as the "Poet Laureate" on Russell Brand's infamous Radio show, he's toured the world & had his work featured in The Times & The Guardian. He presented "Bespoken Word", "Rhyme & Reason" & "Poetic Justice" all on Radio 4, the latter of which focused on his extensive prison rehabilitation work. He also featured on BBC 2's BAFTA nominated program "Poetry Between the Lines". He developed a digital art-work called "Bring Me My Firetruck" for the Open Data Institute (showcased at the Tate Britain for their 2020 "Blake Now" series).

Nick Moss

Nick Moss is an ex prisoner who began writing poetry as a way of mapping his experiences in jail. He won a Koestler award for his chapbook collection 'The Skeleton Choir Singing.' He was awarded a May Turnbull Scholarship, and his work has been featured in the Proletarian Poetry Magma, the New River Press yearbook, and Poets for Grenfell .He runs poetry workshops with prisoners and is part of the Ealing based Campfire storytelling group and the Willesden Junction Poets. His first book of poems will be published by Smokestack Books in 2021. His work is focused on finding ways to give prisoners a voice through the arts.

Niven Rennie

Having has over 30 years experience as a police officer during which he was heavily involved in the Scottish police reform process and represented the Association of Scottish Police Superintendents throughout the implementation of Police Scotland in 2013. In 2014, he became a Chief Superintendent and President of the Superintendents Association. Following retirement from the police in 2016, Niven became the Chief Executive Officer of South Ayrshire Escape from Homelessness (SeAscape), a charity offering support to those in poverty or housing need in the Ayrshire area. As Director of Scottish Violence Reduction, he is now responsible for the strategic direction of the Violence Reduction Unit and represents the unit on a number of national bodies.

Olivia Dehnavi

Olivia Dehnavi leads on policy and research at Working Chance, a charity which supports women with convictions by preparing them to gain meaningful employment, offering employability skills training, programmes aimed at building confidence, career coaching and in-work mentoring. Olivia advocates for changes to policy and practice that will improve employment outcomes for women with convictions. She has previously worked on women's rights, prisons and access to justice in an international context as a human rights consultant in Cambodia, where she campaigned for the release of political prisoners. While studying law in London, she coached debating in women and men's prisons.

Pete Wallis

"Pete joined Oxfordshire Youth Justice Service as a restorative practitioner in 2000, having previously worked as a teacher, residential care worker, drugs worker and with prisoners and the homeless. He has facilitated hundreds of restorative meetings and is passionate about the power and benefits of restorative justice. Pete has written or co-authored several books on restorative justice and related issues, most recently a graphic novel and resource book on consent. He is founder and current Chair of Trustees of SAFE! Support for young people affected by crime, a charity he set up in 2010 which provides services to young victims across the Thames Valley.

Peter Neyroud

Peter Neyroud is a Lecturer in Evidence-based Policing. He is is the Deputy Director of the M.St. Police Executive Programme. He has been at the Institute since 2010, following a 30-year career in the police service. He has been a Resident Scholar at the Jerry Lee Centre for Experimental Criminology managing a major research programme, Operation Turning Point; a randomised controlled trial testing offender desistance policing. He has taught senior police leaders and advised governments across the world and in the UK on criminal justice reform. His research interests centre on field experiments in policing, pre-court diversion, crime harm and the implementation and leadership of change in criminal justice agencies.

Phil Bowen

Phil Bowen is Director of the Centre for Justice Innovation, which seeks to build a justice system which every citizen believes is fair and effective. Prior to being Director, Phil spent the majority of his career in the British civil service. He worked for the Home Office and Ministry of Justice, before working at HM Treasury and Cabinet Office as a delivery adviser to the Prime Minister on criminal justice reform. During his time in the civil service, he spent 14 months on secondment to the Center for Court Innovation in New York, working at Bronx Community Solutions.

Father Richard Rene

Father Richard René is Director of the St Silas Orthodox Prison Fellowship Society and a priest of the Orthodox Church in America's Archdiocese of Canada.

Rhian Metcalfe

Rhian Metcalf - Probation Officer in Merseyside: I am interested in working on projects that create opportunities for personal development and progression for both our clients and our staff teams. I have an interest in innovative operational changes. I won a Butler Trust Award in 2019. I have a career history working within the National Probation Service since 2012, beginning on temporary contracts and working my way up from a receptionist to a probation officer. I have two degrees, one in humanities and the other in criminal justice and I have recently begun a Prince 2 qualification in project management.

Riana Taylor

Riana Taylor held senior leadership roles in South Africa, the UK, China and Vietnam which includes criminal justice operations and rehabilitative services. She joined Circles UK as CEO in 2016. She finds tremendous fulfilment in this role as she believes that people can change and has a deep commitment to social inclusion and restorative work. She fully relates to the organisation's ethos of preventing further victims, enabling perpetrators of sexual abuse to take ownership of their actions and reintegrate safely and positively back into the community. In her personal life, Riana enjoys gardening, the theatre, traveling, socialising and playing tennis.

Sarah Wilkinson

Sarah has a background in policy, communications and participation roles across the charity/ youth sector, helping organisations – like Nacro, Barnardo's and Catch22 – listen to, communicate and respond to the voices of children and young people. She is a strong advocate of Peer Power's mission to embed empathy, love and relational approaches in social care, justice and health settings. Outside of work she enjoys cooking, socialising and absolutely loves crisps.

Dr Shola Apena Rogers

Dr Shola Apena Rogers is a Registered Practitioner with the HCPC, a Chartered Forensic Psychologist and Lecturer at the University of Birmingham. She is an experienced practitioner and researcher who has worked within various settings, including the Criminal Justice System, Children's Social Care, the NHS, and the voluntary sector. Shola has extensive experience employing evaluation methodology and project management approaches to problem solve social justice issues. Shola is also a Consultant Trainer delivering Motivational Interviewing, Adolescent Mental Health, and Trauma Informed Practice training programmes. Shola is also on the board of Trustees with Street Doctors.

Simon Kenny

Simon Kenny was born in Australia and moved to the UK as a child in 1973. He is a former solicitor and Deputy District Judge who to the great surprise to himself and others found himself in prison at the age of 60. Much of his sentence was spent at HMP Maidstone, a foreign national prison where he became a Listener, Peer Support Worker and Prison Counsel Chairman. He was given the High Sherriff of Kent's Award for Outstanding Contribution. Since leaving prison Simon maintains an interest in prison reform and the plight of foreign prisoners in this "hostile environment."

Tanjit Dosanjh

Tanjit became an optometrist in 2008 and learned of the optical labs in California's prisons. He asked the UK prison service to copy their model but, frustratingly, could not make any headway. So in 2012 he self-funded his optical training lab inside HMP Standford Hill. By 2015 he was awarded £262,000 from the Sainsbury Family Trust, The Paul Hamlyn Foundation and The Triangle Trust enabling him to set up an optical lab in Maidstone. Between 2016–2019 he trained 60 prisoners, 45 whom secured jobs with opticians. He also secured optometry contracts in 60 prisons. Spectacles for prisoners are made by prisoners which makes the organisation financially self-sustaining.

The Tartan Con

Michael served over 4 years in prisons across the country and develops practical solutions grounded in his experience to tackle prisoners' anxiety, stress and frustration. From the first days spent behind bars to the days spent preparing for release, Michael's work helps prisoners to cope with an alien environment, to reduce the staggering toll of self-harm, suicide and violence inside. His approaches have been adopted by every organisation managing prisons in the UK in both public and private sectors. Michael campaigns for a zero target for self-harm in prisons and argues for an approach to criminal justice based on evidence over ideology. Michael blogs and records podcasts under the pseudonym of The Tartan Con.

Tracy Hammond

Whilst coaching horse riders, Tracy became curious about 'what makes people tick'. Driven by this curiosity she started to work with people said to have behaviour that challenged. Tracy concluded that such behaviour was often caused by services and she resolved to be part of the solution rather than add to people's difficulties. Tracy joined KeyRing in 2001 and is currently Research and Innovation Director there. She has an interest in how the Criminal Justice System interacts with people with learning disabilities and is determined that the voices of people failed by the system should be heard by policymakers. "

Trevor Urch

Employed by Birmingham and Solihull Mental Health Foundation, Trevor has been the Recovery and Service User Involvement Lead at HMP Birmingham since 2010. The role is at times challenging but is counter-balanced with its own reward system. He cites one such reward is witnessing the benevolence of the residents that he works with as they aim to engender hope for their peers who are struggling in the setting.

REFERENCES

Introduction: Humane Justice
Lisa Rowles and Iman Haji

Notes

[1] Ministry of Justice (2018) Memorandum on Main Estimate 2018–19, London: Ministry of Justice

[2] Ministry of Justice (2020) Criminal Justice Statistics quarterly, England and Wales, October 2018 to September 2019. London: Ministry of Justice

[3] HM Prison and Probation Service (2019) Annual report and accounts 2018–19, London: HMPPS

[4] Ministry of Justice (2019) Safety in custody statistics quarterly update to September 2018, London: Ministry of Justice

[5] Table Q5.1b and Q5.4, Ministry of Justice (2019) Criminal justice statistics quarterly June 2019

[6] HM Chief Inspector of Prisons, (2020) "Aggregate report on Short scrutiny visits"

[7] Ibid

[8] Ministry of Justice (2020) "National Statistics: Offender Management Statistics Quarterly: April to June 2020" London: Ministry of Justice

[9] Ibid

[10] Ibid

A Kind Prison
Nick Moss

Notes

[1] Question posed to Lucy Frazer www.parallelparliament.co.uk/mp/richard-burgon/written-questions (Accessed 13 October 2020)

[2] Andrea Albutt as quoted in Sommerville, E., "British prisoners 'will die' from coronavirus, top governor warns" (2020) *The Evening Standard* www.standard.co.uk/news/uk/coronavirus-outbreak-prisoners-will-die-andrea-albutt-a4386451.html (Accessed 13 October 2020)

[3] Howard League, "Judicial review: Howard League and Prison Reform Trust issue government with letter before action over its response to coronavirus in prisons" (2020) howardleague.org/news/judicial-review-howard-league-and-prison-reform-trust-issue-government-with-letter-before-action-over-its-response-to-coronavirus-in-prisons/ (Accessed 13 October 2020)

[4] Lord Justice Woolf, "The Woolf Report: A summary of the main findings and recommendations of the inquiry into prison disturbances" (1991) *Prison Reform Trust* www.prisonreformtrust.org.uk/Portals/0/Documents/Woolf%20report.pdf (Accessed 13 October 2020)

[5] Ibid, para 3.54.

[6] Lord Ramsbotham as quoted in "Role of the Prison Officer – Justice Committee" publications. parliament.uk/pa/cm200809/cmselect/cmjust/361/36104.htm (Accessed 13 October 2020)

The Nurseries of Crime – finding kindness, hope and compassion
Malcolm Carter

Notes

[1] Prison Reform Trust, "Mental Health Care in Prisons" www.prisonreformtrust.org.uk/WhatWeDo/Projectsresearch/Mentalhealth#:~:text=25%25%20of%20women%20and%2015,than%20in%20the%20general%20population (Accessed 13 October 2020).

[2] Ibid

[3] Ibid

Kindness, hope and compassion in the criminal justice system: Is it worth it?
Alan Jermey

Notes

[1] PRT 2019: Prison the Facts, Bromley Briefings, Summer 2019 (London, Prison Reform Trust, 2019)

[2] Ibid

[3] MOJ 2018: Education & Employment Strategy: Ministry of Justice, London

Binding our wounds: Compassion and hope in tackling racial disparity
Phil Bowen

Notes

[1] The Lammy Report (2017) assets.publishing.service.gov.uk/government/uploads/system/uploads/attachment_data/file/643001/lammy-review-final-report.pdf (Accessed 14 October 2020)

[2] Release, "The Numbers in Black And White: Ethnic Disparities In The Policing And Prosecution Of Drug Offences In England And Wales" (2013) www.release.org.uk/publications/numbers-black-and-white-ethnic-disparities-policing-and-prosecution-drug-offences (Accessed 14 October 2020)

[3] Centre for Justice Innovation, "Building Trust How our courts can improve the criminal court experience for Black, Asian, and Minority Ethnic defendants" (2017) justiceinnovation.org/sites/default/files/media/documents/2019-03/building-trust.pdf

[4] Government Response to the Lammy Review (2017) assets.publishing.service.gov.uk/government/uploads/system/uploads/attachment_data/file/881317/tackling-racial-disparity-cjs-2020.pdf

[5] Ministry of Justice, "Tackling Racial Disparity in the Criminal Justice System: 2020 Update" (2020) assets.publishing.service.gov.uk/government/uploads/system/uploads/attachment_data/file/881317/tackling-racial-disparity-cjs-2020.pdf

We are doing the best we can with a very bad system
Marianne Moore

Notes

[1] Hatton, Jean 2005. Betsy: The dramatic Biography of prison reformer Elizabeth Fry. Monarch: Oxford. Pp. 160-163

[2] Hatton, Jean. 2005. Betsy: The dramatic Biography of prison reformer Elizabeth Fry. Monarch: Oxford. Pp. 170-174

[3] Hatton, Jean. 2005. Betsy: The dramatic Biography of prison reformer Elizabeth Fry. Monarch: Oxford. Pp. 174-180

[4] Hatton, Jean. 2005. Betsy: The dramatic Biography of prison reformer Elizabeth Fry. Monarch: Oxford. P. 180

[5] Elizabeth Fry quoted in Hatton, Jean. 2005. Betsy: The dramatic Biography of prison reformer Elizabeth Fry. Monarch: Oxford. P. 124

[6] Elizabeth Fry quoted in Hatton, Jean. 2005. Betsy: The dramatic Biography of prison reformer Elizabeth Fry. Monarch: Oxford. P. 205

[7] Fry, Elizabeth. 1827. *Observations on the visiting, superintendence, and governance of female prisoners.* Hatchard & Son: London p. 3.

[8] Hatton, Jean. 2005. *Betsy: The dramatic Biography of prison reformer Elizabeth Fry.* Monarch: Oxford. P. 190

[9] Fry, Elizabeth. 1827. *Observations on the visiting, superintendence, and governance of female prisoners.* Hatchard & Son: London pp. 4-5

[10] Fry, Elizabeth. 1827. *Observations on the visiting, superintendence, and governance of female prisoners.* Hatchard & Son: London p. 3.

[11] Hatton, Jean. 2005. *Betsy: The dramatic Biography of prison reformer Elizabeth Fry.* Monarch: Oxford. P. 220

[12] Elizabeth Fry quoted in Hatton, Jean. 2005. *Betsy: The dramatic Biography of prison reformer Elizabeth Fry.* Monarch: Oxford. P. 263

[13] Elizabeth Fry quoted in Hatton, Jean. 2005. *Betsy: The dramatic Biography of prison reformer Elizabeth Fry.* Monarch: Oxford. P. 272

[14] Hatton, Jean. 2005. *Betsy: The dramatic Biography of prison reformer Elizabeth Fry.* Monarch: Oxford. P. 275

[15] Elizabeth Fry quoted in Hatton, Jean. 2005. *Betsy: The dramatic Biography of prison reformer Elizabeth Fry.* Monarch: Oxford. P. 316

[16] Charlotte Newman's letter to Elizabeth Fry, 17th February 1818 quoted in Hatton, Jean. 2005. *Betsy: The dramatic Biography of prison reformer Elizabeth Fry.* Monarch: Oxford. P. 192

Compassionate Custody?
Dave Nicholson

Notes

[1] Webb, S. & Webb, B.P. (1922) *English local Government: English prisons Under Local Government* (with Preface By Bernard Shaw). London. Longmans, Green and Co.

[2] Opperman, G. (2012) Doing Time: Prisons in the 21st Century. Epsom. Bretwalda Books.

[3] Skotnicki, A. (2019) *Conversion and the Rehabilitation of the Penal System: a Theological Rereading of Criminal Justice.* Oxford. Oxford University Press, p58

[4] Ibid, page 76

[5] Huxley, A. (1945) The Perennial Philosophy. London. Chatto & Windus.

[6] Skotnicki, note 3

[7] Maruna, S. (2001) Making Good: How Ex-Convicts Reform and Rebuild Their Lives. Washington. American Sociological Association

[8] Giordano, P. C. et al (2002) Gender, Crime, and Desistance: Toward a Theory of Cognitive Transformation, American Journal of Sociology 107, no. 4: 990–1064.

[9] Braithwaite, J. (1989) Crime, Shame and Reintegration. Cambridge. Cambridge University Press.

[10] Ibid

[11] Turley, C. et al. (2013) *Enabling Features of Psychologically Informed Planned Environments.* London. Ministry of Justice Analytical Series

[12] Skotnicki, note 3, at p 78

[13] Ibid

[14] Toch, H. (1997) Corrections: A Humanistic Approach. New York. Harrow and Heston.

[15] Giordano, P. C. et al (2008). A life-course perspective on spirituality and desistance from crime. Criminology: An Interdisciplinary Journal, 46(1), 99–132

[16] Johnson, B. (2012) Can a Faith Based Prison Reduce Recidivism? Corrections Today. Volume:73 Issue:6. Pages:60-62.

[17] Burnside, J. et al (2005) My Brother's Keeper: Faith-based Units in Prisons. Cullompton: Willan.

[18] Skotnicki, note 3 at p130

[19] Rawlings, B. & Haigh, R. (2017). Therapeutic communities and planned environments for serious offenders in English prisons. BJPsych Advances, vol. 23, 338–346.

[20] Weaver, B. & Nicholson, D. (2012) 'Co-producing Change: Resettlement as a Mutual Enterprise'. The Prison Service Journal. 204, pp 9-17.

[21] Bird, L. (2011), The Belief in Change Programme: leading offenders to a better life, International Journal of Leadership in Public Services, Vol. 7 No. 2, pp. 119-130.

[22] Kainos Community (2020) https://kainoscommunity.org/challenge-change/ Accessed 02/05/2020.

[23] Rawlings, B. & Haigh, R. (2017). Therapeutic communities and planned environments for serious offenders in English prisons. BJPsych Advances, vol. 23, 338–346.

[24] Stevens, A. (2011) A "Very Decent Nick": Ethical Treatment in Prison-Based Democratic Therapeutic Communities, Journal of Forensic Psychology Practice, 11:2-3, 124-150

[25] Winstone, J. (ed.) (2016) Mental Health, Crime and Criminal Justice: Responses and Reforms. Basingstoke. Palgrave Macmillan.

[26] Snow, D. A. & Machelek, R. (1984) The Sociology of Conversion. Annual Review of Sociology. Vol. 10:167-190

[27] PRI. (2015) Preventing Radicalisation in Prisons: Developing a coordinated and effective approach. (International expert roundtable, December 2015, Amman, Jordan)

[28] Ibid

[29] Ibid

[30] Ibid

[31] Ibid

A brighter future: the role of hope in women's rehabilitation
Olivia Dehnavi

Notes

[1] Howard League for Penal Reform

[2] National Audit Office

[3] John H. Laub, Daniel S. Nagin and Robert J. Sampson, 'Trajectories of change in criminal offending: Good marriages and the desistance process', *American Sociological Review*, 63 (1998)

[4] Filip Sosenko, Glen Bramley & Sarah Johnsen, *Gender Matters: Gendered patterns of severe and multiple disadvantage in England* (2020)

⁵ The Lammy Review: An independent review into the treatment of, and outcomes for, Black, Asian and Minority Ethnic individuals in the Criminal Justice System (2017); Bromley Briefings Prison Factfile, Winter 2019

⁶ Bromley Briefings

⁷ Martin Seligman, *Flourish: A Visionary New Understanding of Happiness and Well-being*, Nicholas Brealey Publishing (2011)

⁸ workingchance.org

⁹ Martin Seligman, Learned Optimism, Nicholas Brealey Publishing (2006)

¹⁰ SAMHSA's Concept of Trauma and Guidance for a Trauma-Informed Approach (2014) store.samhsa.gov/product/SAMHSA-s-Concept-of-Trauma-and-Guidance-for-a-Trauma-Informed-Approach/SMA14-4884>

¹¹ Ryan T. Motz, J.C. Barnes, Avshalom Caspi, Louise Arseneault, Francis T. Cullen, Renate Houts, Jasmin Wertz, Terrie E. Moffitt, *Does contact with the justice system deter or promote future delinquency? Results from a longitudinal study of British adolescent twins*, Criminology (2019) onlinelibrary.wiley.com/doi/full/10.1111/1745-9125.12236>

¹² Brené Brown, *I Thought It Was Just Me (but it isn't): Making the Journey from "What Will People Think?" to "I Am Enough"*, Gotham Books (2008)

¹³ Nacro, *Using an Identity Lens: Constructive working with children in the criminal justice system* (2020) 3bx16p38bchl32s0e12di03h-wpengine.netdna-ssl.com/wp-content/uploads/2020/01/Using-an-identity-lens-toolkit.pdf>

¹⁴ Ray Paternoster and Shawn Bushway, 'Desistance and the Feared Self: Toward an Identity Theory of Criminal Desistance', *Journal of Criminal Law and Criminology*, 99 (2009); Barry R Schlenker, 'Identity and self-identification' in B. R. Schlenker (ed.), *The self and social life*, McGraw-Hill (1985)

¹⁵ S. Farrall, & A. Calverley, *Understanding Desistance from Crime: Theoretical Directions in Resettlement and Rehabilitation*, Open University Press (2006); K. Martin & L. Stermac, 'Measuring Hope: Is Hope Related to Criminal Behaviour in Offenders?', in *International Journal of Offender Therapy and Comparative Criminology*, 54(5) (2010)

¹⁶ David Scott, *Against Imprisonment: An Anthology of Abolitionist Essays*, Waterside Press (2018)

¹⁷ Megan R. Gunnar, 'Social Buffering of Stress in Development: A Career Perspective', Perspectives on Psychological Science (2017) journals.sagepub.com/doi/full/10.1177/1745691616680612>

¹⁸ Paul Growcoot, 'An essay on identity work and desistance' (2019) discoveringdesistance.home.blog/2019/02/11/an-essay-on-identity-work-and-desistance/>

¹⁹ Hope Is A Discipline feat. Mariame Kaba, *Beyond Prisons Podcast* www.stitcher.com/podcast/beyond-prisons/e/53864185?autoplay=true>

Understanding and changing the narrative
Shola Apena Rogers

Notes

¹ McAdams, D. P. (1993). The stories we live by: personal myths and the making of the self (Vol. null).

² Presser, L. (2009). The narratives of offenders. Theoretical Criminology, 13(2), 177-200.

³ Maruna, S. (2001). Making Good: How Ex-convicts Reform and Rebuild Their Lives: American Psychological Association.

[4] Presser, L. and S. Sandberg (2015). What is the story? Narrative Criminology: Understanding Stories of Crime. L. Presser and S. Sandberg. New York, NYU Press: 1-20.

[5] Liddle, M., Boswell, G., Wright, S. and Francis, V. Perry, R. (2016) Trauma and young offenders a review of the research and practice literature. Beyond Youth Custody.

[6] Baglivio, M, T., Wolff, K. T., Piquero, A. R., & Epps, N. (2015). The Relationship between Adverse Childhood Experiences (ACE) and Juvenile Offending Trajectories in a Juvenile Offender Sample, *Journal of Criminal Justice*, 43, 3, 229-241.

[7] McKendy, J. P. (2006). 'I'm very careful about that': narrative and agency of men in prison. Discourse & Society, 17(4), 473-502.

[8] Inbau, F., Reid, J., Buckley, J., & Jayne, B. (2001). Criminal interrogation and confessions (4th edn). Gaithersburg, MA: Aspen.

[9] Soukara, S., Bull, R., Vrij, A., Turner, M. and Cherryman, J. (2009) 'What really happens in police interviews of suspects? Tactics and confessions', Psychology, Crime & Law,15:6,493 — 506

[10] Building resilience through witnessing clients overcome adversity demonstrating an immense capacity to heal, which has a positive effect on the practitioner

[11] Cooley, B. N., Moore, S. E., & Sample, L. L. (2017). The role of formal social control mechanisms in deterring sex offending as part of the desistance process. Criminal Justice Studies, 1-22. doi:10.1 080/1478601X.2017.1299335

Ensuring restorative justice goes viral – time for a second surge?
Dr Belinda Hopkins

Notes

[1] Restorative Justice was first used, in the UK at least, just over 25 years ago. Its origins go back much further than that, with elements of restorative practice found in indigenous communities over many hundreds of years.

[2] Thank you to Robyn Hromek for the initial inspiration for this essay. Her book Planting the Peace Virus – Early Intervention to Prevent Violence in Schools (2004) Sage Publications is recommended.

[3] G. Johnstone ed. (2003) *A Restorative Justice Reader*; Cullompten, Devon; Willan Publishing .....

[4] H. Zehr (1990) Changing Lenses; Scottdale, PA; Herald Press

[5] Charles K. B. Barton (2003) *Restorative Justice: The Empowerment Model*; Alexandria, Australia; Hawkins Press; restorativejustice.org.uk/what-restorative-justice

[6] restorativejustice.org.uk/what-restorative-justice

[7] www.why-me.org

[8] www.restorativejustice.org

[9] Private conversation Richard Monkhouse ex Chair of the Magistrates Association

[10] Restorative Justice is the name usually given to the restorative ethos, principles and practice in the criminal justice system; when applied more widely, and often more informally the term 'Restorative Practice' is used

Restorative justice, putting the heart into the criminal justice system
Pete Wallis

Notes

[1] Ward,T.,Mann,R.E.,& Gannon,T.A.(2007).Thegoodlivesmodelofoffenderrehabilitation:Clinical implications.Aggression and Violent Behaviour, 12,87–107.doi:10.1016/j.avb.2006.03.004

[2] ACEs are traumatic events that happen to a child before they reach 18. ACEs include all types of abuse and neglect and parental separation, substance misuse, mental illness, incarceration, and domestic violence

Charity, kindness, hope and compassion
Anne Fox

Notes

[1] Prison Reform Trust, "Bromley Briefings: Prison Factfile Winter 2019" (2019) http://www. prisonreformtrust.org.uk/portals/0/documents/bromley%20briefings/Winter%202019%20 Factfile%20web.pdf (Accessed 15 October 2020)

[2] Ibid

[3] Ibid

[4] HMPPS, "Guidance: Desistance" https://www.gov.uk/guidance/desistance#:~:text=Desistance%20 is%20the%20word%20for,come%20to%20abstain%20from%20crime.&text=This%20is%20 to%20understand%20common,us%20in%20helping%20people%20desist.

[5] Gibbs, P., et al., "'Tough On Crime' – Why Beliefs Shape Policy" in Fox, A., and Frater, A., "Crime And Consequence: What should happen to people who commit criminal offences?" 3rd Edn [Monument Fellowship: London, 2019) pp 97-102

Kindness in prisons
Gerard Lemos

Notes

[1] The Samaritans. 2012 *A Listener Lives Here: The Development of Samaritans' Prison Listener Scheme* see also Jaffe, M. 2012 The Listener Scheme in Prisons: Final Report on the Research Findings, Presented to the Samaritans July 2012. Keele University

[2] Ibid.

[3] Ibid.

[4] Listener from HM Prison/YOI Feltham quoted in The Samaritans 2012 *A Listener Lives Here: The Development of Samaritans' Prison Listener Scheme*

Meeting Shame with Kindness, Hope and Compassion
Charlie Rigby

Notes

[1] Gilligan, J. Violence: reflections on our deadliest epidemic. London: Jessica Kingsley Publications Ltd; 1999.

[2] Schneider, C. Shame, exposure and privacy. London: W. W. Norton & Co; 1992.

[3] Brown, B. The power of vulnerability: teachings on authenticity, connection and courage. Colorado: Sounds True; 2013.

Kindness: A compelling virtue in the criminal justice and desistance trajectory
Revd Dr Carver Anderson

Notes

[1] As Zelig Pliskin puts it: Having a kindness consciousness will enable you to understand seemingly puzzling occurrences. The less you want to be in a certain place, the more you should be on the lookout for opportunities to make a difference. Pliskin, Z. (2000). *Kindness: Changing people's lives for the better.* New York: Shaar Press. p. 18).

[2] Anderson, C. (2020). Black Young Men: Problematisation, Humanisation and Effective Engagement. In: Parsons, J. M. and Chappell, A. (eds). *The Palgrave Handbook of Auto/Biography.* Switzerland: Palgrave Macmillan, pp 577-598, and Glynn, M. (2014) *Black men, invisibility and crime: towards a critical race theory of desistance.* London: Routledge.

[3] Brown, G., Bos, E., and Brady, G. Hear our voices: Exploring How Bringing Hope's Damascus Road Second Chance Prison and Community Programme Supports Black Men in Prison and in the Community. Coventry: Coventry University, 2016

[4] Lewis, J 2018, *When you see something that is not is not right, you have to speak up,* video recording, You Tube, viewed 10 August 2020, ://www.youtube.com/watch?v=A7xggPgdi3s.

[5] see Furbey et al., *Faith as social capital: Connecting or dividing?* Bristol, Policy Press, 2006, chapters 1-3

[6] Brown, G., Bos, E., and Brady, G. Hear our voices: Exploring How Bringing Hope's Damascus Road Second Chance Prison and Community Programme Supports Black Men in Prison and in the Community. Coventry: Coventry University, 2016

[7] Glynn, M., Black men, invisibility and crime: towards a critical race theory of desistance. London, Routledge, 2014).

[8] Ross Deuchar, Gangs and Spirituality: Global Perspectives, Switzerland, Springer, 2018

[9] Paul Grant, Saving Our Sons: Strategies and Advice for the Parents of Afrikan Teenage Sons

Love Actually: Why we need love and empathy in services and systems
Sarah Wilkinson & Anne-Marie Douglas

Notes

[1] Our Young Partners are children, young adults and teenagers aged 10–25 who have experienced injustice and inequality. They are passionate about using their experiences in positive and powerful ways to improve social care, justice and health services by voicing issues for and with other young people.

[2] Anne-Marie Douglas. 'Towards a System that Heals. Exploring Empathy and its application to youth justice, and children's education, health and social care services'. Winston Churchill Memorial Trust Fellowship. To be published later in 2020.

[2] Peer Power Experts - Message from young people for young people in the secure estate. What is COVID-19 www.peerpower.org.uk/message-from-young-people-for-young-people-what-is-covid-19/

[4] Julia Unwin CBE (2018) 'Kindness, emotions and human relationships: The blind spot in public policy'. Carnegie Trust. www.carnegieuktrust.org.uk/news/julia-unwin-report-examines-role-of-kindness-in-public-policy

Circles of Support and Accountability: reducing shame, bringing hope and preventing further victims of sexual abuse
Riana Taylor, CEO of Circles UK

Notes

[1] Tewksbury, R. and Jennings, W.G. 2010. Assessing the Impact of Sex Offender Registration and Community Notification on Sex-Offending Trajectories. Criminal Justice & Behavior, 37, 570–582.

[2] Carich, M., Wilson, C., Carich, P. and Calder, M. (2010). Contemporary Sex Offender Treatment: Incorporating Circles of Support and the Good Lives Model. In J. Brayford, F. Cowe and J Deering (eds) What Else Works? Creative Work with Offenders. Cullompton, Willan Publishing - p202

[3] Lussier, P. and Beauregard, E. 2018. Sexual offending, a criminological perspective. Routledge / Taylor & Francis, Abingdon, UK.

[4] Kernsmith, P. D., Craun, S. W. and Foster, J. (2009). Public attitudes toward sexual offenders and sex offender registration. Journal of Child Sexual Abuse, 18, 290–301.

[5] Higgins, E. M. and Rolfe, S. M. (2016). "The sleeping army": Necropolitics and the collateral consequences of being a sex offender. Deviant Behavior.

[6] Kaufman, G. (1989). The Psychology of Shame – Theory and Treatment of Shame Based Syndromes. Springer, New York, NY

[7] Carvicchia, S. (2010). Shame in the coaching relationship: reflections on organisational vulnerability. Journal of Management Development, vol 29, no. 10, pp 877-890. Emerald Group Publishing Limited, p882

[8] Ibid

[9] Fox, K.J. (2014). Behavior theorizing community integration as desistance-promotion. Criminal Justice and Behavior. Published online 25 September 2014.

[10] Pranis, K. (2007). Restorative values. In Johnstone, G and Van Ness, D (Eds), Handbook of Restorative Justice. Willan Publishing.

[11] Duwe, G. (2018). The Promise and Potential of Circles of Support and Accountability - A Sex Offender Reentry Program. American Enterprise Institute.

The complexity of compassion
Alice Dawnay

Notes

[1] Names have been changed to preserve confidentiality

'The transformative power of recognising suffering'
Jo Hobson & Kezia Poutney

Notes

[1] His Holiness the Dalai Lama; L.L. Lapointe, 'Compassion Fatigue' *Journal of Medical-Special Speech Pathology:: Voices: Collected Essays on Language Laughter and Life* p.25

[2] C. Goodman (2009) *Consequences of Compassion: an interpretation and defence of Buddhist Ethics* (Oxford University Press, USA) p.172

[3] Women in Prison website, Key Facts accessed 29.04.20 www.womeninprison.org.uk/research/key-facts.php

⁴ Cambridge Dictionary accessed 24.04.20 dictionary.cambridge.org/dictionary/english/kindness.

⁵ Random Acts of Kindness website, accessed 07.05.20 www.randomactsofkindness.org/kindness-quotes/131-constant-kindness-can-accomplish-much

⁶ European Court of Human Rights, Case of Vinter and Others v. the United Kingdom, Judgment Strasbourg, 9 July 2013 hudoc.echr.coe.int/eng?i=001-122664#{%22item id%22:[%22001-122664%22]}

⁷ www.bbc.co.uk/news/uk-25574176

⁸ Dirk van Zyl Smit, 'Even life prisoners should have hope and a chance to change' 3rd Jan 2014 www.theguardian.com/commentisfree/2014/jan/03/life-prisoners-david-cameron-100-year-sentence

⁹ Dirk van Zyl Smit, 'Even life prisoners should have hope and a chance to change' 3rd Jan 2014 www.theguardian.com/commentisfree/2014/jan/03/life-prisoners-david-cameron-100-year-sentence

¹⁰ His Holiness the Dalai Lama, Archbishop Desmond Tutu and Douglas Abrams, *The Book of Joy: Lasting Happiness in a Changing World* (2016) p122

¹¹ ibid

On kindness as "being solid": visible presence and icons in institutional caring
Father Richard Rene

Notes

¹ St Matthew, 1:23

² Three Treatises on the Divine Images. "Treatise 1.16"

³ See 2 Peter 1:4

Searching for hope, kindness and compassion in the Criminal Justice System? Find your local women's centre
Angela Collins

Notes

¹ Corston, J. (2007) The Corston report: a report by Baroness Jean Corston of a review of women with particular vulnerabilities in the criminal justice system: the need for a distinct, radically different, visibly-led, strategic, proportionate, holistic, woman-centred, integrated approach. London Home Office

² Annison et al. (eds.) (2015) Women & Criminal Justice: From the Corston Report to Transforming Rehabilitation Bristol: Policy Press

³ MoJ (2010) Breaking the Cycle Effective Punishment, Rehabilitation and Sentencing of Offenders, London

⁴ MoJ (2013) Transforming Rehabilitation: A Strategy for Reform, London

⁵ Hunter, G. and Radcliffe, P. (2013) Are magistrates doing justice to women?, Criminal Justice Matters, 92, 34-5

⁶ Roberts, J. (2015) Criminal justice in times of austerity, Centre for Crime and Justice Studies www.crimeandjustice.org.uk/resources/criminal-justice-times-austerity (Accessed 16 October 2020)

How can kindness and compassion shape probation?
Rhian Metcalfe

Notes

[1] Kirton, G., and Guillaume, C., "Employment Relations and Working Conditions in Probation after Transforming Rehabilitation: With a Special Focus on Union Effects" (2015) www.napo.org.uk/sites/default/files/BR%20112-2015%20Appendix%20A%20-%20Gill%20 Kirton%20Report.doc

[2] HMIP (2018) Quality and Impact of Inspection. The Effectiveness of Probation Work by the National Probation Service in London. Available at www.justiceinspectorates.gov.uk/hmiprobation/ wp-content/uploads/sites/5/2018/01/London-NPS-QI.pdf

[3] Phillips, J (2001) Target, Audit and Risk Assessment, Cultures in the Probation Service. European Journal. 64(3) 209-225

[4] Seti, C. L. (2008). Causes and treatment of burnout in residential child care workers: A review of the research. Residential Treatment of Children & Youth, 24(3), 197-229. doi:10.1080/08865710802111972

[5] Westaby, C., Philips, J. and Fowler, A. (2016) Spillover and work-family conflict in probation practice: Managing the boundary between work and home life. European Journal of Probation, 8(3) 113–127

[6] Knight, C. and Modi, P. (2014) The Use of Emotional Literacy in Work with Sexual Offenders. The Probation Journal, 61(2) 132–147

[7] Ibid

[8] Phillips, J (2001) Target, Audit and Risk Assessment, Cultures in the Probation Service. European Journal. 64(3) 209-225

[9] Burke and Collett as cited in ibid.

[10] Mawby, R. C. and Worrall, A. (2013) Doing Probation Work: Identity in a Criminal Justice Occupation. Routledge: Taylor and Francis Group

[11] Ibid

[12] Ibid

[13] Teater, M., and Ludgate, J., "OVERCOMING COMPASSION FATIGUE A Practical Resilience Workbook" [USA, Pesi Publishing & Media, 2014]

A therapeutic lens on compassionate care: Encountering the inner child in a forensic mental health setting
Belinda Sherlock

Notes

[1] Feldman, C., (2005). Compassion: Listening to the Cries of the World. Berkeley, CA: Rodmell Press.

[2] Nhat Hanh, Thich, (2010). Reconciliation: Healing the Inner Child. Berkeley, CA: Parallax Press.

[3] hooks, b., (2001). All About Love: New Visions. New York: HarperCollins.

[4] Harris, T. A., (1995). I'm OK – You're OK: A Practical Guide to Transactional Analysis. London: Arrow Books.

[5] Gilligan, J., (2001). Preventing Violence. New York: Thames & Hudson.

[6] Gilbert, P., (2015). The Compassionate Mind. 3rd ed. Croydon, UK: Robinson.

[7] Ricard, M., (2015). Altruism: The Power of Compassion to Change Yourself and the World. London: Atlantic Books.

[8] Ibid

[9] Van Dernoot Lipsky, L. with Burk, C., (2009). *Trauma Stewardship: An Everyday Guide to Caring for Self While Caring for Others*. Oakland, CA: Berrett-Koehler

[10] Gilbert at note 6

[11] Chödrön, P., (2005). Start Where You Are: how to accept yourself and others. London: Element

[12] Van Dernoot Lipsky, note 9

[13] Bowlby, J., (1988). A Secure Base: Clinical Applications of Attachment Theory. 2nd ed. New York: Routledge.

[14] Van der Kolk, B., (2015). The Body Keeps the Score. London: Penguin Random House.

[15] Seebolm. H., (2011). ' On bondage and liberty: the art of the possible in medium-secure settings'. In: Dramatherapy and Destructiveness. 1st ed. Hove, UK: Routledge, pp. 120–132